In The Word

by

Leon du Preez &
Maartin Bezuidenhout

28 Days in the word

by Leon du Preez & Maartin Bezuidenhout

ISBN 978-1-990978-67-8

All scriptures are quoted from the New King James version of the Bible unless otherwise stated.

Copyright © 2023 by Leon du Preez International.

Published by Scarlet House Publishing.

Table of Contents

Section 4: The Poetic Books:

Job — The Book of Ultimate Testing and Deliverance
Psalms — The Book of Prayer and Praise
Proverbs — The Book of Wisdom
Ecclesiastes — The Preacher
Song of Solomon — The Book of Covenant Love

Section 5: The Major Prophets:

Isaiah — The Evangelical Prophet
Jeremiah — A Call to Repentance
Lamentation — The Sorrows of a Prophet
Ezekiel — God Strengthens
Daniel — God is Sovereign

Section 6: The Minor Prophets:

Hoshea — The Faithful Husband
Joel — Jehovah is God
Amos — A Burden-Bearer
Obadiah — A Servant of the Lord
Jonah — The Saviour of a Nation
Micah — The Mighty Evangelist
Nahum — The Righteous Judgement of God
Habakkuk — Fearless Faith
Zephaniah — God's Approaching Judgement
Haggai — The Lord's House
Zechariah — Yahweh Remembers
Malachi — Sending a Messenger

28 Day Reading Plan

SECTION 1

KEYS ON HOW TO STUDY THE BIBLE

The Apocrypha and Lost Books of the Bible

"An Overview"

Are there any missing books from the Bible as we know it? — This is a common question asked amongst believers when they start to study the Word.

Now when we discuss what books belong in the Bible then it's important to understand the term canon.

The word canon has a Greek origin and means a ruler or standard of measurement. We, therefore, refer to the canon of the Bible as a unique list of books, inspired by God. And seeing that it's inspired by God means that it belongs in the Bible.

Then we have what is known as non-canonical books that is uninspired, meaning that it does not belong in the Bible.

It is important to remember that the canon is determined by God and not by man. So, asking the question whether a book belongs in the Bible means that we need to determine whether that book is one of God's inspired books or not.

That being said, we find several books that have historical value but not included in the canon of the Bible. Many of these books called the Apocrypha (Hidden), have been accepted by the Roman Catholic Church but never held as part of the canon during the early history of the Church.

The Apocrypha contains ideas and doctrines that are not in line with the Word of God and have a selection of negative characteristics written by unreliable sources.

What Is The Apocrypha?

All the Apocryphal books are believed to have been written between the time of Malachi and Jesus known as the silent four hundred years.

The Table Of Contents Found In The Apocrypha:

- 1 & 2 Esdrasand
- Tobit
- Judith
- Editions to Esther
- Wisdom of Solomon
- Ecclesiastical book
- Letter of Jeremiah
- The song of the three children
- The history of Susanna (Added to Daniel)
- Bel and the Dragon (Added to Daniel)
- The prayer of Manassas
- 1 & 2 Maccabees

Reason Why These Books Were Left Out:

- It was not in any way hinted nor quoted by Jesus.
- The style of writing was not inspired to be divine.
- It was not written by divine people, like prophets, Moses etc. (Regarded uninspired)
- It does not line up with main doctrine/main scripture.

Lost Books: Old Testament (Some of the books, not exhaustive list)

- Book of Enoch
- Lost Book of Eden
- The Book of Jasher
- The Book of Wars
- The Book of Adam and Eve

Main Reason It Was Taken Out:

- Was too late after Old Testament was compiled and too early for New Testament.
- When searched on google, you find that there are multiple versions which are mostly made up.
- Cannot look at it as main context of scripture.
- It was to fantasy like.
- It is not part of inspired speech, if God wanted it in the Bible, it would have been there.

Lost Books: New Testament (Some of the books, not exhaustive list)

- Gospel of Judas
- Gospel of Thomas
- Gospel of Peter
- Gospel of Nicodemus

Main Reason It Was Taken Out:

- They do not carry the idea of the person of Jesus Christ.
- It promotes Gnosticism.

The Conclusion?

If there were inspired letters God chose not to preserve, or not to add to the Bible then it's because we do not need them, therefore, lets keep our Bible Study with what we believe was inspired by God, The Bible.

The **Bible**

"To Read or Study"

A shocking statistic shows that only 20% read their Bibles four times per month, which means that 80% don't even read their Bibles – this does not even take studying into consideration.

The truth, however, is that the only way to gain spiritual depth and substance is when we study the Bible. That's why it is important to understand that there is a difference between reading and studying.

So, what does it truly mean to study the Bible?

First, we need to understand that the Bible is the only book that is always relevant, as its diversity impacts every age and every circumstance.

Secondly, we need to understand that the Bible is inspired by the Holy Spirit, and so is always alive and powerful, as found in **2 Timothy 3:16** and **Hebrews 4:12**

> *16 "All Scripture is God-breathed and is useful for teaching, rebuking, correcting and training in righteousness"*

2 Timothy 3:16 (NIV)

> *12 "For the word of God is living and active and full of power [making it operative, energizing, and effective]. It is sharper than any two-edged sword, penetrating as far as the division of the soul and spirit [the completeness of a person], and of both joints and marrow [the deepest parts of our nature], exposing and judging the very thoughts and intentions of the heart."*

Hebrews 4:12 (AMP)

Now these verses are filled with revelation, but for the purpose of illustrating the difference between reading and studying, let's take a look at the phrase "God-breathed" from **2 Timothy 3:16**

The Hebrew word for "Holy Spirit" is "Ruach ha-kodesh."

Ruach means "Wind" or "Breath"
Kodesh is from Kadosh, which means "Holy"

This forms the phrase "Holy Wind" or "Holy Breath". This speaks of the force of wind that went forth as God spoke and created the heavens and the earth with His Words.

Now, this completely changes the way that we look at **2 Timothy 3:16,** as it states that all scripture is filled with the Holy Wind or Breath of God, meaning that all scripture is infused and inspired by the Holy Spirit, therefore, making the Bible alive, active and powerful, continually operative in the life of a believer.

Note, we would never have known this by simply reading the verse. This revelation came through studying.

It will, therefore, require a study of the Bible in order for us to access the vaults of revelation that are in Heaven.

Bible reading makes you full, but Bible study is the principle that will bring you into a place of revelation, and revelation is the thing that will cause you to move from a place of darkness — which is ignorance — into a place of light — which is truth.

It is therefore imperative that we study the Word, so that we can rightly divide the Word of Truth.

[14] "Remind them of these things, charging them before the Lord not to strive about words to no profit, to the ruin of the hearers. [15] Be diligent to present yourself approved to God, a worker who does not need to be ashamed, rightly dividing the word of truth. [16] But shun profane and idle babblings, for they will increase to more ungodliness."

2 Timothy 2:14 – 16 (NKJV)

Paul is writing this letter to Timothy, giving him instructions on how to deal with the gossip that is growing like a cancer in the church.

Paul further explains to Timothy that in order for him to effectively deal with this situation, that he must study the Word. This was to ensure that after he has preached to them, that he will not be found ashamed.

We need to understand that the one preaching will stand accountable for the words they have preached.

Now many might think that they stand clear of this judgement, yet the Lord Jesus Christ has left us all with the Great Commission saying; *"Go into all the world and preach the gospel to every creature" Mark 16:15 (NKJV).*

It is therefore imperative that we become students of the Word, in order to be ready in and out of season.

"Therefore I run thus: not with uncertainty. Thus I fight: not as one who beats the air. But I discipline my body and bring it into subjection, lest, when I have preached to others, I myself should become disqualified"

1 Corinthians 9:26 (NKJV)

In the above verse, Paul is saying that he disciplines his body so that he will not be disqualified at any given time by putting his flesh into subjection, through **studying** the Word.

7

We will all stand naked at the judgement seat, with our actions and words fully exposed. For example, if you have preached to others that they must study the Word and pray, but you yourself do not, you will be exposed in this.

Studying the Word, therefore, causes us **not** to be ashamed on the day of judgement.

Thirdly, we need to understand that the Word of God must be read and studied in fellowship with the Holy Spirit, for the bible says that the letter kills, but the Spirit gives life.

I want to encourage you, as you are about to go on a journey through the Word of God — both reading and studying a story like none that you have ever heard, with unlimited power at your fingertips and many treasures waiting to be unlocked — to make the Holy Spirit a part of your journey. Ask Him to lead, guide, teach and counsel you as you read and study the Bible.

Bible **Study**

"Power of Meditating on the Word"

[8] *"This Book of the Law shall not depart from your mouth, but you shall meditate in it day and night, that you may observe to do according to all that is written in it. For then you will make your way prosperous, and then you will have good success."*

Joshua 1:8 (NKJV)

Meditation of God's Word forms an integral part of Bible study.

This is an extremely powerful principle that every believer must apply to their lives in order to live a life of dominion and glory.

The word "*meditate*" in **Joshua 1:8** is from the Hebrew word "*hagah*" which means to imagine, mutter and roar, which gives us three dangerous dimensions of meditation.

The Three Dangerous Dimensions of Meditating on God's Word:

1. Visualise the Word of God as you Study It:

This is where we tap into the thought dimension as we ponder on the Word of God through imagination, meaning that we think of God's Word in pictures.

And so, as these pictures run through our minds over and over, they get infused with our spirit beings becoming a part of us.

This then moves us into the second dimension of meditation called "Mutter"

2. Mutter God's Word:

Another definition of the word "*meditate*" is to "*mutter*", which means to speak something under your breath over and over again.

This is where you take a verse or chapter from the Bible, and memorise it, then you speak that chapter or verse over and over until it saturates every fibre of your being.

This then moves us into the third dimension of meditation called "*Roar*"

3. Roar God's Word:

Here we start to speak the Word of God out loud. The Word has now become alive and real to you, causing you to speak it with boldness.

The purpose of this dimension is to annihilate every lie, deception, and suggestion that the devil has sent to kill, steal, and destroy. The truth that you now know will crush every lie of the enemy, causing you to walk in power and dominion.

You will find that as you now start to speak the Word of God out loud that it will increase your measure of faith, also causing you to see things from a heavenly perspective as your mind is being renewed.

10 Benefits Connected with Meditating on the Word of God:

1. The Word Renews Your Mind

In order for us to be effective in our spiritual walk, we need to know the good, acceptable and perfect will of God. For us to gain knowledge of this means that we will need to be transformed from a current state of being (a carnal state) into a new state of being (spiritual state). For this transformation to take place, we need to change the way we think and perceive things.

This renewal of mind can only take place through meditating on the Word of God. Meditation is what moves the Word from your mind and infuses it to your spirit.

Romans 12:2 (NKJV)

2. The Word Increases Faith

The bible says that without faith, it is impossible to please God. Faith is, therefore, of the utmost importance in a believer's life. Faith gives the believer the ability to walk in the things that are not, as if they are, and to speak the things that are not, as if they are.

Faith is the substance of heaven that will cause you to move in a dimension of infinite possibilities. Faith comes in measure, and therefore can be increased. The way that you increase faith is by hearing the Word of God.

Meditation, therefore, is what will give you Rhema, which is the spoken Word of God in any situation that you might be facing, and Rhema comes by meditating on the Graphe written Word of God.

Hebrews 11:1 & 6 (NKJV)
Romans 10:17 (NKJV)

3. The Word Is A Weapon That We Have Been Given to Stand Effectively Against the Wiles and Schemes of The Enemy:

The book of Ephesians shows us that we need to be strong in the Lord and in His mighty power, because our battle is not against flesh and blood but against the rulers, against the principalities and against the powers of this dark world and against spiritual forces of wickedness in high places.

The most effective weapon we have to be victorious in this battle is the Word of God.

The Bible says that the Word of God is living and powerful, sharper than any two-edged sword; therefore, when used correctly, it can resolve any problem, both physically and spiritually.

It is when we study the Word, and it becomes a part of us, that we now become powerful weapons in the hands of God.

It is meditation on the Word of God that will cause us to become living Epistles as Paul said in the book of Corinthians, causing us to now function as light.

Ephesians 6:10 – 18 (NKJV)
Hebrews 4:12 (NKJV)

4. The Word Is the Greatest Source of Hope

It is undeniable that if you can give someone hope, you give them life. There are more than 7,000 promises recorded in the Word of God, and as a child of God, you qualify for each and every one of them.

The Word generates hope; hope generates expectation and expectation generates a response - and we serve a God that is more than capable of responding!

Romans 15:13 (NKJV)

5. The Word Gives Wisdom

The Bible says that wisdom is the principal thing, meaning that it is the highest thing. In fact, wisdom is regarded as one of the greatest qualities that we can possess.

Wisdom will cause you to live a long, prosperous, and healthy life. Wisdom gives you the ability to see things from a heavenly perspective, and so to see things the way that God sees things. It gives you the ability to discern between right and wrong choices, which is of the utmost importance when it comes to both natural and spiritual matters.

Psalm 19:7 (NKJV)
Proverbs 4:7 (NKJV)
Proverbs 9:10 – 11 (NKJV)

6. The Word Brings Prosperity and Success

To prosper means to live in abundance in every dimension of your life, not just financially.

It means to prosper in your career, in your studies, in your relationships, in your marriage, spiritually and financially.

The Word of God is filled with keys that will give you the capacity to generate wealth in every sphere of your life. The Bible is clear when it states that we should follow and apply everything written in it, because if we do this, then we will have good success and be prosperous.

Joshua 1:8 (NKJV)
John 10:10 (NKJV)

7. The Word is a Source of Healing

The Bible says that death and life are in the power of the tongue, and those who love it shall eat the fruit thereof.

The Bible also says that the Word of God is alive, operative, and energising — meaning that the moment we open our mouths and speak the Word of God by faith, then His supernatural power goes into operation, and healing is evident as the natural environment around you now becomes subject to the words that you release from the supernatural.

Psalm 107:20 (NKJV)
Proverb 18:21 (NKJV)
Mark 16:15 – 18 (NKJV)
Hebrews 4:12 (AMP)

8. The Word Empowers Us

The key to be empowered by the Word of God is not just in hearing but applying it.

The Bible says that faith by itself — if it is not accompanied by action — is dead. So, hearing the Word generates faith, but taking action is what generates power.

When you take the Word of God and believe every word wholeheartedly, you become unshakable.

Luke 6:46 – 19 (NKJV)
James 2:17 (NKJV)

9. The Word Gives Direction

It is evident that in your spiritual walk, you will face many valleys and hit many lows.

There will be times that you will feel that darkness has crept in from all sides and that you are slowly drowning in an ocean of despair. It is in these moments that we need to hold on to every word of God, because His word destroys darkness and will lead you into victory every single time.

The answers to every question you have is locked up in the Word, so if you find yourself at a place not knowing what to do, it simply means that you need more Word.

Psalm 23:1 – 6 (NKJV)
Psalm 119:105 (NKJV)
Proverbs 3:5 – 6 (NKJV)

10. The Word Reveals Calling and Purpose

The Bible says that God knows the plans that He has for us, plans of peace and not of evil, to give us an expected end.

It is imperative that we acknowledge and understand that God has placed us on this earth to fulfill a very specific assignment. Therefore, we should make every effort to find out what is our God-given call and purpose. Once we do this, then we shall never fall.

These plans can be revealed to us in many ways, through Prophecy, through prayer, through visions and dreams and of course, through studying the Word.

Jeremiah 29:11 (NKJV)
2 Peter 1:10 (NKJV)

Now that we understand the importance of studying the Word, let's have a look at the next chapter which reveals some powerful methods and guidelines that we can follow and apply, on how to study the Bible effectively.

Study Keys

"The Four Power Keys on How to Unlock Your Bible"

Now there are a few keys that we need to take into consideration if we want to study the Bible effectively.

Key 1: Understanding the Three Different Translation Categories:

a. **Translation Category 1: Word for Word**

The following Bible translations are best suitable for studying the Word:

- **King James Version (KJV)** – This is the most accurate translation from the original Hebrew and Greek manuscripts.
- **New King James Version (NKJV)** – This translation is the 2nd most accurate and has been modernised more.
- **English Standard Version (ESV)**
- **Holman Christian Standard Bible (HCSB)**
- **Amplified (AMP)**
- **Revised Standard Version (RSV)**
- **New American Standard Bible (NASB)**

b. **Translation Category 2: Thought for Thought**

It is not advised to use one of the following versions for Bible study, however, they are extremely useful to bring through the thought of a passage of scripture.

- **New International Version (NIV)**
- **New Living Translation (NLT)**
- **Good News Bible (GNB)**
- **New Century Version (NCV)**
- **New American Bible (NAB)**
- **New Revised Standard Version (NRSV)**
- **New English Translation (NET)**

17

c. Translation Category 3: Paraphrased

The following translations make the Word relatable to you, however, it is also not advised to use one of these translations for Bible Study.

- **The Message Bible (MSG)**
- **Passion (TPT)**
- **The Living Bible (TLB)**

Key 2: How to Choose the Best Study Bible:

- First, you need to make sure that the Bible is a Word for Word translation.
- You must be comfortable with the Bible – something that you can easily carry around.
- The commentaries should be accurate. Always remember that commentaries never replace the Word of God, it's simply a theologist's point of view and therefore will still need to be tested.
- Although many have adapted to reading and studying the Bible online, it is still recommended to get a physical copy of the Bible, as it is easier to make notes and to remember.
- The Dake and the Thompson Chain currently prove to be two of the best study Bibles available today.

Key 3: The Three Rules of Bible Study:

1. Observation:

When we look at the word "observe", it means to scrutinise and inspect something closely with the intent to learn or gain greater knowledge.

This should always be the mindset that we read the Bible with; to gain a greater understanding of the bigger picture and even more, to grow in accuracy of the Lord God Almighty, this is accomplished through paying close attention to the detail.

As you read through the Word of God, ask the Holy Spirit to sharpen your spiritual sight, to see what it is that He wants to reveal to you. When the Holy Spirit becomes a part of your Bible Study, it becomes interesting. This is when your Bible Study becomes a journey of discovery, as you find the Word suddenly become alive before your very eyes.

And so, in the first rule of Bible Study, you read the Word of God with the intention to set your heart to understanding, and will then find that the Holy Spirit will cause certain verses or chapters to stand out.

The majority of people simply open the Word and start to read with no purpose or intent, hoping that something will make sense. This is dangerous and can cause you to become despondent towards the Word of God. It is imperative to plan your Bible reading, meaning there needs to be purpose behind the method. This will cause your Bible reading to become intentional – then most of all, your Bible-reading must be led by the Holy Spirit.

To observe the Word means to slow down as you dissect every part of scripture with the intent to gain understanding. Observation cannot be rushed. When observation is rushed, you might draw the wrong conclusion.

Observation generates understanding and establishes context, which is of the utmost importance.

Once a verse or passage of scripture stands out, we need to write them down. This is where we move into the second part of observation, called interrogation of scripture.

We need to understand that there is so much information that one can take out of a verse or passage of scripture when trained on what to look for, that will make you a professional when it comes to Bible Study.

The first thing that we need to identify after we have written the scriptures down are the major key words and key phrases, that will lead us into deeper revelation. This can easily be accomplished by asking ourselves the following questions as we intently ponder and meditate on those specific verses or passages of scripture.

- Who is speaking?
- Who are the main characters?
- Who is the author?
- What are the main events?
- What are the main circumstances?
- What is the main subject?
- When was this written?
- When will or did this happen?
- Where did or will this happen?
- Where was this said or written?
- Why was thisa written?
- Why is this said?
- How will or did something happen?
- How is the truth illustrated?

Once all the key words and phrases have been identified, we are then ready to move into the second rule of bible study called interpretation.

2. Interpretation:

Interpretation means to give a clear understanding of what a scripture or passage of scripture truly means – setting aside any of our own preconceived ideas with the ultimate goal to understand the writer's original intent.

Interpretation and observation are intertwined with one another where the one depends on the other, meaning the quality of interpretation depends on the quality of observation.

Interpretation is the second stage to establish context, and can be done by applying the following steps:

2.1. Pre-Context and Post-Context:

Pre and Post context means to read the verse/chapter before and after the verse/passage of scripture being studied.

E.g. Let's say that **2 Timothy 3:16** is the verse that we study. Pre-context means to read and observe **2 Timothy 3:15** and post context means to read and observe **2 Timothy 3:17**.

2.2. Identify the Theme of The Book:

We must understand the intention of the book. Reading the introduction of each book, which many seem to bypass, will give you a greater understanding of its background.

The theme of each book in the Bible is normally set out either in the beginning or at the end of each book. Alternatively this information can be found in this book.

2.3. Time and Dispensation:

It is important to know the dispensational language of each book of the Bible. In other words, to understand the timeline in which the book was written as well as the timeline we are in currently – the dispensation of grace. This can be done by using Google or the Dakes Bible.

2.4. Know the History, Manners and Customs of the Books:

There are various different types of software available that will aid us in gaining the information that we need.

a. Basic Software:

- Logos Bible Study
- Olive Tree
- eSword

b. Websites:

- Bible Hub – This site gives both Hebrew and Greek definitions and has various Lexicons and Concordances available.
- Blue Letter Bible
- Bible Study Tools
- Precept Austin

2.5. Read Commentaries, Dictionaries, Lexicons, and Always Cross Reference:

Commentaries, Dictionaries, and Cross References are all excellent resources to help you to understand things in context.

a. Commentaries:

How can we discern which commentaries are good? When they fall within our statement of faith.

The following are recommended commentaries that can be used for effective Bible Study.

- Matthew Hendry
- Barnes Commentary
- Clarkes Commentaries
- Expositors Biblical Commentary
- Guzik Commentaries
- JFB: Jameson Fausset and Brown
- Pulpit Commentaries
- Geneva Commentaries

b. Good Cross Reference:

Cross References gives you the ability to select a verse, and then sets out all the other verses in context.

- TSK – Treasury of Scripture Knowledge

c. Bible Dictionaries:

- Smith Bible Dictionary
- Easton Bible Dictionary
- Vines Dictionary
- TDNT – Theological Dictionary of the New Testament
- Tyndale Bible Dictionary

d. Greek and Hebrew Lexicons:

Lexicons give you the ability to select an English word, and then give you the Hebrew and Greek meaning.

A good lexicon must be able to do 3 things:

- One must be able to provide the Strong's Number and get the Greek word.
- You must get the meaning of the Greek word.
- You must get the meaning of the Hebrew word.

The following are recommended Lexicons:

- Strong's Exhaustive Lexicon – Basic Root Lexicon
- Vines
- Mounce
- TDNT
- Thayers
- BDAG

e. Concordances:

- The Dake Concordance
- Thompson Chain Concordance

2.6. The Bible Must Always be Taken Literally:

Even when the Bible makes use of parables, try to find the literal meaning in them.

2.7. Scripture Never Contradicts Itself:

When you find a contradiction in scripture, it simply means that it has not yet been opened up to you, and needs further study.

3. Application:

Once you have observed the verse or passage of scripture, and can now give a proper interpretation thereof, you then need to ask yourself the following questions to establish how you can take the verse or passage of scripture and apply it to yourself.

- What command was given?
- What instruction was given?
- What are the conditions?
- What are the promises?

Key 4: Different Bible Study Methods:

a. Chronological Bible Study:

The Bible consists of various writings, that were compiled over thousands of years, making up the different books of the Bible; these books are structured into two main divisions; The Old and New Testament.

Divisions of the Old Testament: 39 Books

- **The Pentateuch:** The first five books of Moses.
  Genesis to Deuteronomy
- **The Twelve History Books:**
  Joshua to Esther
- **The Five Poetic Books:**
  Job to Song of Solomon
- **The Five Major Prophets:**
  Isaiah to Daniel
- **The Twelve Minor Prophets:**
  Hosea to Malachi

Divisions of the New Testament: 27 Books

- **The Four Gospels:**
  Matthew to John
- **One History Book:**
  Acts
- **Fourteen Letters of Paul:** The Paulene Letters
  Romans to Hebrews
- **Seven General Epistles:**
  James to Jude
- **One Book of Prophecy:**
  Revelation

The Bible was carefully structured into the above format so that the reader will be able to follow the sequence of events as they took place, from the beginning of creation right through to the Book of Revelation.

This, however, is not in chronological order; meaning that the order of the books as given above are not all in sequence of when they have actually taken place on the timeline.

For example, as you go through the Bible and reach the Book of Isaiah, you might think that it is the next sequence of events that follow right after Song of Solomon on the timeline, which in fact, is not the case.

The events recorded in the Book of Isaiah, for example, actually happened during the same time of Uzziah, Jotham, Ahaz, and Hezekiah, all kings that reigned over Judah, recorded in the Second Book of Kings.

A Chronological study will place everything in the same timeline that they actually occurred, and as an example, will read as follows:

E.g. 2 Chronicles 28 then **2 Kings 16 – 17** then **Isaiah 13 – 27** jumping back **to 2 Kings 18:1 – 8.**

To read the Bible in Chronological order is also a powerful method in order to understand things in context.

b.   Topical Bible Study:

This is where you take a topic e.g. Angels, and study everything on that topic.

This can be thoroughly done by applying the three rules of Bible Study under **Key 3**.

c.   Character Bible Study:

Here you take specific individual — for example Moses, Joshua, David etc. — and do a complete study on their personalities, strengths, weaknesses, successes, and failures. There is valuable information locked up in the lives of many great men and women recorded in the Word of God that have paved the way for us that we can learn from.

This can be thoroughly done by applying the three rules of Bible Study under **Key 3**.

d.   Book Study:

This is where you take a book, for example, Genesis, and do a complete study on that Book.

The following are main keys that one has to be able to answer in order to know a book:

- Who is the author?
- What date is the setting for the book?
- What is the purpose of the book?
- To whom is the book written?
- What is the theme of the book?
- Identify the main places in the book?
- Who are the main characters of the book?
- What are the main key passages in the book?

e. Word Study:

This is where one takes a verse and breaks it open word for word, by looking up the Hebrew or Greek meaning of each word of the verse.

This is a very effective way to get to the root meaning of a specific word and so to understand both the right interpretation and context of the word.

This is where digital studies also come in. The following are some websites that have free resources and are good for beginning use:

- www.Blueletter
- www.Bible.org
- www.Biblehub.com

To do a more in-depth study go to:

- www.preceptaustin.org

f. Read Through the Bible:

If you have never read through the entire Bible then this is definitely the place where you want to start your journey. This can easily be accomplished by following a basic Bible reading plan.

Now, you might be wondering why this is important:

When we read through the entire Bible from cover to cover it gives us a panoramic view of the Word, thus giving us an understanding of everything in context.

And context is of the utmost importance when it comes to studying the Bible, as previously discussed.

And so, this book was carefully designed and put together exactly for that purpose; to help you gain a clear understanding and complete overview of the Old Testament in 28 Days.

Impossible? Not quite...

Notes:

- *This book does not in any form or way replace the Bible, but rather complements it, and so, for best results, it is advised that this book be read in conjunction with the Word.*
- *The last section of this book also contains a Bible reading plan with attainable goals that are set out for every day.*

NOTES

SECTION 2

THE PENTATEUCH

Table of Contents

Genesis — The Book of Beginnings
Exodus — The Birth of a Nation
Leviticus — The Law of a Nation
Numbers — The Wilderness Wonderings
Deuteronomy — The Laws Reviewed

Book of **Genesis**

"The Book of Beginnings"

Genesis is the first book of the Bible and was written by Moses. Genesis literally means "Beginning". The book of Genesis is foundational to the understanding of the rest of the Bible and is supremely a book of the relationship between God and nature, God and man, and thirdly, between man and man.

The book of Genesis clearly states that there is only one true living God. It directly opposes the idea of many Gods (polytheism), that there is no God at all (atheism) and that everything is divine (pantheism). This book teaches us that the One true God is sovereign over all that exists and so introduces how God makes covenants with His chosen people, standing fast to His unconditional love and faithfulness towards them.

Through the entire book of Genesis, we are taken on a journey from the creation and formation of the heavens, the earth, the seas and everything within them to the creation and formation of man. From here, we see man's encounter with the serpent, leading to the fall of man and God casting them out from the garden of Eden.

From this point forward, we can see God's relentless pursuit of restoration with man and His unconditional love for us. We see God never giving up but continually and faithfully making a way for the once glorious relationship man used to have with God to be restored.

The book of Genesis can be divided into two main categories:

Genesis 1 – 11

This category speaks about four major events.

1. **Creation: Genesis 1 & 2**
2. **The Fall: Genesis 3**
3. **The Flood: Genesis 4 – 10**
4. **The Tower of Babel: Genesis 11**

Genesis 12 – 50

This category speaks about four major lives.

1. Abraham: Genesis 12 – 22
2. Isaac: Genesis 24 – 27
3. Jacob: Genesis 27 – 36
4. Joseph: Genesis 37 – 50

HIGHLIGHTED EVENTS IN GENESIS
CHAPTER 1 - CHAPTER 11:

1. **Creation**
   Genesis 1:1 – 31 (NKJV)

The book of Genesis begins with the revelation of God - the Creator of the heavens and the earth. This was followed by the stages in which God created everything over a period of six days.

Some believe that the six days were literal 24-hour days, and others say they were indefinite periods. However, several factors support the first interpretation more than the second, making this is a topic well worth further study.

The six days included:

- **Day 1:** Revealing of day and night.
- **Day 2:** The setting of the firmament, which God called Heaven
- **Day 3:** The revealing of dry land and the gathering together of the water, called sea. The revealing of grass, herb yielding seed and fruit trees bearing fruit after their kind.
- **Day 4:** Creation of the two great lights (sun and moon) to divide the day from night and the creation of the stars.
- **Day 5:** Creation of every living creature that the waters brought forth and every winged fowl after their kind.
- **Day 6:** Creation of the beasts of the earth, cattle, and every creeping thing that creeps on the earth. Then, the creation of man in God's own image.
- **Day 7:** God rests from all the work that He has done.

Note: *Every time the Bible says, "And God said", something happened directly afterwards. This shows us the creative power of the spoken Word of God. It also shows us that God created everything by His speech. Every time God spoke, something was created and formed according to what He said.*

Genesis 2:1 – 25 (NKJV)

After the six-day creation period, the author reveals the layout of the garden of Eden — a place created and prepared by God in which He placed man to live. In the midst of the garden, we find two important trees to take note of that will define the very course of history — the tree of life and the tree of the knowledge of good and evil.

Here, God gives His first command to the man that if broken, there would be severe consequences. God said that man may freely eat of any tree found in the garden, except from the tree of the knowledge of good and evil. In the day that he shall eat of this tree, he shall surely die. The exemption — of course — also included the tree of life.

Note: *Until this point, Adam was alone with no helper comparable to him. God saw that it is not suitable for man to be alone. As a result, God caused a deep sleep to fall upon Adam, took one of Adam's ribs, closed his wound, and from his rib — God formed a woman.*

2. **The Fall**
   Genesis 3:1 – 24 (NKJV)

Through the following verses, we discover how evil came into the world. Here, the author reveals the serpent for the first time, exposing his deceptive, false, and rebellious nature. Therefore the devil (satan,) who disguised himself as a serpent, was later referred to as "that old serpent", as seen in the book of **Revelation 12:9; 20:2**.

The following events caused significant damage to the relationship between God and man, man and nature and man and man, which was once glorious. The serpent deceived the woman by doubting in God's word, so that she eats of the forbidden tree of the knowledge of good and evil.

35

After the woman ate from the tree, she also gave some of the fruit to her husband to eat. The scripture records that both their eyes were opened.

The Bible further reveals the consequences that were unlocked due to their disobedience to the Word of God. As a result, God cursed the serpent, multiplied the sorrow and conception of the woman, cursed the ground for man's sake, and said that in toil, he shall now eat of it, all the days of his life.

As a direct result of sin, death came in, and man could no longer live forever. So there will come a time when every man will return to the dust they came from. God then drove Adam and Eve out from the garden of Eden, placing two Cherubims at the garden entrance preventing man from gaining access to the tree of life, which will only later on become available again through God's redemption in Christ.

3. The Flood
Genesis 4 – 10 (NKJV)

Through the following chapters, we unravel the events leading up to Noah's flood. After Adam and Eve were driven out from the garden of Eden, he knew his wife, and she conceived and bore Cain and Abel.

Here we find the first recorded murder in the Bible when Cain and Abel brought offerings unto God. The Bible states that God accepted Abel's offering but not Cain's.

Cain's anger and jealousy consumed him so much that it drove him to the point where he murdered his brother, Abel. Yet again, an action was taken that unlocked another severe consequence as God then drove Cain out, marking him as a fugitive and vagabond.

Adam then knew his wife again, and she bore him yet another son named Seth. From here, we can follow the descendants of Adam right through to Noah and his three sons, Shem, Ham and Japheth.

At this stage, man began to multiply greatly upon the face of the earth. Many daughters were born unto man, leaving a world that no longer worshipped the Lord God Almighty. The sons of God then saw the daughters of men and took them for wives.

The events that follow have devastating results, as we see in:

Genesis 6:4 – 6 (NKJV)

It is here that God decided to destroy both man and beast, every creeping thing and birds of the air. God chose to spare only Noah and his family, as he had found grace in the sight of God. The reason for Noah having found grace in the sight of God is worth taking note of as the Bible states that Noah was a just man — who was perfect in his generations and that he *walked* with God.

Now because all flesh was corrupt and violence was increasing upon the earth, God came unto Noah, instructing him to build an ark — even revealing to him the exact design of the ark. God told Noah that He will send a flood to remove all wickedness from the face of the earth.

When the rain started, God instructed Noah to go into the Ark - with his wife, sons, and their wives – together with seven of every clean animal, male and female, two of each animal that is unclean, male and female, seven of each type of bird, male and female, and of every creeping thing that creeps on the earth. This was to keep the species alive on the earth after the flood, which was to last for forty days and forty nights. After all the animals had entered the Ark according to God's instruction, God then shut the door and caused the rain to begin.

And so, the Bible records that the entire face of the earth was covered with water. All flesh that had breath in them — of both man and animals alike - which remained upon the earth died.

After forty days and forty nights, the rain stopped and God caused a strong wind to pass over the earth, causing the water to subside.

Once all the water subsided, the Ark rested on the mountains of Ararat, upon which God instructed Noah and his family and all the living creatures to come out of the Ark. Then, God commanded them to be fruitful and multiply on the earth again.

Noah then built an altar to the Lord and made burned sacrifices in this place. The Bible says that the Lord smelled a soothing aroma and said in His heart:

"I will never again curse the ground for man's sake, although the imagination of man's heart is evil from his youth; nor will I again destroy every living thing as I have done."

Genesis 8:21 (NKJV)

And so, God established the following covenant with creation, which we read in the scripture referenced below.

Genesis 9:8 – 13 (NKJV)

Noah then became a farmer, where he planted a vineyard. The Bible then records yet another event with devasting results.

Noah drank of the wine of the vineyard and became drunk and uncovered in his tent. The Bible stated that Ham saw the nakedness of his father and exposed his father to his other two brothers. Shem and Japheth — refusing to look at their father's nakedness out of the pureness of their hearts — took a garment, placed the garment upon their shoulders and walked backwards towards their father to cover his nakedness.

When Noah woke up, he knew what his son Ham had done and so cursed him, saying that he will be a servant of servants to his brothers. It is here that Canaan was born, as the Bible shows us that Ham is the father of Canaan. Therefore, we read that this word came to fulfilment when the Israelites later entered the promised land, subduing all the inhabitants of the land.

4. The Tower of Babel

This is an event that clearly expresses the power of unity and imagination. The event also shows the birth of different languages and nations.

At this stage, man greatly multiplied upon the face of the earth, and the whole earth was of one language and one speech. From the pride of their hearts, the people decided to build a city and a tower that would reach the heavens.

Now the Bible says that the Lord came down and saw the city and tower that the sons of men had built and said:

"... Behold, the people is one, and they have all one language; and this they begin to do: and now nothing will be restrained from them, which they have imagined to do."

Genesis 11:6 (KJV)

God then decided to go down and confuse their language so they could no longer understand each other. As a result, they could no longer build the city and the tower. After that, we read that the people were scattered abroad over the face of all the earth.

From this point, we follow Shem's descendants to Abram, bringing us to the first major life — the life of Abraham.

**HIGHLIGHTED LIVES IN GENESIS:
CHAPTER 12 – CHAPTER 50:**

1. **Abraham**
   Genesis 12 – 22 (NKJV)

Genesis 12 opens up by revealing a previous conversation that the Lord had with Abraham, as seen in **Acts 7:2**, meaning that God is repeating His original command, but this time revealing more detail concerning that initial conversation.

Here, we read that God makes a promise unto Abram. A promise that carries a sevenfold blessing:

a. I will make you a great nation.
b. I will bless you.
c. I will make your name great.

    d.   You shall be a blessing.

    e.   I will bless those who bless you.

    f.   I will curse those who curse you.

    g.   In you, all the families of the earth shall be blessed.

Abram then took his wife Sarai, Lot, his brother's son, and all their possession and departed to the land of Canaan.

In Canaan, the Lord appeared unto Abram for the second time, stating that He will give his descendants the land. God continued to bless Abram in all his ways until he grew very rich in livestock, silver, and gold.

Now Lot also had flocks, herds, and tents, and their possessions were so great that the land could not support them both. This caused much strife between Abram's herdsmen and Lot's herdsmen. And so, Abram suggested that Lot take all his possessions and depart to a place of his choice. At that, he decided to go to Sodom and Gomorrah, which were well watered. However, the men of the city of Sodom were wicked and sinful against the Lord. This is the same city that God later destroys (in **Genesis 19**) because of its great wickedness and sin.

After Lot departed from Abram, the Lord appeared to him for the third time, telling him to lift his eyes and look northward, southward, eastward, and westward. God said that as far as he could see, God would give unto his descendants forever. This is when God further instructed him to walk in the land - through its length and width — for where his feet touch the ground, God will give it unto him and his descendants.

Later Sodom and Gomorrah went to war, and it came to Abram's attention that Lot had been taken captive. At this, Abram took three hundred and eighteen armed servants and went in pursuit of Lot to save him.

Abram managed to overtake and overthrow the army who took Lot captive and so brought back all the goods — including Lot.

It is after this rescue mission that tithing is mentioned for the first time in the Bible. Abram met Melchizedek, king of Salem, who represented the personage of the Lord Jesus Christ – as better explained in **Hebrews 7**. Melchizedek blessed Abram, and the Bible says that Abram gave unto him a tithe of all. **Genesis 14:18 – 20**

The word of the Lord then came unto Abram for the fourth time, recorded in the Bible saying, *"Fear not, I am your shield and exceeding great reward"*. At this stage, Abram started to plead with God regarding his offspring. At this, God reaffirmed His promise by instructing Abram to go outside and see if he could count the stars because so shall his descendants be.

The Bible then says something relating to Abrams's response that is worth taking note of, stating,

> *"And he believed in the Lord, and He accounted it to him for righteousness"*

> **Genesis 15:6 (NKJV)**

God then established his covenant with Abram, changing his name from Abram to Abraham, meaning *"father of many nations"*.

At one hundred years old, God fulfilled His promise to Abraham! A son was born unto him, and they named him Isaac.

After waiting so long for this promise to be fulfilled, Abraham had to pass the greatest test of faith when God instructed him to take his only son and offer him as a burnt sacrifice.

Abraham chose to be obedient to the voice of God, and just before slaying his only son, an angel of the Lord called out from Heaven, commanding him not to lay a hand on his son.

This was proof that Abraham truly feared the Lord. As a result of his obedience and willingness, God responded with a very powerful blessing, as seen in:

Genesis 22:11 – 18 (NKJV)

2. **Isaac:**
   Genesis 24 – 27

When Abraham was well-aged, he sent one of his eldest servants to go to his country and choose a wife for Isaac. The servant chose Rebekah for Isaac, whom he married at the age of forty.

After being married to Isaac for many years, Rebekah still hadn't given Isaac any children, as she was barren. Isaac pleaded with the Lord concerning Rebekah that she would be able to conceive.

Rebekah then gave birth to two boys, Esau and Jacob. The Bible states that Isaac loved Esau, but Rebekah loved Jacob.

The Conspiracy

When Isaac was old and blind, he requested for his son Esau to go hunt game and prepare venison, such as he loved, so that he could eat and then bless him.

Rebekah overheard the conversation between Isaac and Esau. She then quickly instructed her son, Jacob — Esau's brother — to take two choice kids of goats so that she could make savoury food for Isaac.

Rebekah further instructed Jacob to clothe himself with his brother Esau's clothing, and to cover his hands and neck with the skins of the goats, so that Isaac would not be able to tell that it was Jacob. Isaac would be led to believe that it was Esau, as Esau was a hairy man. And so, Jacob took the food to Isaac, deceiving his father by disguising himself as his brother.

Isaac then blessed Jacob, thinking it was Esau. Thus, the Bible records that Jacob stole Esau's blessing, and Jacob became Isaac's primary heir, placing Esau in an inferior position.

When Esau realised what had happened, he hated Jacob and devised in his heart to kill him after the mourning of their father.

3. **Jacob:**
   Genesis 27 – 36

As a plan to escape Esau's wrath, Jacob departed to his father's home country in Haran to find a wife. It is here that Jacob meets Laban, his mother's brother. Jacob requested to marry Laban's younger daughter, Rachel. Jacob agreed to serve Laban for seven years to be given Rachel in marriage. After seven years of service, Laban deceived Jacob and gave Jacob his elder daughter, Leah.

Jacob then served Laban for another seven years to receive Rachel. After seven years, Rachel was finally given to him.

After working twenty years for his uncle, Jacob finally made his way back home to his father, Isaac. On the journey back home, Jacob encountered God and wrestled with Him through the night. Here, God blessed Jacob and changed his name from Jacob to Israel.

Jacob reconciled with his brother, Esau, and together they buried their father, Isaac.

Unto Jacob was born Rueben, Simeon, Levi, Judah, Dan, Naphtali, Gad, Asher, Issachar, Zebulun, Joseph, and Benjamin. The same became the twelve tribes of Israel.

4. **Joseph:**
   Genesis 37 – 50

Joseph was Jacob's eleventh son, Jacob's first son from his favoured wife, Rachel. The Bible also reveals that Jacob loved Joseph more than his other sons, as he was born to him in his old age. So, the Bible records that Jacob made a tunic of many colours for his son, Joseph.

The fact that Jacob loved Joseph more than his other sons caused them to harbour great jealousy and hatred in their hearts towards Joseph. And so, to fuel the hatred of his brothers even more, Joseph would share his dreams with them, indicating that one day he would rule over them.

Their anger and hatred caused them to conspire against Joseph, whom they then planned to kill in the wilderness. Rueben objected to the murder and suggested that they only cast him into a nearby pit with the intent to save him later.

In Reuben's absence, Judah suggested to selling Joseph into slavery. They then took Joseph's robe, tore it, and dipped it in blood so that it would appear as if he had been eaten by a wild animal.

The merchants then sold Joseph to Potiphar, a high-ranking officer in Egypt. Here, Joseph became the supervisor over Potiphar's household.

Joseph continued to have favour with Potiphar and was very successful until Potiphar's wife tried to seduce him.

Out of honour for Potiphar and out of the purity of his heart, being in right standing with God, Joseph refused all her attempts to be with him. One day, she caught Joseph by his garments, coming unto him again, and so he was forced to run away, leaving his garments behind.

Because of Joseph's continual refusal and denial of her proposition, she became angry and accused him of rape, using the garment that Joseph left behind as evidence.

As a result, Joseph was cast into jail. But God continued to show him favour and success. In prison, he interpreted two dreams – a dream of the cup bearer and a dream of the baker, of which both came to pass shortly after.

Two years after the cupbearer was released, Pharaoh had disturbing dreams that needed interpretation. The cupbearer remembered Joseph and his gift to interpret dreams. Immediately, Pharaoh called for Joseph.

Joseph accurately interpreted Pharaoh's dreams, and with great wisdom, he advised Pharaoh on how to deal with the seven years of plenty and seven years of famine.

Because of his great wisdom, Joseph was instated as ruler over Egypt — second to the king.

When the seven years of famine struck the land, Israel sent his sons to Egypt to buy grain, where Joseph was then reunited with his brothers. Joseph showed them mercy, forgiving them for what they had done to him, responding in a way that is well worth taking note of as he said to his brothers not to be angry or grieved because they sold him but that it was God that sent him beforehand, to preserve the way for them.

Joseph then requested that his brothers bring his father, Jacob, and the remainder of his household to come and live in Egypt.

And so, in Egypt, Jacob's descendants lived for 400 years until the time of Moses.

PROPHETIC DECLARATIONS:

1. **Genesis 1:26 — 27 (NKJV)**

²⁶ Then God said, "Let Us make man in Our image, according to Our likeness; let them have dominion over the fish of the sea, over the birds of the air, and over the cattle, over all the earth and over every creeping thing that creeps on the earth."

I declare and decree in the name of Jesus that whatever atmosphere I enter and wherever my feet touch the ground, that ground and atmosphere will become subject to me as it recognises the authority of God upon my life.

2. **Genesis 12:2 — 3 (NKJV)**

² I will make you a great nation; I will bless you
And make your name great; And you shall be a blessing.
³ I will bless those who bless you, And I will curse him who curses you; And in you all the families of the earth shall be blessed."

I declare and decree that by faith, I reach into eternity and receive every blessing that God has prepared for me and call it into fruition right now in Jesus' name.

NOTES

Book of **Exodus**

"The Birth of a Nation"

Exodus is the second book written by Moses and means "exit" or "departure". The book of Exodus is foundational to the understanding of God and the way that He reveals His Name, His attributes, His redemption, His laws, and how to worship Him.

Exodus is a continuation of Genesis, approximately four hundred years after Joseph. There is a period of two hundred years from the death of Joseph to the rise of a new king who knew not Joseph. This new king made the lives of the Israelites bitter with bondage, oppressing them as slaves.

It is, however, reassuring to know that God remembers and is concerned about His people, as revealed through this book. The book of Exodus reveals the power of standing in covenant with the true living God, and the theology of salvation in God is greatly amplified throughout this book.

God reveals Himself as a fearless Warrior fighting for His chosen people. It shows God redeeming them from the hands of their oppressor by performing His mighty signs, miracles, and wonders, restoring Israel and fulfilling the covenant He made with His servants — Abraham, Isaac and Jacob. This was done through a mediator, Moses, who led them to the promised land.

The book of Exodus can be divided into the following four major events:

1. **Oppression of Israel and the birth of Moses: Exodus 1– 6**
2. **The Redemption of a Nation: Exodus 7 – 12**
3. **The Exodus: Exodus 13 – 18**
4. **New Law and Worship Instructions: Exodus 19 – 40**

HIGHLIGHTED EVENTS IN EXODUS

1. **Oppression of Israel and the Birth of Moses**
    Exodus 1– 6 (NKJV)

The Bible says that the children of Israel were fruitful and increased abundantly. Scripture tells us that they multiplied and grew exceedingly mighty so that the land was filled with them.
Exodus 1:7

A new king arose during this time over Egypt that did not know Joseph and was greatly troubled by the multitudes of the Israelites. He feared that in the event of war, they might turn against them and leave the land.

The king then set taskmasters over the Israelites, afflicting them with burdens and hard labour. But they continued to grow and multiply no matter how much they were afflicted.

As a result, the king of Egypt ordered the midwives of the Hebrew women to kill any newborn child if it was a son but to spare the child if it was a daughter. The midwives, being God-fearing women, decided to go against the king's orders. They spared all the male children using the excuse that the Hebrew women gave birth before they could get to them. God dealt well with the midwives because of their faithfulness, providing them with households, and so the Israelites continued to grow mightily.

Pharaoh — now becoming more disturbed by the matter — ordered his people, commanding them to cast every son being born into the river and to spare only the daughters.

It was during this distressful time that Moses was born and so also escaped death, being hidden by his mother from the Egyptians for three months.

When they could no longer hide him, his mother took a basket made of bulrushes, dipped in asphalt and pitch, placed the child in it and laid him in the reeds by the riverbanks.

God, being a Master-Strategist, intervened. We see in the events that followed how God's grand design unfolded. Pharaoh's daughter found the baby boy in the river and decided to keep him as one of her own. She named him Moses, and so Moses grew up in the Egyptian palace.

When Moses was fully grown, he saw an Egyptian beating one of his Hebrew brethren. He looked around to ensure no one was looking, and he killed the Egyptian, hiding him in the sand. When Pharaoh gained knowledge of the event, Moses's life was in danger yet again, as Pharaoh sought to kill him.

Moses fled for his life from Egypt and dwelt in the land of Midian. Here, Moses meets his wife Zipporah and tends to Jethro's flock.

The Burning Bush
Exodus 3

While tending to the flock, an Angel of the Lord appeared to Moses in a flame of fire from the midst of a bush. Here, Moses looked closely and noted something out of the ordinary: the bush was burning with fire but was not consumed.

The Bible says that Moses stopped and decided to go and take a look at this incredible sight, not knowing that he was about to encounter the true living God. It is here that God called Moses from the bush, commanding him to remove his sandals, for the place upon which he stood was Holy ground.

God then revealed himself unto Moses as the Great I Am, the Lord God of his fathers — Abraham, Isaac, and Jacob. God revealed to Moses His plans to deliver His people from the hands of the Egyptians and to bring them to a land overflowing with milk and honey. God commanded Moses to go and tell Pharaoh to let His people go.

Moses was reluctant at first and gave God excuses as to why he could not perform this great task. God reassured Moses that He will be with him no matter what challenges he faced. God performed two signs as proof that He will be with Moses, guiding him through the process.

These signs were to be used when he met Pharaoh as proof that he was sent by the living God.

First Sign:

God told Moses to throw the rod in his hand on the ground, which turned into a serpent. When he picked the serpent up, the serpent turned back into a rod.

Second Sign:

God instructed Moses to place his hand in his bosom and take it out again. When he took his hand out, it was leprous. God then instructed him to put his hand back into his bosom, and when he took it out the second time, his hand was completely healed.

Third Sign:

This sign was only given as an instruction from God if Pharaoh refused to believe the first two signs. God instructed Moses to take water from the river and pour it on dry ground, and then the water would turn to blood.

So, God revealed to Moses that through him, He will stretch out His hand and strike Egypt with all His wonders. God said that after this, Pharaoh would let His people go.

2. **The Redemption of a Nation**
   Exodus 7 – 12 (NKJV)

After numerous attempts to confront Pharaoh to let God's people go and performing the signs given by God, Pharaoh still hardened his heart and did not heed to their demands, as the Lord had said.

The Ten Plagues

Pharaoh's hardened heart, refusing to listen to God, unlocked some of the greatest wonders recorded in the Word of God to go into operation. God stretched forth His hand against all of Egypt, striking them with the following ten plagues.

a. First Plague: Water into Blood – **Exodus 7:14 – 25**
b. Second Plague: Frogs – **Exodus 8:1 – 15**
c. Third Plague: Lice – **Exodus 8:16 – 19**
d. Fourth Plague: Flies – **Exodus 8:20 – 32**
e. Fifth Plague: Livestock Diseased – **Exodus 9:1 – 7**
f. Sixth Plague: Boils – **Exodus 9:8 – 12**
g. Seventh Plague: Hail – **Exodus 9:13 – 35**
h. Eighth Plague: Locusts – **Exodus 10:1 – 20**
i. Ninth Plague: Darkness – **Exodus 10:21 – 29**
j. Tenth Plague: The Passover and Death of the Firstborn – **Exodus 11 & 12:1 – 30**

The Passover

The Lord, who was about to perform His last wonder before Israel's redemption, came to Moses announcing that at midnight, He will go through all of Egypt and all the firstborn in the land shall die. This would include all from the firstborn of Pharaoh, to the firstborn of the female servants, to the firstborn of all the animals.

God then gave Moses instructions to follow concerning the children of Israel. This was so He would pass over them and not strike them down when He passed through the land.

Passover Instructions

- Every household was to choose a lamb, known as the Passover lamb.
- The lambs were to be slain at an elected time, and blood was to be placed on the two doorposts and lintel of every house.
- Every household was to eat its flesh, roasted in the fire, with unleavened bread and bitter herbs.
- They were not allowed to eat it raw or boiled.
- Nothing was to remain until morning, and whatever remained must be burned with fire.
- It was to be eaten with a belt around their waist, sandals on their feet, and a staff in their hand.

When God would pass through the land of Egypt, He would strike all the firstborn of the land, so the blood on the doorposts would be a sign for God to pass over that house.

And so it came to pass that the Lord struck all the firstborn of the land of Egypt, passing only over the houses with blood on the doorposts. So, Pharaoh arose to a great cry that went throughout the land. There was not a house from all his servants and of all the Egyptians where there was not one found dead.

Pharaoh finally agreed to release the children of Israel. That night, the children of Israel went to bed as slaves but woke up being set free.

3. The Exodus
Exodus 13 – 18 (NKJV)

And so, the Israelites embarked on a journey like none other, making their way to the promised land, led by a divine navigation system. God went before them by day in a pillar of cloud and by night in a pillar of fire.

Once again, God hardened Pharaoh's heart. With bitterness, hatred, and anger, he pursued after the children of Israel in the wilderness with all his horses and chariots, seeking to kill them. At the red sea, the Egyptian armies managed to overtake the children of Israel, who now found themselves entrapped between the red sea and the Egyptian armies.

Here the children of Israel began to fear for their lives. They started to murmur and complain, with an unbelieving nature showing a characteristic of doubt and disbelief in God. They were a stiff-necked people, quickly forgetting all the powerful signs, miracles and wonders that God had performed before their eyes, continually delivering them from the hands of their oppressors.

Once again, God revealed His mighty power to them by instructing Moses to stretch forth his hand over the sea. God then caused a strong east wind to divided the waters, making a path of dry land through the sea.

And so, the children of Israel passed through the red sea with a wall of water on their right and left, with the Egyptian armies pursuing them. Once all the Israelites made their way to the other side of the sea, Moses stretched forth his hand according to God's instruction, causing the waters to enclose upon the Egyptian armies, destroying them.

And so, the Lord overthrew the Egyptians amid the sea. Israel — being stiff-necked — continued to murmur and complain as God led them through the wilderness to the promised land while still performing many mighty wonders.

4. New Law and Instructions for Worship
Exodus 19 – 40 (NKJV)

The Israelites continued their journey until they came to Mount Sinai. It is here on Mount Sinai that Moses spent forty days and forty nights in the manifest presence of God. Here was where he received the ten commandments, with divine laws to be followed by the children of Israel as God's chosen people.

10 Commandments: Exodus 20:1 – 17

a. You shall have no other gods before Me.
b. You shall not make idols.
c. You shall not take the name of your Lord God in vain.
d. Six days you shall do labour, but on the seventh, you shall rest. It is the Sabbath of the Lord your God.
e. Honour your father and mother.
f. You shall not murder.
g. You shall not commit adultery.
h. You shall not steal.
i. You shall not bear false witness against your neighbour.
j. You shall not covet.

Laws

a. Law concerning Servants – **Exodus 21:1 – 11**
b. Law concerning Violence – **Exodus 21:12 – 27**

  c. Animal Control Laws – **Exodus 21:28 – 36**
  d. Responsibility for Property – **Exodus 22:1 – 15**
  e. Moral and Ceremonial Principles – **Exodus 22:16 – 31**
  f. Justice for All – **Exodus 23:1 – 9**
  g. The Law of Sabbaths – **Exodus 23:10 – 19**

Moses then further gave the Israelites these instructions concerning the design and layout of the tabernacle, the tent where the priests will meet with God on behalf of Israel, the ark of the covenant and the appointment of priests and instructions concerning worship.

PROPHETIC DECLARATIONS:

0Exodus 14:24 — 25 (NKJV)

[24] Now it came to pass, in the morning watch, that the Lord looked down upon the army of the Egyptians through the pillar of fire and cloud, and He troubled the army of the Egyptians. 25 And He took off their chariot wheels, so that they drove them with difficulty; and the Egyptians said, "Let us flee from the face of Israel, for the Lord fights for them against the Egyptians."

I declare and decree that according to Exodus, every plan of the enemy formed against me shall be dismantled and be taken apart. It shall not come nigh my dwelling place but will flee into every direction. I call forth the fire of God against every plan, weapon, device, and assignment against me, my family, and my ministry to be consumed, devoured and disintegrated in the name of Jesus.

NOTES

NOTES

Book of **Leviticus**

"The Law of a Nation"

Leviticus is the third book written by Moses and means "relating to the Levites".

The book of Leviticus does not only focus on the special duties of the Levites, but it was also given this name because the basis of the book centres around the worship at the tabernacle, which the Levitical priests conducted.

Leviticus was written so that the Israelites could better understand the infinite holiness of God, which also forms the key thought of this book. Leviticus reflects spiritual holiness as physical perfection.

God's desire for Israel is for them to act in a holy manner, as after the covenant at Mount Sinai, Israel became the representation of God's Holy Kingdom here on earth.

To accomplish this task, God left them with many instructions to carry out. In so doing, they were established as God's Holy people.

According to all that God had commanded Moses, he began to instruct the Levitical priests on how they were to conduct offerings, ceremonies, and celebrations.

The word "Holy" is mentioned more in this book than in any other book of the Bible. Therefore, special attention was given to Israel's religious rituals to teach them in holiness.

1. **Leviticus 1 – 7:** Through these scripture passages, Moses gives explicit instruction concerning the altar of sacrifice and different offerings to be made to God.

2. **Leviticus 8 – 10:** Moses ordains his brother Aaron, and their sons, as priests to oversee, attend to, and serve in the tabernacle. Moses also gives clear instructions concerning the Levitical priesthood.

3. **Leviticus 11 – 15:** God's purpose with these chapters is to protect Israel from various diseases and illnesses, and to give clear instructions on how to deal with food, unclean animals, birth, sicknesses, infected clothing, infected households, dead bodies, and many more — all that are sources of different illnesses and diseases.

4. **Leviticus 16:** Moses gives clear instructions on how the High Priests were to clean and prepare themselves ceremonially to meet with God. This was known as the day of atonement that took place once every year, where the High Priest would go into the Holy of Holies and offer sacrifices unto God for sins on behalf of Israel.

5. **Leviticus 17 – 27:** These chapters deal mainly with the moral laws necessary to live holy lives. These included sexual morality, ceremonial laws, penalties for breaking the law, re ligious festivals and celebrations, the Sabbath year, and the year of Jubilee.

PROPHETIC DECLARATIONS:

1. Leviticus 19:18 (NKJV)

[18] **"You shall not take vengeance, nor bear any grudge against the children of your people, but you shall love your neighbor as yourself: I am the Lord."**

I declare and decree according to the commandment of God that His true love, compassion, mercy and grace shall flow through my life, continually changing those around me. I declare to reflect nothing but the perfect and flawless character, likeness, and image of Christ and, in doing so, to continually establish the authority of God here on earth.

NOTES

NOTES

Book of **Numbers**

"The Wilderness Wanderings"

Numbers is the fourth book written by Moses and is a record showing Israel's preparation to enter the promised land. It reveals God as a Master-Organiser and a God of order, as He structured a crowd of more than two million people.

Numbers began where God assembled Israel into military camps. After the events at Sinai, Israel marched as God's conquering army with God as their Head, ready to establish His Kingdom in the promised land.

This book further reveals the consequences of Israel's disobedience, rebellion, murmuring, and complaining — especially towards God — when they breached covenant by refusing to enter Canaan. However, despite their disobedience, God remained faithful to His Word concerning His chosen people.

Note: *The events in Leviticus took place over a period of one month, and therefore, Numbers is simply a continuation of where Leviticus left off.*

The book can be divided into three sections:

1. The Old Generation: Numbers 1 – 14

The focus point of this section is mainly on the old generation and the various preparations, ceremonies and laws that God gave them.

The first four chapters reveal three important groups of people:

a. Warriors: Numbers 2

In Chapter one, the first census was taken up. In Chapter two, the people were being prepared and arranged into tribes; out of the tribes, all able men were numbered for warfare.

b. Priests: Numbers 3

In the first part of this chapter, Moses anointed Aaron and his sons as priests, according to God's instruction.

c. Levites: Numbers 3 & 4

In the second part of this chapter, and continuing into chapter four, God numbered and prepared the Levites for service in the tabernacle.

Note: *This is very similar to the lives of believers - even today! The first group speak about warfare, the second group speaks about worshippers, and the last group speaks about service. We understand that you cannot have worship without warfare, or warfare without worship, or worship and warfare without service. As a believer, you need a perfect balance of the three categories in your life.*

2. The Wanderings: Numbers 15 – 20

This section covers a period of thirty-eight years, where the Israelites wandered in the wilderness because of their unbelieving, rebellious hearts.

3. The New Generation: Numbers 21 – 36

After forty years in the wilderness, a new generation finally rose who entered the promised land, according to God's Word.

HIGHLIGHTED EVENTS IN NUMBERS

Murmuring of the Israelites
Numbers 11:1 – 3 (NKJV)

After the Israelites had done all the preparations and the tribes had been structured, each with their specific duties, it seemed that Israel was now ready and equipped to advance towards the promised land, as found at the end of **chapter ten**.

Whenever God's presence lifted from the tabernacle, it was a sign for Israel to pack up according to the instructions given by God and to start marching. When His presence came down upon the tabernacle, there they were to set up camp again and rest.

The people regressed to their disloyal complaints three days after departing from Sinai. These were the same complaints they had expressed a year earlier, flaring up only three days after their deliverance at the Red Sea.

As a result, the Lord's anger burned against their disloyal hearts and rebellious attitudes, consuming some of them in the uttermost parts of the camps. The people cried out to Moses once again. Then he prayed to God, and the fire was quenched.

At this stage, Moses became so discouraged and frustrated with the people's continual complaints and disobedience that he complained to God, saying it would be better to kill him than deal with their wretchedness.

God then gave Moses a clear strategy. He instructed Moses to choose seventy elders, upon which God then took of the Spirit upon Moses and placed it upon them to help Moses carry the burden of the people.

Murmuring of Aaron and Miriam
Numbers 12:1 – 16 (NKJV)

In this Chapter, God revealed the dangers of familiarity and speaking against God's anointed, as seen when Aaron and Miriam spoke against Moses, that he was married to an Ethiopian woman. They further voiced their disagreements towards Moses, saying that he was not the only one that could hear from God. They stated that they could also hear, upon which the Bible says that the Lord heard them.

Note: *Moses did not marry a second time. This was still the same wife that Aaron and Miriam all of a sudden had a problem with. Moses, however, did not react nor respond to their accusations. Instead, God intervened and stood up for him.*

69

Aaron and Miriam were about to experience the devastating results of their actions as God summoned Moses, Aaron and Miriam to come before the tabernacle of meeting, saying:

Read Genesis 12:6 – 8 (NKJV)

And so the anger of the Lord was aroused against Aaron and Miriam, so that Miriam became instantly leprous upon which Aaron repented and asked for forgiveness, pleading for Miriam to be healed.

Moses then brought Aaron's request before the Lord that instructed Miriam to be exiled from the camps for seven days and that after the seven days, she is to return and then only can Israel advance.

Murmuring of the Spies Sent Into Canaan
Numbers 13 & 14 (NKJV)

Israel now stood on the verge of their breakthrough, about to enter the promised land, yet they delayed their promise again because of their unbelieving and rebellious hearts.

Upon Moses's instruction, twelve spies were sent into the land of Canaan — a leader from each tribe — to see the land's condition.

Ten of the twelve spies came back with a negative and bad report and, in doing so, negatively influenced the children of Israel. This caused a death sentence to come upon them after hearing that the land is indeed fruitful but that the land devours its inhabitants. As a result, Israel will not be able to take it because the people who occupy the land are stronger than them. They further revealed that their cities were fortified and very large and that they saw giants in the land, and when they saw them, they looked like grasshoppers in their own sight. So, the Bible says that so they became in their enemy's sight.

Two spies, Joshua and Caleb, came back with an excellent report. They tried to persuade the people not to lose hope but to take courage, believe in God and keep faith in His Word. They reminded the people that He has said that He will go before them and drive out the inhabitants of the land before their very eyes. They further tried to persuade and encourage the people to go and take the land immediately and not to wait, for God is with them. They reminded the people that God had already given the land into their hands. Upon hearing these things, the people wanted to stone Joshua and Caleb.

At this, the glory of the Lord appeared on the tabernacle before all of Israel, where God spoke to Moses. God was planning to kill the entire nation because of their unbelieving hearts. God further states that He will start over with Moses and that He will make of him a nation mightier than they. Moses then quickly pleads with God not to go ahead with the plan for His name's sake.

It is interesting to see that God heeded to Moses's plea, but their actions still came with a devastating price.

God revealed that this old generation would not go into the promised land but would die in the wilderness. And that once this generation had been phased out, their children — a new generation — shall then rise and go into the promised land. The only two exempts from this death sentence were Joshua and Caleb, who, with the new generation, entered into the promised land.

Numbers ends with Joshua stepping in as the successor of Moses to lead the new generation into the promised land.

Moses left a new generation with final instructions from God on how Israel was to advance into the land and take it. He ended with how the land of Canaan was to be divided amongst the twelve tribes and then appointed leaders to divide the land.

PROPHETIC DECLARATIONS:

1. Numbers 6:24 – 26 (NKJV)

[24]**"The Lord bless you and keep you;**
[25] **The Lord make His face shine upon you, And be gracious to you;**
[26] **The Lord lift up His countenance upon you, And give you peace."**

I declare and decree the blessings of God shall rest upon me all the days of my life. I declare and decree that His face shall always be upon me and that I will always find favour in the eyes of God. I declare and decree that the peace of God shall surround me on every side and that my family and I will know no harm for as long as we live in Jesus mighty name.

NOTES

Book of **Deuteronomy**

"The Laws Reviewed"

Deuteronomy concludes the last book written by Moses and means "The Second Law". Moses wrote this book to remind the children of Israel of everything God had done for them and to remind them of all the laws they were to follow as instructed by God. Therefore, Moses wrote this to reiterate the law a second time.

The book expressed the last three sermons of Moses and targeted the new generation who entered the promised land.

The book can be divided into three sections:

1. **The First Sermon: Deuteronomy 1 – 4**
2. **The Second Sermon: Deuteronomy 4 – 26**
3. **The Third Sermon: Deuteronomy 27 – 34**

Deuteronomy can be divided into two main parts:

Part 1: Deuteronomy 1 – 11

These chapters focus on past events, as the Israelites reflected on everything that had happened so as not to make the same mistakes. Here Moses taught the new generation essential principles that they would need to understand to possess the land of Canaan.

Two important principles that God teaches this new generation to enter the promised land are the power of words and the power of imagination.

At the end of **Deuteronomy 2:24 – 25**, God commanded them to advance because He had *already* given Sihon and his land into their hands. God further assured them that this would be the beginning of where He would set the fear of them upon the nations under the whole heaven, that shall hear the report of them and so tremble, and be in anguish, because of them.

God, being faithful to His Word, delivered Sihon, a powerful king, into Israel's hand.

Then a second time in **Deuteronomy 3:2 – 3**, they went up to Bashan, facing Og king of Bashan, where the Lord again assured them that He had *already* delivered this king and his land into their hands. According to the word of the Lord, Israel defeated king Og and all his people, according to all that God has said.

Note: *Every time God spoke to them, it was in the past tense, saying that He had already given them power over. This was to encourage them, but more importantly, to develop their imagination. God knew that if they could see it, they would be able to accomplish it. The right frame of mind would also cause them to speak the right words.*

Part 2: Deuteronomy 12 – 34

These chapters focus on what God still had in store for Israel, giving certain precautions and warnings. Moses further reviewed specific laws, feasts, judges to be appointed, property boundaries, principles concerning warfare, and offerings of first fruits and tithe.

In Deuteronomy 28, Moses revealed two fundamental categories that are applicable even today:

    a. **Blessings of Obedience: Deuteronomy 28:1 – 14 (NKJV)**
    b. **Curses of Disobedience: Deuteronomy 28:15 – 68 (NKJV)**

The book of Deuteronomy ends with Moses announcing his successor, Joshua, who would lead the new generation into the promised land. He then released a final blessing over Israel before going to Mount Nebo, where he then passed on.

PROPHETIC DECLARATIONS:

1. **Deuteronomy 20:4 (NKJV)**

[4] **"for the Lord your God is He who goes with you, to fight for you against your enemies, to save you."**

I bring every battle I am faced with under the authority of God and so declare in the name of Jesus that I stand victorious as God is the One that goes before me, fighting for me to give me victory.

2. **Deuteronomy 31:6 (NKJV)**

[6] **"Be strong and of good courage, do not fear nor be afraid of them; for the Lord your God, He is the One who goes with you. He will not leave you nor forsake you."**

I declare and decree in the name of Jesus that fear is not my portion. I take courage in the Lord God Almighty and choose to walk by faith and not by sight.

NOTES

NOTES

SECTION 3

THE HISTORY BOOKS

Table of Contents

Book of **Joshua**

"The Promised Land"

The book of Joshua is a direct continuation of Deuteronomy, as he is the successor that courageously followed through with the conquest into the land of Canaan.

Joshua comes from the Hebrew name "Yehoshua", meaning "the Lord saves". The same name in the Greek form, which is "Jesus", was given to Mary's first-born Son, who became the Saviour of the World.

Joshua was known for his unwavering trust in God. He was a warrior with incomparable courage who accomplished greatness in the face of adversity.

He lived through slavery in Egypt, where he saw and experienced firsthand the supernatural wonders of God, as God delivered them from the hands of their oppressors.

He stood witness as God divided the waters of the Red Sea, allowing them to pass through on dry ground. He saw God leading them by a pillar of cloud by day and a pillar of fire by night.

Joshua continued to live through many other signs, wonders and miracles as God continued to reveal His mighty power to Israel, even in the wilderness, where they wandered for forty years. Through all of Israel's rebellion and unbelief, Joshua continued to demonstrate his faith in the Lord. He picked up the leadership responsibility over the second generation, leading them through many victories as they conquered the land of Canaan, with God as their Head.

The book of Joshua reveals some of the greatest battles and victories recorded in the Bible and can be divided into three major events.

HIGHLIGHTED EVENTS IN JOSHUA:

1. **Entering the Promised Land:**
   Joshua 1 – 5

At this stage, the twelve tribes were still stationed on the east side of the Jordan River. Therefore, the first few chapters are focused on God commanding Israel to move forward and pass through the river Jordan on dry land to enter the land of Canaan. At this point, it seemed as though history was repeating itself.

Upon the instructions given by God, Joshua commanded the people to prepare and make provisions for themselves, as they would cross the river in three days.

While preparing to cross the River Jordan, Joshua decided to send out two spies to go and view the land — especially Jericho, as this was a highly fortified city. They were unmatched and unbeatable, as every army that had ever laid siege against it had failed. This was the perfect setting for God to reveal His mighty power once again!

   a. **Rahab and the Spies**
      Joshua 2 (NKJV)

News of Israel and of a God who delivers all their enemies into their hands with His mighty hand was now quickly spreading through all the nations. This left the surrounding nations on high alert — especially the inhabitants of Canaan.

Here, at Jericho, the spies came to a Harlot named Rahab, where they decided to lodge for the night. Some had recognised them as they came in and reported the matter to the king of Jericho, stating that they saw men from the children of Israel who came to search the country.

The king of Jericho immediately sent his soldiers to Rahab, commanding her to bring out the men that came to her, as they had come to spy out the land.

The way Rahab responded and the choices she made next changed the course of her life in a way she never expected. Her actions were so profound that she was found worthy of being recorded in the Word of God, along with some of the greatest generals of faith, documented in **Hebrews 11**.

Rahab decided to put her faith in the only true living God. She acted quickly and hid the men in her roof, explaining to the soldiers that the men they sought were, in fact, there but that she did not know where they came from. Rahab further explained that the men left just before the city's gates were shut for the night and might still overtake them if they hurried.

The soldiers left in pursuit of the spies. After they left, Rahab spoke to the men confessing that she knew that the Lord had given Israel the land, that the dread of them had come upon the inhabitants of Jericho.

Rahab explained how they heard of the Lord that dried up the Red Sea when they came out of Egypt and how they defeated the two kings of the Amorites on the other side of the Jordan — Sihon and Og — leaving them utterly destroyed.

As a result, their hearts melted with fear, leaving Jericho without any courage because of Israel, who admitted that the Lord their God alone was God in heaven above, and on the earth beneath.

Rahab further bargained with the spies, requesting that because she had shown them kindness, they would return the favour by sparing her and her family's lives from the wrath that was about to come on the city.

The spies agreed to Rahab's appeal, their lives for her life. If she would conceal their business, then it shall be when the Lord gives them the land they will indeed deal kindly and truly with her.

Rahab's house was on the city wall, so she let the spies down by a rope through her window. Before escaping, the spies gave Rahab critical information regarding Israel's return and the safeguard of both Rahab and her family.

They instructed Rahab to bind the same scarlet cord in the window that she used to let them down with as a sign that when Israel came into the land to take it, they would know to pass by this house because of the red cord in the window.

Rahab was further instructed to ensure that her father, mother, brothers, and all her father's household would be in her house upon their return because if any were caught outside, their blood would be upon their own hands.

The last instruction was that they would be free from their oath if she told anyone of their business. Once the spies left, Rahab immediately tied the cord in the window.

The two men returned to Joshua and told him all that had happened to them. They encouraged Joshua, saying that the Lord truly gave the land into their hands because all the country's inhabitants were sorely afraid and fainthearted because of them.

b. Crossing the Jordan
Joshua 3 (NKJV)

The next morning, Joshua assembled the armies to set out to Jordan where they stayed for the night. After three days, the officers went through the camp giving strict instructions concerning how they were to cross over the Jordan.

The Levites were to take the ark of the covenant, taking the lead, going before the people. The men were to set out the moment they saw the Levites carry the ark of the covenant of the Lord their God, making sure they kept a safe following distance between themselves and the ark.

The Lord revealed to Joshua that this would be the day He would exalt him in the sight of all of Israel and that the people would know He was with him, just as He was with Moses.

God further instructed Joshua to command the priests who bore the ark of the covenant that when they come to the edge of the water, to stand in the Jordan. It shall then be that when the soles of their feet touch the water of the Jordan, that the waters coming down from upstream shall be cut off and stand as a heap.

So, it was when they came to the Jordan that the priests went before the army, according to the instruction God had given to Joshua. The moment they dipped their feet in the water of the Jordan, the stream flowing down from upstream was cut off, thus allowing Israel to cross over on dry ground.

2. Possessing the Promised Land: Joshua 6 – 12

The book further reveals a series of victories where Israel overtook and conquered central, northern and southern Canaan, giving Israel complete control over the hill country and the Negev.

Joshua further proved to be a great military strategist in the way that he waged war, being led by God, and also an excellent statesman in the way he governed the tribes.

a. The destruction of Jericho Joshua 6 (NKJV)

At this stage, Jericho was under complete lockdown because of the children of Israel. No one came in, and no one went out.

As explained earlier, Jericho was one of the most fortified cities - superior in battle. Everyone that had ever laid siege against the city failed, yet they had found themselves in a position where they were afraid and without courage. For the first time, they were unsure of the outcome when faced with a nation being led by the only true living God.

How was a city to be taken that seemed to be impenetrable?

A challenge that God gladly rose to, as He gave Joshua the following instructions:

- God first spoke to Joshua, saying, "...*See! I have given Jericho into your hand, its king, and the mighty men of valour" Joshua 6:2 (NKJV)*

Note: *God gave Joshua a command saying "SEE". This is a fundamental principle that we need to understand. God knew that if Joshua could see it, he would be able to attain it. God brought the battle to Joshua's thought dimension, causing him to see the battle as already over and that victory was already theirs by adding, "I have already".*

Joshua knew that God was faithful to His Word, having said this before, and every time coming through for them. This removed all doubt and fear.

- Then all the men of war were to march around the city of Jericho for six days, once per day. **Joshua 6:3 (NKJV)**
- Seven priests bore seven trumpets of rams horns before the ark, and on the seventh day, they should circle the city seven times and the priest blow the trumpets. **Joshua 6:4 (NKJV)**
- When all the people hear the trumpets, they are to shout with a great shout; then the wall will fall down flat. **Joshua 6:5 (NKJV)**

So, it came to pass on the seventh day; they marched around the city seven times. On the seventh time, the priests blew the trumpets, and the army shouted with a great shout according to God's command, and the wall fell down flat.

Joshua further instructed them to remember to spare Rahab and all her household, for she protected the spies when they had come into the city.

They were further instructed to leave all the accursed things of the city because if they brought them into the camps of Israel, it would cause the camp to become accursed. They were only to take all the silver and gold, vessels of bronze and iron, to be consecrated unto the Lord. These things were to go into the treasury of the Lord.

And so, God delivered the city into their hands, and they took the city. They killed everyone in it, destroyed all the accursed things and took only the gold and silver, vessels of bronze and iron. They also spared the life of Rahab and all her household, where she continued to live with Israel according to God's instruction.

And the Lord was with Joshua that his fame spread throughout the country.

Israel continued to take territory by defeating Ai and making a peace treaty with the Gibeonites. News of the Gibeonites having made peace with Israel quickly reached the Amorites, leaving them filled with fear because Gibeon was a great city. It was one of the royal cities and was greater than Ai, which the Israelites had already destroyed.

The Amorites decided to join forces with four other kings going up against the Gibeonites for having made peace with Joshua and the children of Israel. The Gibeonites, now completely outnumbered, requested help from Joshua and Israel to save them.

b. The Sun Stands Still
Joshua 10 (NKJV)

The following event reveals the God of impossibilities step from eternity into time, intervening on Joshua's behalf. Joshua – who had unshakable faith – commanded a mighty miracle and wonder.

Once again, the Lord told Joshua not to fear them because He had already delivered the Amorites into his hands, that not a man shall stand before him.

The Lord then routed them before all of Israel, who killed them with a great slaughter at Gibeon. As they fled from Israel and were on the descent at Beth Horon, the Lord caused large hailstones to come down from heaven on them, killing many. More died from the hailstones than the children of Israel killed with the sword.

Joshua saw they needed more time to defeat these kings and did something extraordinary. He spoke to the Lord saying the following, in the sight of Israel:

"...Sun, stand still over Gibeon; And Moon, in the Valley of Aijalon.
[13] So, the sun stood still, And the moon stopped, Till the people had revenge upon their enemies"

Joshua 10:12 – 13 (NKJV)

The Bible further states that there had never been any day like that, before it or after, that the Lord listened to man's voice as the Lord fought for Israel.

Joshua took the five kings hiding in a cave and commanded his army commanders to come forward and place their feet upon their necks. He instructed Israel not to be afraid but to be strong and of good courage, for this is what the Lord will do to all the enemies they are going to fight.

He then killed them and hanged them from five trees until the evening before casting them back into the cave they had been hiding in.

Joshua and all of Israel continued to overtake and conquer from the Southland to the Northern parts of Canaan.

3. **Allocation of the Promised Land:**
   Joshua 13 – 24

The book of Joshua ends with God instructing Joshua with specific tribal allotments concerning Israel.

Joshua – finally, at his old age - after the Lord had given them rest from all their enemies, addressed Israel. He reminded them of all that the Lord had done for them, to keep the laws of the Lord their God, because by doing this, they would always prosper.

Joshua then died at the age of one hundred and ten, being buried in the portion of his inheritance.

PROPHETIC DECLARATIONS:

1.   Joshua 10:24 & 25 (NKJV)

[24] **So it was, when they brought out those kings to Joshua, that Joshua called for all the men of Israel, and said to the captains of the men of war who went with him, "Come near, put your feet on the necks of these kings." And they drew near and put their feet on their necks.** [25] **Then Joshua said to them, "Do not be afraid, nor be dismayed; be strong and of good courage, for thus the Lord will do to all your enemies against whom you fight."**

I declare and decree in the name of Jesus that every enemy sent out against me shall find themselves under my feet and that I will not stagger at the promise set before me, for it is the Lord God Almighty that shall bring them to pass in my life.

NOTES

NOTES

Book of **Judges**

"The Theocracy"

The Book of Judges narrates the leaders of Israel – from the time of the elders who outlived Joshua to the time of the monarchy.

The book expounds on Israel's continual rebellion and frequent sin, departing from God's Word. It shows how quickly they forgot about all the mighty works God had done and how He delivered them by constantly driving out their enemies from before them with His mighty hand. They further disregarded the fact that God had given them the land as His people, having chosen them to be His army and His charge to expel all the wickedness from the land.

Instead of obeying God, Israel chose to attach themselves to Canaan's people, their morals, gods, and religious practices. This was what brought about their destruction, time and time again!

The book reveals a pattern whereby Israel would constantly fall back into sin. Then, as soon as they fell into destruction due to their sinful acts, they would cry out to God for help. God graciously forgave them every time they cried out, only for them to repeat the same mistakes.

During these times of great peril, Israel would cry to the Lord for deliverance from their oppressors. God would then raise judges, through whom He would cast down their oppressors and restore their peace.

The book is best described in:

"Nevertheless, the Lord raised up judges who delivered them out of the hand of those who plundered them."

Judges 2:16 (NKJV)

The focus of the book is primarily on the following fourteen judges:

HIGHLIGHTED EVENTS:

Judge #1: Othniel – Judges 3:5 – 11 (NKJV)

The anger of God burned against Israel because, yet again, they did evil in the eyes of God by serving the Baals and Asherahs. As a result, God sold them into the hands of Cushan-Rishataim, king of Mesopotamia, whom they served for eight years.

Then the children of Israel remembered the Lord God, again crying out to Him for deliverance from their oppressors. God heard their cry and chose Othniel – Caleb's younger brother – to deliver them.

The Bible records that the Spirit of the Lord came upon Othniel to judge Israel. He went to war against the king of Mesopotamia, stating the Lord delivered them into the hands of Israel. As a result, Israel had peace for forty years until Othniel died.

Judge #2: Ehud – Judges 3:12 – 30 (NKJV)

After Othniel's death, the children of Israel fell back into their old ways – again, sinning greatly against the Lord.

As a result, God strengthened Eglon, king of Moab, to rise against Israel. Eglon joined forces with the people of Ammon and Amalek, who together went to war against Israel and took possession of the City of Palms.

Israel then served Eglon, the king of Moab, for eighteen years.

After the eighteen years, Israel remembered the Lord their God again, crying unto Him for deliverance from Eglon. God responded to their cry, raising a left-handed man named Ehud to deliver them.

Ehud then made a double-edged dagger, forty-five centimetres in length. He strapped this dagger to his right thigh, underneath his clothes. He intended to assassinate Eglon, king of Moab when he presented the king with a tribute.

After Ehud presented the tribute to Eglon, he sent the people who carried the tribute out. Then Ehud turned back to the king, telling him he had a secret message, and the king commanded everyone to leave.

Here, Ehud told Eglon that he had a message from God. Eglon then arose from his seat, presenting Ehud with the perfect opportunity to assassinate the king. Ehud wasted no time. He reached down with his left hand, took the dagger, and plunged it into Eglon's belly. Eglon was overweight, and history records that the dagger was plunged so deep that even the hilt went in after the blade, causing his fat to close over the blade.

Ehud then escaped quickly through the porch, locking the doors behind him so it would appear as if the king was attending to his business. Later, his servants found him dead in his room.

The Bible then states that Ehud assembled the armies of Israel, killing about ten thousand Moabite men, with not one being able to escape – including their men of valour. And so, Israel subdued Moab, and the land had peace for eighty years.

Judge #3: Shamgar – Judges 3:31 (NKJV)

Shamgar killed six hundred men of the Philistines with an ox goad and delivered Israel.

Judge #4 and #5: Deborah and Barak – Judges 4:1 – 24 (NKJV)

After Ehud's death, the children of Israel again fell back into their old ways and sinned greatly against the Lord.

As a result, God strengthened Jabin — king of Canaan — to rise against Israel. What followed was Israel being oppressed by them terribly for twenty years.

After twenty years, Israel remembered the Lord their God yet again, crying out to Him for deliverance from Jabin, king of Canaan. At that time, a prophetess named Deborah was judging Israel and called for Barak, giving him instructions from God, saying:

> *6 ..."Has not the Lord God of Israel commanded, 'Go and deploy troops at Mount Tabor; take with you ten thousand men of the sons of Naphtali and of the sons of Zebulun; 7 and against you I will deploy Sisera, the commander of Jabin's army, with his chariots and his multitude at the River Kishon; and I will deliver him into your hand'?"*

Judges 4:6 – 7 (NKJV)

Barak agreed to go on this mission if Deborah decided to go with him. Deborah's acceptance came with a price, as she said there would be no glory for Barak on this journey because the Lord will sell Sisera into the hands of a woman.

Barak then summoned Zebulun and Naphtali for the journey, marching with ten thousand men under his command, and Deborah went with him.

When Sisera, commander of Jabin's army, gained knowledge of the Israelite armies assembling against them, he immediately gathered all his chariots. He gathered nine hundred chariots and all the people with him to go up against Israel.

When the right time presented itself, Deborah instructed Barak to get up for this was the day that the Lord had given Sisera and his army into his hands, further encouraging him by saying, **"Has not the Lord gone before you"** *Judges 4:14 (NKJV)*

The Lord routed Sisera and his chariots by the sword before Barak, causing Sisera to abandon his chariot. He escaped on foot and fled to the tent of Jael — the wife of Heber — where his fate was sealed.

Jael then took Sisera, pretending to show kindness towards him by allowing Sisera to hide in her tent. Sisera was thirsty and requested a little water to drink. She gave him a glass of milk and then covered Sisera with a blanket.

When Sisera fell asleep, Jael took a tent peg with a hammer and drove the nail through Sisera's head, pinning him to the ground.

Barak, in pursuit of Sisera, met Jael outside the tent, where she revealed the body of Sisera unto him with the peg driven through his temple.

That day, the Lord subdued Jabin — king of Canaan — before all of Israel, destroying them. After that, the land had forty years of peace.

Judge #6: Gideon – Judges 6 – 8 (NKJV)

After forty years of peace, the children of Israel again sinned greatly against the Lord. This time the Lord delivered them into the hand of Midian for seven years.

Because of the Midianites, the children of Israel were forced to live in caves and strongholds in the mountains. Every time Israel would sow, the Midianites would come and destroy all their produce, leaving them with no substance, sheep, ox, or donkey.

Once again, Israel found themselves in ruin, crying out to God for deliverance from the hands of their oppressors. God then sent a prophet through whom He reminded Israel that He is the One who brought them up from Egypt, delivering them from the hands of all their oppressors, commanding Israel not to be afraid of the inhabitants of the land where they dwell. But they had not obeyed the voice of the Lord God.

At this, an angel of the Lord came unto Gideon while he was threshing wheat in the winepress, saying:

"The Lord is with you, you mighty man of valor!"

Judges 6:12 (NKJV)

The Lord further revealed to Gideon that he was the one chosen to deliver Israel out of the hands of the Midianites.

Gideon felt incapable and unworthy of the task set before him and requested that God give him a sign that it was indeed God speaking to him.

First Sign:
The Offering — Judges 6:18 – 21 (NKJV)

Gideon presented an offering of meat, unleavened bread and broth to the Angel of God, who then commanded Gideon to place the offering on a rock and to pour out the broth.

Then the Angel took the end of his staff, touching the meat and unleavened bread, and fire came out of the rock consuming the meat and unleavened bread. After this, the Angel of the Lord departed from Gideon.

The Lord then assured Gideon that His peace will be with him and that he should not be afraid because he shall not die.

Then God gave Gideon the following instructions:

- Gideon was to take his father's bull — the one that was seven years old — and tear down the altar of Baal and cut down the wooden images beside it.
- Then he was to build an altar of the Lord God on top of the rock, take the bull and offer a burnt sacrifice with the wood of the image that he shall cut down.

Gideon then took ten of his servants and did all according to the commandment of the Lord. But, because he was afraid of the city's men, he decided to do at by night.

The next morning, when the men of the city saw the altar of Baal was torn down, the wooden images cut off and a new altar was erected upon which the second bull was offered, they desired to kill Gideon.

Gideon's father, named Joash, quickly intervened and persuaded them not to do it. He said that Baal could plead for himself and deal with Gideon, as he was the one who had torn down Baal's altar.

The Midianites and Amalekites then gathered together and encamped at the valley of Jezreel, preparing to plunder the Israelites.

When Gideon blew the trumpet, the Spirit of the Lord came upon him, and the Abiezrites gathered behind him, together with Manasseh, Asher, Zebulun and Naphtali.

Second Sign:
The Wet Fleece – Judges 6:36 – 38 (NKJV)

Gideon, who was now about to go into battle again, asked God for a sign that He would save Israel through his hands.

For a sign, Gideon took a fleece of wool and placed it on the threshing floor and requested that dew would only be found on the fleece, but all the ground around it shall be dry. The sign happened according to Gideon's request.

Third Sign:
The Dry Fleece – Judges 6: 39 – 40 (NKJV)

Gideon then requested one last sign that the fleece now be dry and all the ground around be full of dew, and it happened the next morning that Gideon found the fleece completely dry, but the ground around it was full of dew.

Gideon's Brave Three Hundred:
Judges 7:1 – 25 (NKJV)

The Lord then appeared to Gideon, stating that the men with him are too many for Him to give the Midianites into their hands because they will take glory for themselves, saying this victory was accomplished through their own hands.

God then instructed Gideon to proclaim before all the men that those afraid to go into battle could turn around and return to Mount Gilead, upon which twenty-two thousand soldiers returned, leaving only ten thousand.

The remaining ten thousand were still too many, so God further instructed Gideon to bring the men down to the water so that He could test them there. The ones who lapped the water on their knees as a dog laps his water were to be separated from those who lapped the water by putting their hands to their mouth.

The ones using their hands added up to three hundred men. The rest all got down on their knees to drink water. And so the Lord said unto Gideon,

"By the three hundred men who lapped I will save you, and deliver the Midianites into your hand. Let all the other people go, every man to his place."

Judges 7:7 (NKJV)

That night, God commanded Gideon to go down against the Midianites as He had already given them into his hands.

The Dream:
Judges 7:13 – 14 (NKJV)

Gideon was still afraid and was further instructed by God to take his servant Purah and go down into the camp. God said that there he would hear something that would greatly encourage and strengthen him to face the battle at hand.

Upon arrival, Gideon overheard a man sharing a dream with his companion, stating that he saw a loaf of barley bread tumble into the camp of Midian and that it came to a tent and struck it so that it overturned, and the tent collapsed.

Immediately his companion interpreted the dream revealing that this can only be the sword of Gideon, a man of Israel and that God has without a doubt delivered Midian into his hands.

When Gideon heard the interpretation, he worshipped God and immediately assembled the Israelite army.

The Divine Battle Strategy:
Judges 7:16 – 25 (NKJV)

Gideon then divided the three hundred men into three separate companies. He gave each man a trumpet in one hand and an empty jar with a torch in the other, leaving them with precise battle instructions.

Gideon instructed them to watch him closely and so to imitate him exactly. He explained that when they see him at the edge of the Midianite camp, he will blow his trumpet, and then everyone with him shall blow their trumpets on every side surrounding the camp and shout, "*The sword of the Lord and of Gideon.*"

So Gideon and the three hundred men blew their trumpets and broke their jars on every side surrounding the Midian camps – with their torches in their left hands, holding the trumpets in the right, shouting *"The sword of the Lord and of Gideon!"*

At that moment, great confusion struck the Midianite camp to such an extent that every man turned his sword against their companion. This caused the Midianites to flee to the borders of Abel Meholah.

Israel now had the upper hand and immediately pursued after them, sending messengers to Ephraim to come down and seize the Midianites at the water places.

And so, they captured two Midianite princes, Oreb and Zeeb, where they executed Oreb at the rock of Oreb and Zeeb at the winepress of Zeeb. They pursued the Midianites to the Jordan, where Gideon and the three hundred crossed over.

Gideon's Victory Over The Midianites:
Judges 8:1 – 21 (NKJV)

At this point, the three hundred men were exhausted in pursuing the Midianites. Then Gideon requested loaves of bread for his men from the leaders of Succoth as they were pursuing the two Midianite kings — Zebah and Zalmunna.

But the leaders of Succoth showed Gideon and his men no kindness, treating them with utter disrespect, refusing to help them.

This was a response accompanied by devastating results as Gideon replied, stating that because they treated them so harshly, he would return after the Lord delivered Zebah and Zalmunna into his hand and tear their flesh with the thorns of the wilderness and with briers.

After this, they came to Penuel, where the men from this place treated them the same way as the men of Succoth. Gideon told them he would return after his victory and tear down their tower.

Gideon eventually caught up with Zebah and Zalmunna at Karkor with their armies of about fifteen thousand men remaining. This was after about one hundred and twenty thousand men died after drawing their swords against each other.

The two kings tried to flee, but Gideon pursued and overtook them and also routed the entire army. On the way back, Gideon stopped at Succoth and took their elders – seventy-seven men in total – and beat them with thorns from the wilderness and with briers because they ridiculed him when he asked for bread when his men were weary.

Then he tore down the tower of Penuel and killed the men of the city before drawing his sword, killing both Zebah and Zalmunna.

Gideon then passed on and was buried in the tombs of Joash, his father. After Gideon passed on, the Israelites did not remember the Lord God who had delivered them from the hands of their oppressors and again sinned greatly against the Lord by making Baal-Berith their god.

Judge #7: Abimelech — Judge 9 (NKJV)

Judge #8: Tola — Judges 10:1 – 2 (NKJV)

Tola judged Israel for twenty-three years and then died.

Judge #9: Jair — Judges 10:3 – 5 (NKJV)

Jair judged Israel for twenty-two years before dying and was buried in Camon. Jair had thirty sons who rode on thirty donkeys and possessed thirty towns.

Judge #10: Jephthah — Judges 11 – 12:1 – 7 (NKJV)

Jephthah was a mighty man of valour, the son of Gilead and born in Gilead. However, Jephthah was born of a harlot and was, therefore, cast out by his other brothers. They judged him for being born of a strange woman, not of Gilead's wife, so they did not want him to have part of their father's inheritance.

Jephthah was forced to flee from his brothers to a place called Tob. This was good land where he became the leader of a band of men that joined him in many exploits. Through these exploits, he learnt the art of war.

It then came to pass that Ammon waged war against all of Israel to reclaim their territory, an easy feat as Israel stood without an appointed judge at this time.

At this, the leaders of Israel fetched Jephthah in the land of Tob, requesting that he come and lead them in war against Ammon.

Jephthah rejected their request saying that they had hated him and expelled him from his father's house, yet in their time of distress, they wished to summon his help.

The elders assured Jephthah that the intent of their hearts was to make him head over all the inhabitants of Gilead, leading them in battle against Ammon.

After accepting Jephthah's conditions, they made him head and captain over them, with the Lord as their witness.

Jephthah's Vow and Victory:
Judges 11:29 – 31 (NKJV)

The Spirit of the Lord came upon Jephthah, that assembled his armies before marching to Ammon. Then Jephthah made a vow to God that if He delivers Ammon into his hands, that upon his return in peace from the people of Ammon, whoever comes out of their house to greet him will be sacrificed as a burnt offering to God.

After Jephthah's victory over Ammon, he returned home, fell to the ground, and rent his clothes as his only daughter came out to meet him with timbrels and dancing, celebrating his return.

Jephthah then explained to his daughter the reason for his utter despair and how he made a vow to God that he could not go back on.

His daughter understood the severity of the situation and comforted her father by standing in agreement with the vow. She requested that Jephthah would at least grant her two months to go into the mountains with her friends so that she could bewail her virginity.

Jephthah granted his daughter her request, and after the two months had passed, he fulfilled his vow, and she knew no man.

And so, Jephthah judged Israel for six years before passing on, being buried in Gilead.

Judge #11: Ibzan – Judges 12:8 – 10 (NKJV)

Ibzan judged Israel for seven years and was buried in Bethlehem.

Judge #12: Elon – Judges 12:11 – 12 (NKJV)

Elon judged Israel for ten years and was buried in Aijalon.

Judge #13: Abdon – Judges 12:13 – 16 (NKJV)

Abdon judged Israel for eight years and was buried in Pirathon.

Judge #14: Samson – Judges 13 – 16 (NKJV)

After this, the children of Israel sinned greatly – yet again – against the Lord. As a result, God delivered them into the hands of the Philistines for forty years.

Gracefully, God would always remember His people and make a way to redeem them, even through their repetitive processes of rebellion.

At this, God raised yet another judge to deliver Israel, known as Samson.

Samson was born in Zorah from the Danites and called as a Nazarite, which came with the following conditions:

Nazarite Call

Nazarite comes from the Hebrew word "nazir", meaning "consecrated" or "separated" - **Wiki**

1. No razor shall come upon their head, meaning they were not allowed to cut their hair.
2. They were not allowed to eat anything from the vine, including alcohol, grapes and raisins.
3. They were not allowed to make any contact with corpses or graves, even those of family members, as this would make them spiritually impure.

Samson was a mighty man of valour, known for his boldness and extraordinary strength. He performed twelve great exploits every time the Spirit of God would come mightily upon Him.

a. Rending the Lion with Bare Hands:
Judges 14:5 – 9 (NKJV)

Samson was on a journey to Timnath with his father and mother to attend a seven-day feast. This feast was prepared for Samson's upcoming marriage, where he was about to marry a Philistine woman. They passed by a vineyard in Timnath where a young lion came out and roared against Samson.

The Bible says that the Spirit of the Lord came mightily upon Samson so that he tore the lion apart with his bare hands, as one would have torn a young goat.

Samson decided to keep the matter private, not even mentioning the incident to his parents. It is interesting to note that this is the same lion that Samson passed by again later on when he saw the carcass with a swarm of bees and honey in it.

b. Vengeance on the Thirty Men:
Judges 14: 15 – 20 (NKJV)

At the feast, Samson presented them with a riddle. If they could solve this riddle correctly within the seven-day feast, he would be accountable for giving them thirty linen garments and thirty changes of clothing.

¹⁴ So he said to them:

"Out of the eater came something to eat,
And out of the strong came something sweet."

Now for three days they could not explain the riddle.

Judges 14:14 (NKJV)

When the Philistines saw that they would not be able to solve the riddle in the time, they went to Samson's wife and threatened her, stating that if she did not disclose the answer to the riddle, they would burn her with her father's house.

To protect herself and her family, she manipulated Samson into telling her the answer to the riddle, which she then disclosed to the Philistines. On the seventh day, before the sun went down, they gave Samson the answer to the riddle, saying:

…"What is sweeter than honey?
And what is stronger than a lion?"

And he said to them:
"If you had not plowed with my heifer,
You would not have solved my riddle!"

Judges 14:18 (NKJV)

Because they attained the answer by being deceitful, the Spirit of the Lord came mightily upon Samson, strengthening him to take vengeance on the Philistines, killing thirty of their men in Ashkelon to repay his debt.

After that, he took the spoils from them and gave them to the men that expounded the riddle. Samson's anger was greatly aroused, so he returned to his father's house.

c.   **The Three Hundred Foxes:**
     Judges 15:3 – 5 (NKJV)

After this, Samson went back to be with his wife, only to find out that his wife was now given by her father to one of his friends to marry. Her father explained that he thought Samson now hated her because of what she had done, proposing that he marry her younger sister instead.

Yet again, they kindled Samson's anger who went out and caught three hundred foxes, tying their tails together, placing a torch in the knot connecting the two tails.

Samson then set the torches on fire, letting loose the foxes in the standing corn of the Philistines, destroying the shocks, the standing corn, the vineyards and olive groves.

When the Philistines learned who had done this, they took his wife and her father and burned them with fire.

d.   **The Great Slaughter:**
     Judges 15: 7 – 10 (NKJV)

The wicked actions of the Philistines caused Samson to respond with vengeance, this time attacking them hip and thigh with a great slaughter.

After overthrowing the Philistines, Samson went down to Etam, where he dwelt in the cleft of the rock.

The Philistines became vexed as a nation because of Samson and decided to set themselves against Judah. Judah – now in an attempt to avoid conflict with the Philistines – sent three thousand men down to the rock to arrest Samson in order to hand him over.

Samson agreed to be given over to the Philistines on the condition that the men of Judah would not kill him. They assured him they would only bound him securely and then hand him over.

e-g. Breaking Two New Ropes, Slaying One Thousand Men with the Jawbone of a Donkey and Water Out of the Jaw bone: Judges 15: 13 – 20 (NKJV)

The men of Judah then took two new ropes and bound Samson before delivering him into the hands of the Philistines.

When Samson came to Lehi, where the Philistines were waiting for him, the Spirit of the Lord came mightily upon him. He broke the two new ropes as if they were flax burned with fire.

Samson then found a fresh jawbone of a donkey and killed one thousand men with it, saying:

…"With the jawbone of a donkey,

Heaps upon heaps,
With the jawbone of a donkey

I have slain a thousand men!"

Judges 15:16 (NKJV)

After this great victory, Samson became very thirsty and called out to God for help. God caused water to come out from the hollow place that was in the jaw, from which Samson drank, and his spirit was revived.

And so, Samson judged Israel twenty years in the days of the Philistines.

h. Breaking Out and Carrying the City Gate and Door Post Up the Hill: Judges 16:3 (NKJV)

On numerous occasions, the Philistines would try and capture Samson by conspiring with a woman named Delilah, a harlot with whom Samson had fallen in love. She was offered eleven hundred pieces of silver to entice Samson in trying to uncover the secret to Samson's strength, but every attempt ended in failure.

The first time that Samson came into Delilah, the men of the city recognised him and planned an ambush against him at the city gate. Samson waited till midnight, then took the city gates with the two gateposts, pulled them out bar and all, placed them upon his shoulders and carried them to the top of the hill that faced Hebron.

i. **Breaking Seven Fresh Bowstrings:**
    Judges 16: 6 – 9 (NKJV)

Delilah then asked Samson to reveal the secret to his strength and if one wanted to capture and overpower him with what they could bind him. Samson then told Delilah that if they took seven freshly braided bowstrings that had not yet been dried and tied him with the seven strings, his strength would leave him, and he would become like any other man.

The Philistines then gave Delilah the strings that she then used to bind Samson with, and when the Philistines came in, she yelled,

"...The Philistines are upon you, Samson!"

Judges 16:9 (NKJV)

Samson then broke the strings with ease, leaving the secret to his strength hidden.

j. **Broke New Ropes:**
    Judges 16: 10 – 12 (NKJV)

Delilah felt embarrassed and pressed even harder for Samson to reveal his secret. This time, he explained that if he is bound with new ropes that have never been used, he will become weak like any other man.

After binding Samson with the new ropes, the Philistines came in and again, Delilah yelled,

"...The Philistines are upon you, Samson!"

Judges 16:12 (NKJV)

Again, Samson broke the ropes as if they were normal pieces of string, leaving his secret hidden.

k. Breaking Free from the Batten and the Web from the Loom: Judges 16:13 – 14 (NKJV)

Delilah was now growing frustrated. She asked Samson yet again to be truthful in revealing the secret to his strength. He then explained that if she weaves the seven locks of his hair into the web of the loom, then he will be weakened like any other man.

She then did everything according to Samson's explanation and then again yelled,

"...The Philistines are upon you, Samson!"

Judges 16:14 (NKJV)

Samson then simply pulled out the batten and the web from the loom, leaving his secret hidden.

l. Pulling Apart the Pillars, Destroying Three Thousand Men and Woman: Judges 16:15 – 31 (NKJV)

Delilah became desperate to reveal the secret of Samson's strength. She pressed even harder this time, aggravating him for days on end, to the point where his soul was in terrible anguish.

Samson then finally gave in to Delilah's continual pestering, revealing his heart to her by disclosing the secret of his strength. He explained that if his hair were to be cut, then his strength would surely leave him.

That night Delilah called for a man to shave the seven locks of his head while Samson was asleep, and again, she yelled,

"...The Philistines are upon you, Samson!"

Judges 16:20 (NKJV)

Samson then thought he would just escape like in previous times but did not know that the Lord had already departed from him.

The Philistines then took Samson captive and gouged his eyes out before binding him with bronze fetters, forcing him to work as a grinder in prison.

And it came to pass that the lords of the Philistines came together to offer a sacrifice unto dagon – their god – to rejoice over their victory, saying:

> [23]... *"Our god has delivered into our hands Samson our enemy!"*
> [24] *When the people saw him, they praised their god; for they said:*
> *"Our god has delivered into our hands our enemy, The destroyer of*
> *our land, And the one who multiplied our dead."*

Judges 16:23 – 24 (NKJV)

They then began to celebrate, calling for Samson to come and entertain them, and so stationed him between two pillars.

After a while, Samson spoke to the one holding him by his hands, asking if he may rest upon one of the pillars supporting the temple for a moment.

Samson then called out to the Lord one final time, asking Him to remember him and strengthen him once again so that he could take vengeance on the Philistines for his two eyes with one blow.

Samson then took hold of the two pillars shouting, *"Let me die with the Philistines" (Judges 16:30),* and so pushed with all his strength until the pillars gave way, causing the entire temple to collapse, killing more than three thousand Philistine men and women.

Samson was then buried between Zorah and Eshtaol in his father's tomb.

After this, there was no king to rule over Israel, and every man did what was right in his own eyes.

PROPHETIC DECLARATIONS:

1. Judges 6:12 (NKJV)

¹² And the Angel of the Lord appeared to him, and said to him, "The Lord is with you, you mighty man of valor!"

I declare and decree in the name of Jesus that I am clothed with righteousness and stand as a mighty warrior filled with the Holy Spirit of the true Living God. All evil will be cast down, stripped of all authority and power where I go. My presence as a child of God will bring deliverance, healing and restoration in the name of Jesus.

NOTES

NOTES

NOTES

Book of **Ruth**

"Destiny Unlocked"

The book of Ruth is set in the same period as the Judges when there was peace between Moab and Israel and carries important genealogy.

The book mainly revolves around three main characters - Naomi, Ruth, and Boaz.

The book's purpose is to demonstrate God's unconditional love and faithfulness toward us, especially when we persevere in loyalty and obedience.

HIGHLIGHTED EVENTS:

1. **Elimelech's Family Goes to Moab and Naomi Returns with Ruth: Ruth 1:1 – 22 (NKJV)**

When there was a famine in the land, Elimelech from Bethlehem, Judah, took his wife Naomi and his two sons and went to the country of Moab to sojourn there to escape the wrath of the famine.

Naomi's two sons then chose for themselves wives from the women of Moab to marry – Ruth and Orpah.

After that, in about ten years, Naomi's husband and two sons died. Naomi then decided to return to Judah, as it was revealed to her that the Lord had blessed His people with bread.

Before leaving the place where they dwelled, Naomi instructed her two daughters-in-law to return to their own homes as she no longer had anything to offer them.

Orpah then kissed Naomi and left. Ruth's response, however, wrote the very course of history as she stayed loyal to Naomi – her mother-in-law – insisting that she would not leave but go with Naomi back to her home country.

Naomi again tried to persuade Ruth to rather return to her own house, but she refused, saying:

> *16 ..."Entreat me not to leave you, Or to turn back from following after you; For wherever you go, I will go; And wherever you lodge, I will lodge; Your people shall be my people, And your God, my God. 17 Where you die, I will die, And there will I be buried. The Lord do so to me, and more also, If anything but death parts you and me."*

Ruth 1:16 – 17 (NKJV)

Naomi realised that Ruth was determined about the situation, willing to leave all she knew, and allowed her to come with.

2. Ruth Meets Boaz:
Ruth 2:1 – 23 (NKJV)

Then it came to pass during the time of harvest that Ruth was gleaning the field of Elimelech's relative, Boaz, a man of great wealth.

Ruth immediately found favour with Boaz, knowing all she had done and sacrificing for her mother-in-law. Boaz, out of obedience to the law and compassion for Ruth, not only allowed her to glean his field but also blessed her by leaving extra grain for her to collect.

3. Ruth's Redemption:
Ruth 3:1 – 18 (NKJV)

Naomi, who perceived the nature of the situation, urged Ruth to pursue marriage with Boaz as a kinsman-redeemer. Naomi educated Ruth, leaving her with clear instructions on what to do and say when the time presented itself.

Ruth obeyed Naomi and requested her rights, to which Boaz agreed after the steps to the "Kinsmen Redemption" were fulfilled.

4. **Boaz the Kinsmen Redeemer:**
   Ruth 4:1 – 22 (NKJV)

Boaz then proceeded with the process to redeem Ruth, which consisted of the following seven steps.

Seven Steps – Kinsmen Redemption:

   a. Get a witness to confirm all parties involved as possible re
      deemers.
   b. Agreement on who shall be the redeemer.
   c. The one who gives away his right to redemption to another
      had to take off his shoe as a witness that he forfeits his rights.
   d. Kinsmen to redeem the inheritance.
   e. The redeemer to marry the wife of the deceased to raise up
      seed to ensure the continuation of his legacy.
   f. Agreement of witnesses to the transaction taking place.
   g. The married couple to be blessed.

And so, after all these things, Boaz and Ruth were married. Later, she conceived a son, which they named Obed. Obed begot Jesse, the father of David, the lineage of Christ Jesus our Savior.

PROPHETIC DECLARATIONS:

1. Ruth 2:3 (NKJV)

³ **"Then she left, and went and gleaned in the field after the reapers. And she happened to come to the part of the field belonging to Boaz, who was of the family of Elimelech."**

I declare and decree in the name of Jesus that I will suddenly stumble into my destiny with ease and without any resistance. I command my life to align with God's perfect will and so to walk in what He has prepared for me.

NOTES

First Book of **Samuel**

"Birth of the Monarchy"

To understand the full message of Samuel, one must view 1 & 2 Samuel as one book. The book of first Samuel was initially combined with the second book of Samuel.

These books were compiled from 1204-1035 B.C in Palestine by authors Samuel, David, Nathan, and Gad. The final edition, which caused this book to divide into two books, was compiled later by Prophet Isaiah about 743-683 B.C, which is now presented in its final form as we know it today.

These books have varied many times in titles, having been designated "The First and Second Books of Kingdoms" (Septuagint); "First & Second Kings" (Vulgate); and "First and Second Samuel" (Hebrew tradition and most modern versions as we know them today).

The setting of 1 Samuel portrays the establishment of Kingship in Israel. Samuel births the start of a new age by changing the structure of the theocracy (God's Rule) and developing it into the start of the Monarchy (The Reign of Kings).

There are four key events in the first book of Samuel that portrays the theme, which consist of the rise and fall of the first Monarchy under the guidance of King Saul and then later the rise of King David.

The book of 1 Samuel can be divided into the following four major events:

1. Historical Setting for Israel's Kingship Establishment:
   1 Samuel 1 – 7
2. The Birth of the Monarchy: **1 Samuel 8 – 12**
3. Saul's Failure as King: **1 Samuel 13 – 15**
4. David's Rise to the Throne; Progressive Deterioration and End of Saul's Reign: **1 Samuel 16:1 – carrying into 2 Samuel**

HIGHLIGHTED EVENTS IN 1 SAMUEL:

1. **Historical Setting for Israel's Kingship Establishment:
    1 Samuel 1 – 7 (NKJV)**

The first focus of 1 Samuel is Samuel's birth, youth, and calling as a Prophet. It is interesting to note that even though this book deals for the most part with the reign of Israel's first two Kings, Saul, and David, the author did not feel the need to write and include the birth of these men.

The author focuses on describing the birth of their forerunner and the one to anoint them, the Prophet Samuel. The author also sets the importance of Samuel's role in the following events. This is to bring a point across that flesh and blood are still to be subordinated to the Word and Spirit in the process of establishing Kingship in Israel.

One should also note the cry of a mother in this regard, Hannah, a wife to Elkanah, whose womb was shut by God. Her biggest desire was to bear a son, but because of her barrenness, she became bitter in her soul. Hannah's breakthrough came when she made a vow to God.

And so, Hannah vowed a vow.

Note: *The meaning of this in Hebrew is to Promise a Promise. This exceeds far greater than just a vow. To vow a vow, a promise must be met by another promise. Hannah vowed to God that she would give Him a Prophet if He gave her a son.*

This promise was met by God through the Prophet Eli when he heard the cry of Hannah to the Lord and said:

> ¹⁷ *... "Go in peace, and the God of Israel grant your petition which you have asked of Him."*

1 Samuel 1:17 (NKJV)

This caused Samuel to go into his calling as a Prophet much younger than the standard Jewish customs of the time.

Eli then trained Samuel in his calling as a Prophet from a very young age and on how to accurately discern the voice of God, as seen in **1 Samuel 3:9.**

Now the Bible says that Samuel grew in the Lord and that the Lord was with him so that none of his words would fall to the ground.

The Ark of the Covenant Captured:
1 Samuel 4:1 – 11

And so, Israel went to battle against the Philistines, losing about four thousand men that day, causing them to act ignorantly when they saw that this battle was not in their favour and so decided to bring the Ark of the Covenant to the battlefield under the instructions of the elders.

This was a decision with devastating results as Israel lost a further thirty-thousand foot soldiers and the Ark of the Covenant.

It was also in this battle that Eli's two sons, Hophni and Phinehas, died, thus fulfilling the Word of the Lord spoken by a man of God, as seen in **1 Samuel 2:34**

The Death of Eli:
1 Samuel 4:12 – 18

Now the moment when Eli received knowledge that his two sons had died and the Ark of the Covenant was taken captive by the Philistines, he fell backwards by the side of the gate, breaking his neck and causing his death.

Eli judged Israel for forty years before he passed on.

Ichabod:
1 Samuel 4:19 – 22

It then happened that when the wife of Phinehas received the knowledge of her husband who died in battle and of the ark of God that was captured, labour pains came upon her, and she gave birth to a son.

She then called the boy Ichabod, meaning *"The glory has departed from Israel"*.

The Ark with the Philistines:
1 Samuel 5

And so, the Philistines took the ark of God to Ashdod, where they placed the ark of God by dagon, their god, only to find the following morning that dagon was fallen on his face before the ark of God.

They then placed dagon back in its place, only to find dagon again the next morning on his face before the ark of God. This time with its head and both the palms of its hands broken off. Only dagon's torso was left on the threshold.

This was only but the start of the calamity to befall Ashdod and its territory, as the Lord further destroyed and struck them with tumours for their trespass, upon which the Philistines decided to move the ark of God to Gath, only for the people of this city to face the same fate.

The ark of God was then moved from Gath to Ekron. Now because the hand of the Lord was heavy throughout all of the cities, causing many to die and those who did not die to be stricken with tumours, the Ekronites cried out of fear to rather send the ark of God back to its own place, lest any more people lose their lives.

The Ark of God Returned:
1 Samuel 6

And so, after seven months, the Philistines called for their priests and diviners, enquiring what to do with the ark of God.

The priests then gave the Philistines instructions concerning the necessary preparations to be made for the ark of God to be restored to its rightful place.

These instructions, if followed, would bring healing and were to be conducted in the following manner:

- The Ark of God was to be returned with a trespass offering.
- The trespass offering consisted of making five golden tumours and five golden rats, according to the number of the Philistine lords that were all stricken with the same plague.
- They were then to give glory to the God of Israel so that God might lift this affliction upon them.
- A new cart was to be built, with two milk cows that had never been yoked fastened to the cart.
- The Ark of God was then to be placed on the cart with all the golden articles given as a trespass offering in a chest next to the Ark of God.
- The ark was then to be sent away, only driven by the cows. If the ark then goes straight to its own territory, without turning to the left or right, then it means that God did indeed bring this calamity upon them, but if not, then all these things happened to them by chance and were not the hand of God.

They then did all according to the instructions given and watched as the ark of God went straight back to its own territory, not turning to the left nor the right until it reached Beth Shemesh, where the ark was finally restored into the hands of the Levites.

From here, the ark was sent to the house of Abinadab, where Eleazar, his son, was appointed to keep the ark of the Lord.

Judge #15: Samuel
1 Samuel 7

Now the Ark of God remained in Kirjath Jearim for twenty years. During this time, the children of Israel cried out to God for deliverance from the Philistines.

Samuel then judged Israel, charging them with the following:

- Return to the Lord with all your hearts.
- Get rid of all the foreign gods from among you.
- Prepare your hearts for the Lord.
- Serve Him only.

This was a mandate that, if followed, would cause the Lord to deliver them from the hand of the Philistines, who oppressed them.

They then hearkened to the words of Samuel, rid themselves from the Baals and Ashtoreth's, and served the Lord God of Israel with all their hearts.

The children of Israel then gathered at Mizpah, where Samuel prayed to the Lord for all the people as they fasted, consecrating themselves purely unto the Lord, repenting for all their sins.

When the Philistines received knowledge that Israel gathered at Mizpah, they immediately laid siege against them.

This caused great fear to come on the children of Israel, who then went to Samuel to plead with God to save them from the onslaught they were about to face.

Samuel instantly took the battle into the supernatural when he hastily took a suckling lamb and offered it as a burnt offering to the Lord.

The bible says that Samuel then cried out to the Lord for Israel, and the Lord answered him — **1 Samuel 7:9 (NKJV)**

As Samuel was busy with the burnt offering, the Philistines came close to attack, but the Lord thundered aloud upon the Philistines, causing them to become utterly confused, allowing the Israelites to overthrow them completely.

And so, Israel recovered their lost territory from Ekron to Gath, but there was still peace between Israel and the Amorites.

Samuel continued to judge the nation of Israel successfully, every year going on a trip to Bethel, Gilgal and Mizpah, judging in those places before returning to Ramah, where he lived.

2. The Birth of the Monarchy: 1 Samuel 8 – 12 (NKJV)

Samuel's reign ended in his old age, where he made his two sons, Joel and Abijah, judges over Israel, who did not walk in Samuel's ways. They took bribes from the people, gave perverted justice, and turned aside after dishonest gain. This caused great indignation against Joel and Abijah, and as a result, the elders came to Samuel, requesting a king, like all the other nations, to judge them.

This request displeased Samuel greatly, who then brought the matter before the Lord. And the Lord then told Samuel to heed to the people's voice, for they are not rejecting Samuel, but God.

However, the Lord further instructed Samuel to warn the elders of what the devastating behaviour of the king will be that shall reign over them, as found in **1 Samuel 8:11 – 18**

Regretfully, even after hearing the warning, Israel still refused to listen and demanded that a king be appointed over Israel. Samuel then repeated the cry of the people to the Lord, to which the Lord responded, saying:

…"Heed their voice and make them a king."

1 Samuel 8:22 (NKJV)

This decision marked the beginning of a new age for the nation of Israel as the Monarchy was birthed.

1st King over all of Israel: Saul
1 Samuel 9 (NKJV)

In the following events, we see a young man named Saul from the tribe of Benjamin, whose destiny was about to unfold by divine assignation.

The Bible described Saul as:
1 Samuel 9:2 (NKJV)

- A choice, young man.
- Saul was the most attractive man among the sons of Israel.
- Saul was taller than any of the other people from his shoulders upward.

Saul's Journey of Discovery:
1 Samuel 9:3 – 26 (NKJV)

It then came to pass that when the donkeys of Kish, Saul's father, went missing, that he commissioned Saul to choose one of the servants and search for the lost animals.

And so, Saul set out with one of the servants on a journey of discovery, but not the kind that Saul thought, as this was a divine journey established by God, for Saul to step into his destiny.

When they reached the land of Zuph and had been searching for quite some time, Saul suggested that they rather return home, lest Kish now also becomes worried about them.

But by divine design, the servant advised Saul that there was a man of God in the city, that was an honourable man, whose words do not fall void to the ground, but what he speaks comes to pass, and perhaps he can give them some guidance concerning the donkeys.

Knowing that it is not suitable for them to show up empty-handed, they gathered all they could and set out to meet with the man of God.

Now the Lord spoke to Samuel in his ear a day before saying:

¹⁶ "Tomorrow about this time I will send you a man from the land of Benjamin, and you shall anoint him commander over My people Israel, that he may save My people from the hand of the Philistines; for I have looked upon My people, because their cry has come to Me."

1 Samuel 9:16 (NKJV)

And so when Saul came through the gate, the Lord spoke to Samuel, saying that this is the man that shall reign over My people.

Samuel then revealed unto Saul, by revealed knowledge that the donkeys they were looking for, even from three days ago, were found and so not to be worried about them, further stating that all the desire of Israel were upon him and his father's house.

However, Saul's response to Samuel's words revealed much about his self-concept, claiming that he's from the smallest tribe and that his family is the least of all the families of Benjamin, asking why Samuel is speaking such words.

Saul Anointed Privately as Commander over Israel:
1 Samuel 10:1 – 16

Samuel then took a flask of oil and anointed Saul as commander over the Lord's inheritance, further prophesying that the following events would take place on Saul's way back home:

- Saul will meet three men, one carrying three young goats, another carrying three loaves of bread, and another carrying a skin of wine. **1 Samuel 10:3 (NKJV)**
- They will offer Saul two loaves of bread which he must receive. **1 Samuel 10:4 (NKJV)**
- Saul will meet a group of prophets coming down from the high place with a stringed instrument, a tambourine, a flute, and a harp before them, and they will be prophesying. **1 Samuel 10:5 (NKJV)**
- Then the Spirit of the Lord will come upon Saul, and he will prophesy with them and be turned into another man. **1 Samuel 10:6 (NKJV)**

Samuel further charged Saul to wait for him at Gilgal for seven days, where he was to receive further instructions.

And so, Samuel left, and the Bible says that God gave Saul another heart, and all the signs prophesied by Samuel came to pass.

Saul Appointed as King Before all the People:
1 Samuel 10:17 – 27

At Mizpah, Samuel then called for all the tribes to present themselves before the Lord for a king to be elected, at which the tribe of Benjamin were chosen.

Then all the families of Benjamin were to come forward, of which the family of Matri was chosen. Then from this family, Saul, son of Kish, was chosen as king over Israel.

But when they searched for Saul, he was nowhere to be found until the Lord pointed out that he was hiding among the equipment.

Samuel then presented the one the Lord had chosen to which all the people shouted, *"...Long live the king!" 1 Samuel 10:24 (NKJV)*

Saul's First Act as King: Jabesh Gilead Delivered
1 Samuel 11:1 – 15 & 1 Samuel 12

After all these things, Nahash the Ammonite waged war against Jabesh Gilead. All the men of Jabesh immediately tried to establish a covenant with Nahash, explaining that they would serve the Ammonites.

The Bible says that the Spirit of God came upon Saul, who then took three hundred thousand men from Bezek and another thirty thousand from Judah, dividing them into three companies, killing the Ammonites until the hottest part of the day. Further leaving the survivors scattered abroad, not two were left together.

And so, the Lord delivered a great victory into Saul's hands, a triumph that quickly gained the people's trust. After this great defeat, Samuel appointed Saul as king over Israel before all the people at Gilgal.

At this point, it seemed as if Saul was doing well in leading the nation of Israel as their first king, but unfortunately, in the following chapters, we see how Saul's foolishness caused him to make unlawful choices, which ended with devastating results.

3. **Saul's Failure as King - The Beginning of The End:**
   1 Samuel 13 – 15

Illegitimate Sacrifice:
1 Samuel 13

After Saul reigned over Israel for two years, he chose for himself three thousand men, divided into two camps. Two thousand soldiers remained with Saul in Michmash, and a thousand remained with Jonathan in Gibeah of Benjamin.

Jonathan, then attacked the garrison of the Philistines in Geba, causing the Philistines now to retaliate with thirty thousand chariots, six thousand horsemen, and people, so great in number that they seemed like the sand on the seashore.

This caused a terrible fear to come on the people, so they were scattered abroad, hiding in caves, thickets, rocks, holes and pits, with some even crossing the Jordan to the land of Gad and Gilead.

Now Saul was still waiting in Gilgal for seven days according to the time set by Samuel as seen in **1 Samuel 10:8**, but after the passing of the seven days, Saul was uncertain whether Samuel would still come or not.

Saul then took matters into his own hands by presenting an unlawful burnt offering, and just as Saul finished the offering, Samuel arrived and said,

"...You have done foolishly. You have not kept the command of the LORD your God, which He commanded you. For now the Lord would have established your kingdom over Israel forever"

1 Samuel 13:13 (NKJV)

Saul's unlawful act of disobedience was not only the beginning of his destruction but also caused him to now stand on the verge of losing the kingdom.

Jonathan's Victory Over the Philistines:
1 Samuel 14:1 – 23

It then happened that while Saul was sitting on the outskirts of Gibeah with about six hundred men and with Ahijah, the priest that Jonathan took his armour bearer and went out against the Philistine garrison without his father's knowledge.

Jonathan and his armour bearer singlehandedly slaughtered about twenty men on this day. And so, at the same time when Jonathan attacked, God also intervened, causing a great trembling, and shaking to come into the camp of the Philistines, into the field, in the garrison, amongst the raiders and all the people, leaving them scattered in every direction.

Upon receiving a report from his watchmen, Saul instructed the people with him to call the roll and see who departed from their camp, only to find that it was Jonathan and his armour bearer, to their surprise.

And so, while Saul was still busy enquiring of Ahijah the priest, it happened that the noise in the camps of the Philistines only increased. Saul then immediately assembled the armies and set out to the battlefield. Upon arrival, Saul discovered great confusion amongst the Philistines to the extent that they turned their swords against one another.

On this day, the Lord saved Israel, and the battle shifted to Beth Aven.

Saul's Harsh Oath:
1 Samuel 14:24 – 46

Now it happened that while Jonathan and his armour bearer attacked the Philistine garrison that, Saul placed the people under oath, stating:

..."Cursed is the man who eats any food until evening, before I have taken vengeance on my enemies."...

1 Samuel 14:24 (NKJV)

Now Israel, in pursuit of the Philistines, reached the forest where they found honey on the ground but did not dare to eat it because of the oath. But Jonathan, unaware of his father's oath, took the staff in his hands, dipped the edge in the honey, and ate causing his countenance to light up.

One of the men then informed Jonathan of the oath that his father had placed them under, but he thought that this was rather unwise because putting the people under such an oath brought trouble on them, for if they have eaten, then the slaughter of the Philistines would have been much greater.

On that day, the men of Israel drove the Philistines back from Michmash to Aijalon and, because of being faint, rushed on the spoil and ate of the sheep, oxen, and calves with the blood.

This was a great sin against the Lord, to which Saul built an altar to slaughter the animals, instructing the people not to eat with the blood. This was the first altar Saul built for the Lord.

After this, Saul commanded the army to go down after the Philistines and plunder them until morning, leaving no man alive.

Upon the priest's request, Saul then asked the counsel of the Lord whether to go down after the Philistines, but God did not answer him that day.

Saul understood that this could only be because someone sinned, so after casting lots, he discovered that his son Jonathan was guilty.

Jonathan then confessed to eating the honey, leaving his father no choice but to fulfil his oath, declaring that Jonathan must die.

The people then intervened, explaining that surely God has worked with his son Jonathan delivering this great victory into their hands and so should rather be spared.

"...So, the people rescued Jonathan, and he did not die."

1 Samuel 14:45 (NKJV)

Saul then withdrew from pursuing the Philistines and returned to his own place.

Saul's Final Destruction:
1 Samuel 15

The Prophet Samuel then came unto Saul, commanding him to attack Amalek according to the Word of the Lord, for God was about to punish the Amalekites for what they did to Israel when they ambushed them as they came out of Egypt.

Leaving Saul with the following battle instruction:

- Go and attack Amalek and destroy all that they have, and spare no one – **1 Samuel 15:3**
- Kill both man and woman – **1 Samuel 15:3**
- Kill both infant and nursing child – **1 Samuel 15:3**
- Kill all the oxen, sheep, camels, and donkeys – **1 Samuel 15:3**

Saul then set out to destroy the Amalekites according to the Word of the Lord given by the Prophet Samuel. Saul further instructed the Kenites who showed kindness to Israel when they came out of Egypt to depart from among the Amalekites, lest they be destroyed.

And so, Saul and his men laid siege against all the Amalekites from Havilah to Shur — sparing the life of Agag, the king of Amalek, along with all the best of the sheep, oxen, fatlings, lambs, and all that was good and in doing so, completely disobeying the instructions given by God through the Prophet Samuel.

This action caused great indignation against Saul as the Lord told Samuel that:

> [11] *"I greatly regret that I have set up Saul as king, for he has turned back from following Me, and has not performed My commandments." And it grieved Samuel, and he cried out to the Lord all night."*

> 1 Samuel 15:11 (NKJV)

Saul Kingship Revoked:
1 Samuel 15:12 – 35

Samuel then set out to meet with Saul at Gilgal, and upon arrival, Saul greeted Samuel, saying:

> *"Blessed are you of the LORD! I have performed the commandment of the LORD."*

> 1 Samuel 15:13 (NKJV)

Saul then tried to justify his disobedience towards God's original instruction, to which Samuel responded by saying:

> [22] ...*" Has the Lord as great delight in burnt offerings and sacrifices, As in obeying the voice of the Lord? Behold, to obey is better than sacrifice, And to heed than the fat of rams.*

> [23] *For rebellion is as the sin of witchcraft, And stubbornness is as iniquity and idolatry. Because you have rejected the word of the Lord, He also has rejected you from being king."*

> 1 Samuel 15:22 – 23 (NKJV)

Saul's lack of character and inability to lead – seeking man's approval rather than pursuing God's approval, caused him to give in to the demands of his men and therefore sinned greatly against God by deliberately disobeying His commandments.

And so, in a desperate attempt to set things right, Saul pleaded with Samuel to pardon his sin. However, this was a plea of false humility. He further requested that Samuel return with him so that he may worship the Lord – a request that Samuel denied.

Now just as Samuel was about to leave, Saul grabbed the hem of Samuel's garment and tore it, to which Samuel declared that just as his garment was torn, in the same way, God tore the kingdom from Saul and gave it to someone more worthy than him – one who is not double-minded and that will walk in truth.

Samuel then completed the original assignment of God given to Saul by hacking King Agag into pieces before the Lord in Gilgal.

And so, Samuel and Saul both went their own way, never to speak again.

4. David's Rise to the Throne; Progressive Deterioration and End of Saul's Reign: 1 Samuel 16 – 31

David Anointed As King Over Israel:
1 Samuel 16:1 – 13

After this, Samuel took his horn filled with oil and set out on a divine assignment to the house of Jesse in Bethlehem as instructed by God, for there, the Lord chose a new king from among the sons of Jesse.

And so, after Samuel revealed the purpose of his visit – Jesse then presented seven of his sons to Samuel to see who the newly appointed king would be.

Now Eliab, Jesse's eldest son, immediately caught Samuel's attention, thinking surely this is the Lord's chosen one.

But the Lord told Samuel not to look at the outward appearance – for He does not see as man sees but looks at the heart. And so, the Lord rejected all seven sons presented before Samuel.

Samuel knew without a doubt that the Lord had sent him on this mission and asked Jesse if all the young men were present, to which Jesse revealed that the youngest was keeping the sheep.

Samuel then summoned David, to which the Lord instructed Samuel to anoint David as the next king. And so, without delay, Samuel took the horn of oil and anointed David amid his brothers.

From this day forward, the Spirit of the Lord was upon David.

Saul and David Meet for the 1ˢᵗ Time:
1 Samuel 16:14 – 23

> *¹⁴ "But the Spirit of the Lord departed from Saul, and a distressing spirit from the Lord troubled him."*

1 Samuel 16:14 (NKJV)

Now Saul gained knowledge that David, the son of Jesse, could play the harp and so summoned David to come and play for him. David immediately found favour in Saul's sight – Saul even instated David as His armour bearer.

And so it was that the evil spirit would depart whenever David would play the harp, but the moment that he would stop, the spirit would trouble Saul again.

David and Goliath:
1 Samuel 17:1 – 58

Through the following events, we see how David's courage, obedience and response towards a life-defining moment and his trust in the only true living God granted him uncommon favour, breakthrough and victory in every sphere of life.

At the valley of Elah, we witness one of the greatest battles recorded in the Bible as the Philistine armies gathered in battle array on one side of the valley and the Israelite armies on the other side – with the battle in favour of the Philistines. A perfect opportunity for God to reveal His mighty power. For forty days, twice a day, both morning and evening, the champion of the Philistines, a man by the name of Goliath from Gath, would come down into the valley defying, mocking and cursing the armies of Israel.

Now Goliath was a skilled and trained warrior, a giant that the Bible described in the following manner:

- He was six cubits (2.0 meters) and a span in height – **1 Samuel 17:4**
- He had a bronze helmet with a coat of mail, and the weight of the coat was five thousand shekels of bronze. (57 kg.) – **1 Samuel 17:5**
- He had bronze armour on his legs and a bronze javelin between his shoulders – **1 Samuel 17:6**
- His spear was like a weaver's beam, and the iron spearhead weighed six hundred shekels. (7 kg.) – **1 Samuel 17:7**

This man came forward with the following battle conditions:

- Israel was to choose their champion to face him in battle – **1 Samuel 17:8**
- If Israel's champion were to kill Goliath, then the Philistines would become servants to the Israelites – **1 Samuel 17:9**
- If Goliath kills Israel's champion, Israel will become servants to the Philistines. **1 Samuel 17:9**

These battle instructions left the armies of Israel completely discouraged and afraid, as no man was willing to face this giant in battle until David, a shepherd's boy, was divinely set up by God to fight one of the most crucial battles of his life.

And so, David, commissioned by his father Jesse to take some food to his brothers, sets out on a journey, not knowing that he is about to step into his divine destiny.

He arrives at the battle scene only to find the two armies standing in battle formation on either side of the valley, hearing Goliath down in the valley, mocking and cursing the armies of God, and Israel too afraid to act.

Soon after, David starts questioning the situation. And after being rejected by his eldest brother Eliab, David went on asking someone else, where he finally gained insight on the conditions of the battle.

With the Israelites cowering away and no one willing to face Goliath, King Saul finally announces a reward that will be given to the one that will defeat Goliath.

A reward that catches David's attention stating that the victor will be given the following:

- The king's daughter – **1 Samuel 17:25**
- And the victor's father will be exempt from taxes in Israel – **1 Samuel 17:25**

And so, not long after David's conversations with the soldiers, he once again finds himself in the king's presence, boldly stating that the men of Israel do not need to fear because he will go and fight this Philistine that so arrogantly defines the armies of God.

At first, King Saul is hesitant towards David's suggestion stating that he is only a youth and the man that he is about to face was a man of war from his youth.

Irrespective of the king's thought towards David, he stood unwavering at the mission at hand and so, courageously and with all persuasiveness, responded to King Saul by saying,

36 Your servant has killed both lion and bear; and this uncircumcised Philistine will be like one of them, seeing he has defied the armies of the living God."

37 Moreover David said, "The Lord, who delivered me from the paw of the lion and from the paw of the bear, He will deliver me from the hand of this Philistine."
And Saul said to David, "Go, and the Lord be with you!

1 Samuel 17:36 (NKJV)

And so, after David denied the king's armour set down into the valley with nothing but his staff, sling and five smooth stones that he gathered from the brook in the valley, about to change the very course of history.

The moment that Goliath saw David, he continued with his disrespectful and arrogant insults toward David, further stating that he would give his flesh to the birds of the air and beasts of the field.

At this stage, Goliath was utterly unaware that the battle was taken into the supernatural, and the scales tipped into Israel's favour the moment David stepped down into the valley.

Unshaken by Goliath's threats, David responded with words that echoed through eternity, claiming his victory as a son of the true living God, stating that:

46 This day the Lord will deliver you into my hand, and I will strike you and take your head from you. And this day I will give the carcasses of the camp of the Philistines to the birds of the air and the wild beasts of the earth, that all the earth may know that there is a God in Israel.

47 Then all this assembly shall know that the Lord does not save with sword and spear; for the battle is the Lord's, and He will give you into our hands."

1 Samuel 17:46 – 47 (NKJV)

David then took one of the stones, placed it in his sling and struck the Philistine in his forehead with such force that the stone sunk into his forehead, killing Goliath instantly.

The moment the giant fell, David severed Goliath's head with Goliath's sword, causing the Philistines to flee as they saw their champion defeated.

That day the Lord delivered a great victory into the hands of Israel. And so, this event marked the beginning of a new journey for David as he was about to face even a greater challenge.

Saul's Envy Towards David:
1 Samuel 18

David quickly gained Saul's favour and was set as general over the men of war. David would go everywhere that Saul would send him, behaving wisely.

As the story further unfolds, we see David one day coming back after slaughtering the Philistines — on his return, the women start to sing and dance, saying:

> [7] ..."*Saul has slain his thousands,*
> *And David his ten thousands.*"

1 Samuel 18:7 (NKJV)

As a result, Saul's heart became enraged with jealousy towards David, and he now, through various attempts, tries to kill David, but to no avail.

Saul's Attempts to Kill David:

- First and Second Attempt: **1 Samuel 18:10 – 11**
- Third Attempt: **1 Samuel 18:17 – 19**
- Fourth Attempt: **1 Samuel 18:20 – 30**
- Fifth Attempt: **1 Samuel 19:1 – 6**
- Sixth Attempt: **1 Samuel 19:7 – 10**
- Seventh Attempt: **1 Samuel 19:11 – 14**
- Eighth Attempt: **1 Samuel 19:15 – 16**
- Ninth, Tenth and Eleventh Attempt: **1 Samuel 19:17 – 21**
- Twelfth Attempt: **1 Samuel 19:22 – 24**
- Thirteenth, Fourteenth and Fifteenth Attempt: **1 Samuel 20:24 – 42**
- Sixteenth Attempt: **1 Samuel 23:1 – 12**
- Seventeenth Attempt: **1 Samuel 23:13 – 15**
- Eighteenth Attempt: **1 Samuel 23:19 – 29**
- Nineteenth Attempt: **1 Samuel 24:1 – 2**

Jonathan's Loyalty:
1 Samuel 20:1 – 23

David, at this stage, knew without a doubt that his life was in danger and sought Jonathan's counsel regarding the situation as he tried to understand what he had done wrong that Saul wanted to take his life.

Jonathan ignorantly assures David that his perception of the situation is incorrect, stating that surely his father would disclose unto him any plan to take David's life.

But David reminds Jonathan that Saul knows about their close friendship and, as a result, will hide such information from him to spare him from any grief.

Jonathan quickly realises the severity of the situation and assures David that he will stand by his side whatever he decides to do.

And so, David came up with a strategy to confirm Saul's anger towards him, stating that he would be absent from the New Moon feast, not appearing at the king's table for three days as expected.

Jonathan was then given specific instructions on what to say when Saul queries his absence, simply stating that David sincerely requested permission to go and attend a yearly sacrifice with his family in Bethlehem.

If Saul is at peace with the given reason, it will be a sign that David is safe, but if he is angry, it will be a sure sign that Saul indeed wants to kill him.

David's Adventures:
1 Samuel 21:1 – 15

David then went to Nob, to Ahimelech, the priest, stating that he was there on a special assignment as ordered by the king – a visit that would later cost the lives of Ahimelech and his household.

Here David ate the holy bread and took the sword of Goliath before making his way to Achish, the king of Gath.

It then happened that one of the servants of Achish named Doeg recognised David, stating that he was the one that the people would sing about, saying that Saul had slain his thousands but David ten thousands.

And so, out of fear for the king of Gath, David started acting like a madman, scratching the gate doors and letting saliva dribble down his beard.

As a result, Achish rejected David as a madman, inquiring why his servant would bring someone that was insane into his presence.

David and his 400 Men:
1 Samuel 22:1 – 5

From Gath, David escaped to the cave of Adullam, where David's father and brothers joined him with everyone in distress, debt and discontented. And so, David became captain over approximately four hundred men.

From here, David went to the Mizpah of Moab to enquire of the king whether his father and mother could stay there until he gained further knowledge of God concerning his next move – a request accepted by the king of Moab. David was then later instructed by the prophet Gad to leave to the land of Judah.

Saul Murders the Priests:
1 Samuel 22:6 – 23

Doeg, the Edomite who was over Saul's servants – the same Doeg that recognised David in Nob when David went to Ahimelech, the priest – then betrayed David by explaining to Saul that he saw David there enquiring of the Lord.

Now blinded by hatred, jealousy and bitterness, Saul sent for Ahimelech and all of his household, charging them with the death penalty for conspiring against the king.

Note: *Remember that Ahimelech helped David because David told him he was alone on a special assignment for the king. And besides, everyone knew that David was the king's most faithful servant. Ahimelech, therefore, acted out of the purity of his heart, knowing nothing of the actual situation between David and Saul.*

Ahimelech then desperately tried to explain the situation to Saul, how he knew nothing of what he was being accused of, neither little nor much. However, his plea for mercy was to no avail.

Saul then ordered the guards standing with him to turn and kill all the Lord's priest's on false charges, a command they refused to carry out.

Unwilling to let the situation go, Saul turned to Doeg and commanded him to kill the priests.

> *"...So Doeg the Edomite turned and struck the priests, and killed on that day eighty-five men who wore a linen ephod.*
>
> *[19] Also Nob, the city of the priests, he struck with the edge of the sword, both men and women, children and nursing infants, oxen and donkeys and sheep — with the edge of the sword."*
>
> **1 Samuel 22:18 – 19 (NKJV)**

Fortunately, there was one to escape this slaughter, Abiathar, the son of Ahitub, that now fled after David.

Abiathar then explained to David how Saul commanded all the priests be to be killed and that Doeg was the one to carry out the command.

David took full responsibility for what happened, stating it was his fault. David further offered Abiathar a place of safety by taking him in.

David Spares Saul:
1 Samuel 24:1 – 22

In the events that follow, we see an outstanding display of character, honour and mercy that is well worth noting as David reveals a pure heart of integrity by continually sparing Saul's life, even after all Saul has done to him.

The first account of this was set in the Wilderness of En Gedi, where Saul assembled three thousand able men in pursuit of David after he gained knowledge of David's whereabouts.

And so, when Saul came to the sheepfolds by the road, he went into a cave to attend to his needs, the same cave where David and his men were hiding.

David's men immediately thought that this was retribution and said unto David,

> ... *"This is the day of which the Lord said to you, 'Behold, I will deliver your enemy into your hand, that you may do to him as it seems good to you.'" And David arose and secretly cut off a corner of Saul's robe.*

1 Samuel 24:4 (NKJV)

Fortunately, David had a heart after God's own heart. It was, therefore, more important for him to do what was right in the sight of God than to please his men, as David's actions to follow set the tone for what it really means to revere the Lord's anointed.

Even until this point, David still saw Saul as his master and the Lord's anointed and therefore did not allow his men to revolt against Saul.

Even the fact that he cut Saul's robe was a disturbing matter to him, for the bible says that David was troubled in his heart because of what he had done.

After Saul left the cave unharmed, he heard a voice crying from behind him, only to find that it was David with his face bowed down to the earth.

Here, David pleaded with Saul, explaining how the Lord indeed delivered him into his hands. Even after being urged by his men to strike him down, he refused to do so but spared his life, revealing the piece of Saul's robe that he had cut off as evidence that he meant no harm.

David further asked Saul the reason for hunting him down as he has been nothing but faithful towards him. He assured Saul that there was no rebellion nor evil in his heart, stating that God would be judge between them and so deliver him out of Saul's hand.

Now completely perplexed by this unexpected event, Saul asked if it was indeed David speaking and then wept, announcing that David was indeed more righteous than him. Irrespective of the continual evil he planned against David, David would still show mercy and kindness towards him.

From this moment, Saul knew without a doubt that David would be king over Israel and therefore asked David to swear that he would not wipe out his descendants nor remove his name from his father's house, to which David agreed.

And so, Saul returned home, and David and his men returned to the stronghold.

The Death of Samuel
1 Samuel 25:1

And so, the Prophet Samuel died and was buried by the Israelites in Ramah at his home. And after these things, David departed to the Wilderness of Paran.

David, Abigail and Nabal:
1 Samuel 25:2 – 44

The following account of David, Abigail, and Nabal shows the devastating results of being bad-tempered and what can happen when you repay good with evil. In contrast, it also reveals how wisdom, and a kind heart will always contradict, override, and cancel out evil.

Therefore, the following events reveal the truth when Jesus said that with the measure you use, it will be measured to you. – **Luke 6:38**

Now there was a very wealthy man named Nabal who had a business in Carmel. The Bible records that he had three thousand sheep and a thousand goats.

The Bible describes Nabal as:

- Harsh.
- Evil in his doings.
- He was of the house of Caleb.

Now Nabal had a wife whose name was Abigail, and the bible describes Abigail as:

- A woman of good understanding.
- Beautiful in appearance.

It then came to David's attention that Nabal was busy shearing his sheep in Carmel, to which David immediately assembled ten young men to go and greet Nabal in his name with the following message:

- Peace be to you, peace to your house, and peace to all that you have! – **1 Samuel 25:6**
- We protected your shepherds while they were with us and did not take anything from them while they were in Carmel – **1 Samuel 25:7**
- You can ask your men, and they will tell you. May my young men find favour in your eyes as we come to you on a feast day. Please spare whatever you can to your servants and your son David – **1 Samuel 25:8**

Nabal then completely reviled them, asking who David was and why he should give them food. Nabal's refusal to show them any kindness and repaying evil for good had severe repercussions as David now assembled four hundred men to go up against Nabal to kill every male in his household.

One of Nabal's servants then explained the situation to Abigail and how David and his men indeed protected them and Nabal's sheep while they were in the field, nor did they require or took anything for them. Still, in return for their kindness, Nabal treated them harshly.

Abigail then, in a desperate attempt to save her household, acted hastily by gathering the following:

- Two hundred loaves of bread,
- Two skins of wine,
- Five sheep already dressed,
- Five seahs of roasted grain,
- One hundred clusters of raisins,
- And two hundred cakes of figs.

All these items were loaded unto donkeys and escorted by Abigail's servants, who went before her to meet with David. Now Abigail did not disclose any of her doings to Nabal as she knew that he was a scoundrel and would not understand.

And so, Abigail set out on a journey into the unexpected, not knowing what the outcome would be as she took her husband's guilt upon herself.

When Abigail finally made it to David, she bowed down to the ground at his feet, pleading with him to pardon Nabal's offence as indiscretion is with him – further stating that she was unaware of the servants that David had sent.

So, Abigail presented David with the trespass offering she had prepared, asking for forgiveness with the hope that she might find favour in his eyes and that he would oversee Nabal's trespass.

Abigail then further advised David that when God has fulfilled all the good that He has spoken concerning him and appointed him ruler over Israel, this will not be a grief or offence to him because he has not shed blood without cause or even avenged himself but left the matter in God's hands.

And so David responded with favour, blessing the Lord God of Israel for sending Abigail, a woman of good understanding who presented him with Godly advice that kept him from bloodshed and avenging himself with his own hand.

David honoured Abigail's request and courage, sending her in peace after receiving the gift she had prepared for him.

After Abigail revealed all the recent events to Nabal, his heart became like a stone, so after ten days, the Lord struck Nabal, and he died. Thus the Lord has returned Nabal's wickedness on his own head.

And so, after Nabal's death, David requested Abigail's hand in marriage, a proposal she accepted, and so became his wife.

While all this was going on, Saul continued down his path of destruction, this time deciding to give his daughter Michal, David's wife, to Palti, the son of Laish.

David Spares Saul a Second time:
1 Samuel 26:1 – 25

The following event marks the second account of where David spares Saul's life and is set in the Wilderness of Ziph, where Saul yet again assembled three thousand able men in pursuit of David after Saul gained knowledge of David's whereabouts.

And so, David and Abishai went down to the hill of Hachilah at night where Saul was sleeping with his spear firmly fixed in the ground beside his head, encamped with all his men around him along with Abner, the commander of his army.

Saul and his men fell into a deep sleep because of the Lord, enabling David and Abishai to enter the camp undetected.

Once again, leaving David in the tempted position where he could so easily take Saul's life, ending the endless persecution against him.

Abishai even urged David to allow him to pin Saul to the ground with Saul's own spear, ensuring David that it would be swift and that he would not have to strike Saul a second time, stating that this is God who delivered his enemies into his hand.

But David, out of the purity and integrity of his heart, would not allow any harm to befall Saul, especially not by his doing as Saul was still the Lord's anointed in his eyes, stating,

> ..."*Do not destroy him; for who can stretch out his hand against the Lord's anointed, and be guiltless?*" *¹⁰ David said furthermore, "As the Lord lives, the Lord shall strike him, or his day shall come to die, or he shall go out to battle and perish.*

> **1 Samuel 26:9 – 10 (NKJV)**

And so David took the spear and jug of water by Saul's head and departed from the camp, standing on a hill opposite Saul's camp, leaving a great distance between them.

David then called out to the people and Abner, questioning Abner's ability to protect the king, stating that someone came into the camp to destroy the king without him even being aware of the situation, using Saul's jug of water and spear as evidence of this truth.

Saul then recognised David's voice asking if it was indeed him speaking, to which David confirmed — further requesting the reason for Saul still pursuing him and hunting him like an animal as he could understand if there was evil in his hand.

But Saul knew that he acted wickedly and so admitted his foolish actions and sin towards David, further asking for David to come to him, to which David responded that Saul must rather send one of his young men to come and fetch his spear.

After these things, Saul and David went their separate ways.

Saul Consults a Medium:
1 Samuel 28:3 – 25

Saul's life was now completely spiralling out of control as his actions led him down a path of destruction, drawing exceedingly closer to the end of his reign.

It happened that David and the Philistines became allies in a battle against Israel, with Achish telling David that he would make him his chief guardian.

When Saul saw the Philistine army coming up against him, he became frightened in his heart, causing him to act even more wickedly.

After seeing this great army, Saul sought counsel from the Lord through the prophets and the Urim but received no answer from the Lord, not even in his dreams.

As a result, Saul then adds to his guilt by resorting to wicked measures in a desperate attempt to now gain an answer by commanding his servants to find a medium to inquire of.

The servants then explained to Saul that there was a medium at Endor. Saul then disguised himself before going to the medium by night, escorted by two of his men. Initially, the medium was hesitant to help Saul because she thought it was a trap as Saul expelled all the mediums and spiritists out of the land.

But Saul swore to her by the Lord that he meant her no harm and so for her to call up Samuel.

The moment the medium saw Samuel, she became afraid, knowing that Saul was inquiring, thinking that Saul had deceived her by setting up this trap.

Saul then assured her a second time that there was no reason for her to be afraid, asking what she had seen, to which she explained that she saw an old man coming up covered with a mantle. Saul then perceived that it was Samuel and bowed down to the ground.

Samuel then asked Saul the reason for disturbing him, to which Saul explained that he needed council concerning the Philistines laying siege against him and, even more, that he sought God through the prophets but to no avail as God has left him.

> *¹⁶ Then Samuel said: "So why do you ask me, seeing the Lord has departed from you and has become your enemy?"*

> **1 Samuel 28:16 (NKJV)**

Samuel further told Saul that God had torn the kingdom out of his hands and given it to David because of his disobedience, not executing the Lord's fierce wrath upon Amalek.

Samuel then further revealed that God will deliver Israel, including Saul, into the hands of the Philistines and that the next day, both Saul and his sons will die, and they will be with him.

The tragic news caused Saul to fall to the ground and after persuading Saul to eat something, they rose and went their way.

The Tragic End of Saul and His Sons: 1 Samuel 31

The Philistines then attacked Israel prevailing mightily against them, leaving Saul and his sons to flee for their lives.

Saul was severely injured after being hit by an archer to which Saul commanded his armour-bearer to draw his sword and kill him, lest the uncircumcised thrust him through.

But the armour bearer refused to carry out Saul's instruction because he was too afraid. Saul then ended his own life by taking a sword and falling on it. And so when his armour bearer saw that Saul was dead, he also fell upon his sword and died.

And so Saul, his three sons, his armour bearer and all his men died with him on the same day, fulfilling the words spoken by the Prophet Samuel.

The following day the Philistines came to the battlefield and found Saul and his sons fallen to the ground. They then severed Saul's head and stripped off his armour.

They then took Saul's armour, placed it in the temple of the Ashtoreth's and impaled his body on the wall of Beth-Shan.

When news of this tragic event reached the inhabitants of Jabesh-Gilead, all the valiant men went to go and recover the bodies of Saul and his sons. Their bodies were then returned to Jabesh, where they were burned and their bones buried under the tamarisk tree.

After this, the people then fasted for seven days.

PROPHETIC DECLARATIONS:

1.   1 Samuel 3:19 (NKJV)

[19] **"So Samuel grew, and the Lord was with him and let none of his words fall to the ground."**

I declare and decree in Jesus' name that none of my words shall fall null and void to the ground. My words shall be words of Godly wisdom and intelligence carried by the weight of God's glory, saturated with His anointing, hitting every target with pinpoint accuracy, accomplishing every task according to the way God ordained it and according to His perfect will with excellence, perfection, and distinction.

NOTES

NOTES

NOTES

Second Book of **Samuel**

"The Davidic Dynasty"

To understand the whole message of Samuel, one must view 1 & 2 Samuel as one book. The book of first Samuel was initially combined with the second book of Samuel.

These books were compiled from 1204-1035 B.C in Palestine by authors Samuel, David, Nathan, and Gad. The final edition which caused these two books to be divided was compiled later by Prophet Isaiah about 743-683 B.C, which is now presented in its final form as we know it today.

These books have varied many times in titles, having been designated "The First and Second Books of Kingdoms" (Septuagint); "First & Seconds Kings" (Vulgate); and "First and Second Samuel" (Hebrew tradition and most modern versions as we know them today).

The First Book of Samuel introduced the beginning of the monarchy, whilst the setting of the second book of Samuel portrays the establishment of the Davidic dynasty and the expansion of Israel under God's chosen leader.

In the first ten chapters, David is portrayed as a warrior who wins battles, is revered by the people, is kind to the sick and needy, and is righteous in God's eyes. As his men returned home with the ark of the covenant, we witness David dancing before the Lord in the streets of Jerusalem. We also meet Mephibosheth, Jonathan's disabled son, to whom David showed mercy out of concern for Jonathan.

However, biblical writers did not overlook David's flaws as in the chapters that follow; we note David's adultery with Bathsheba being followed by a series of tragic events, which include their child's death, David's daughter Tamar raped by his son Amnon, the murder of Amnon, David's own political overthrown by his son Absalom, and then Absalom's subsequent death.

Despite the turmoil in his latter years, David enjoyed the Lord's forgiveness and favour. His genuine sorrow and regret for his sins were revealed by his repentant heart, a heart that the Lord was well pleased with.

The book of 2 Samuel can be divided into the following three major events:

1. The Triumphs of David and The Temporary Divided Kingdom: **2 Samuel 1 – 10**
2. The Transgressions of David: **2 Samuel 11**
3. The Troubles of David: **2 Samuel 12 – 24**

HIGHLIGHTED EVENTS IN 2 SAMUEL:

1. **The Triumphs of David and The Temporary Divided Kingdom: 2 Samuel 1 – 10 (NKJV)**

The Report of Saul's Death:
2 Samuel 1:1 – 16 (NKJV)

2 Samuel 1 involves a report of King Saul's death, the execution of a messenger, and David's mourning for Saul and his son, Jonathan.

While David was at Ziklag, a young man came to David with his clothes torn and dust on his head, explaining to David that Saul and Jonathan were both dead.

The Amalekite lied, telling a story that would later cost him his life, explaining that he found Saul, who was severely injured, leaning on his spear and that Saul asked him to stand over him and then to kill him, which he then did. He then proceeded to bring Saul's crown and bracelet to David as evidence.

This news deeply grieved David, so he ordered for the Amalekite to be executed as he was not hesitant to raise his hands against the Lord's anointed.

The latter section of this chapter is a lamentation over the death of Saul and Jonathan. David crafted an elegy to express his sorrow over losing his dear friend as well as honouring Saul.

David concealed the king's faults even though Saul tried to kill him numerous times, still keeping a heart of integrity, honouring Saul as the Lord's anointed.

The chapter then ends with a proclamation of brotherly love and honouring soldiers who have fallen in battle.

Temporary Divided Kingdom:

King over Judah — David:
2 Samuel 2:1 – 7

In the events that follow, we see the effects of a temporarily divided kingdom and the early stages of what is yet to come for the nation of Israel.

We also see a quality of David that is well worth taking note of, as he would not make any critical decision without consulting with God first. This quality caused David to live a life of absolute victory.

And so, this chapter starts with David consulting with God concerning his next destination to which the Lord led him and everyone with him to Hebron, where the men of Judah came and anointed David as king over the house of Judah.

It is here that David reigned as king over the house of Judah for seven years and six months.

King over Israel — Ishbosheth:
2 Samuel 2:8 – 11

Ishbosheth, Saul's son, was then made king over the remaining tribes of Israel by Abner, the commander of Saul's army.

Ishbosheth was forty years old when he was appointed king over Israel and reigned for two years.

Israel and Judah at War:
2 Samuel 2:12 – 32

The following battle scene is set at the pool of Gibeon, with Abner and the servants of Ishbosheth on one side of the pool and Joab with the servants of David on the other side.

And so Abner suggested that twelve of his young men compete against twelve of Joab's men, to which Joab agreed.

However, this was to no avail as each man took hold of their opponent's head, piercing their swords into their opponent's side so that everyone fell to the ground together.

A fierce battle then broke out between the two camps. But David's servants prevailed greatly against Abner and the men of Israel, causing them to flee for their lives.

Now Asahel, Joab's brother, a man who was as fleet of foot as a wild gazelle, pursued after Abner. When Abner took note of Asahel chasing after him, he gave Asahel two warnings to stop as he did not want to strike him down.

Unfortunately, Asahel was relentless in his pursuit of Abner and refused to give up, leaving Abner no choice but to strike Asahel in the stomach with the blunt end of the spear, causing the spear to come out of his back, causing his death.

Both Asahel's brothers, Joab and Abishai, also pursued Abner until they reached the hill of Ammah, where the children of Benjamin took a stand behind Abner on top of the hill.

And so, Abner successfully managed to persuade Joab to stop the onslaught as enough blood was shed between brethren.

The battle count was severe for Abner and his men as they lost three hundred and sixty men compared to David's servants, that only lost nineteen men and Asahel.

And so they took Asahel's body and buried him in his father's tomb in Bethlehem before Joab and his men returned to Hebron.

2nd King over all Israel — David (United Kingdom Again): 2 Samuel 3,4 & 5:1 – 5

The war between the house of David and Saul continued for a long time, but the hand of the Lord remained upon David as he only grew in strength, while the house of Saul grew weaker and weaker.

David was now drawing exceedingly closer to fulfilling his Prophetic Destiny in becoming king over all of Israel. We see God's divine plan for David's life shift into the next phase when Abner turns against Ishbosheth and enters a covenant with David stating that he will surrender all of Israel into David's hands.

And so David agreed to this covenant on the condition that Michal, Saul's daughter, be brought back to him. After this, there was peace between David and Abner.

The story then further unfolds with Joab questioning Abner's motive for making this covenant with David and so, without David's knowledge, sent for Abner to meet with him privately with the intent to execute him.

And so, both Joab and Abishai avenged their brother Asahel by stabbing Abner in the stomach so that he died.

Now when David received knowledge of this tragic event, he stated that Abner's blood is not upon him nor his kingdom but rests upon Joab and his household, making the following proclamation:

> *29 "Let it rest on the head of Joab and on all his father's house;*
> *and let there never fail to be in the house of Joab one who has a*
> *discharge or is a leper, who leans on a staff or falls by the sword, or*
> *who lacks bread."*

2 Samuel 3:29 (NKJV)

This tragic event was soon followed by the death of Saul's son Ishbosheth, who was beheaded in his house by two of his captains, Baanah and Rechab.

They then took Ishbosheth's head to David as if they had done a good deed, but their action had severe repercussions as David commanded both to be executed by cutting off their hands and feet before hanging them by the pool of Hebron.

Ishbosheth's head was then taken and buried in the tomb of Abner.

And so, a divided kingdom is once again united with David appointed as king over all of Israel at the age of thirty and he reigned for forty years.

He reigned over Judah in Hebron for seven years, six months, and thirty-three years in Jerusalem over all of Israel and Judah.

The Ark of the Covenant Returned:
2 Samuel 6 – 7

The following event shows the devastating results of when we act, but those actions are not according to the Lord's instructions, even though they might be done with the best intentions.

We see this when David took thirty thousand men to the house of Abinadab to restore the ark of God to Jerusalem.

So they placed the ark of God on a new cart driven by Abinadab's two sons, Uzzah and Ahio, and in doing so, disobeyed the procedures set out by God when transporting the ark.

It then happened that when the oxen stumbled, Uzzah stretched out his hand to prevent the ark from falling, now causing the anger of the Lord to be stirred up against him. The Lord then struck Uzzah so that he died right there by the ark.

This brought the fear of God upon David, who then decided to take the ark of God to the house of Obed-Edom, where it remained for three months.

When David was informed about the great blessing upon Obed-Edom and his household because of the ark of God, with gladness, he set out on a second attempt to bring the ark of God back to the city of David.

This time adhering to all the instructions given by God regarding how the ark was to be transported.

> *13 "And so it was, when those bearing the ark of the Lord had gone six paces, that he sacrificed oxen and fatted sheep."*

2 Samuel 6:13 (NKJV)

Many burnt offerings were made to ensure the Lord would be honoured appropriately, accompanied by a great deal of celebration as the Ark of God was brought into the city.

But when Michal saw David dancing and rejoicing, she despised David in her heart and later voiced her disagreement towards him.

> *21 So David said to Michal, "It was before the Lord, who chose me instead of your father and all his house, to appoint me ruler over the people of the Lord, over Israel. Therefore I will play music before the Lord."*

2 Samuel 6:21 (NKJV)

Michal's disrespectful attitude came at a very high price as she became barren from this moment forward.

After this, God then made the following covenant with David through the Prophet Nathan concerning his seed that shall reign after him:

- That David's own seed will inherit the kingdom after him and that God will establish his kingdom. – **2 Samuel 7:12 (NKJV)**
- He will build a house for God, and his kingdom will be established forever – **2 Samuel 7:13 (NKJV)**
- God will be his Father – **2 Samuel 7:14 (NKJV)**
- God will chasten him if he commits iniquity – **2 Samuel 7:14 (NKJV)**
- God's mercy will never depart from him – **2 Samuel 7:15 (NKJV)**
- God will establish David's house and kingdom forever – **2 Samuel 7:16 (NKJV)**

2. **The Transgressions of David:**
   2 Samuel 11 (NKJV)

David, Bathsheba, and Uriah:
2 Samuel 11:1 – 27

Through the verses that follow, we discover the impact our decisions have on our lives – either for good or bad, depending on whether those decisions line up with God or not.

We find one such example in this passage of scripture when David allowed the lust of the flesh to consume his sound judgement; as one evening, while he was walking on the king's roof, he took note of a woman bathing, and the woman was very beautiful.

And so, David inquired about the woman, only to find that this was Bathsheba, the wife of Uriah.

Then David, against his better judgement, gave in to the temptations of the flesh, instructing messengers to bring Bathsheba unto him. And so, David laid with her, and she conceived.

Now when David received news of Bathsheba being with child — instead of taking responsibility for his actions, he now, through a series of events, acted even more wickedly by conspiring against Uriah, Bathsheba's husband, in an attempt to conceal the situation.

1st Attempt:

The first thing that David did was to instruct Joab to send for Uriah to return from war, hoping that Uriah would go and lie with his wife Bathsheba after a long journey back home.

But David's plan failed as Uriah felt that it would be wrong of him to go back home and to eat and drink and lie with his wife while the ark and Israel and Judah are dwelling in open tents encamped in the open field and so instead slept at the door of the king's house together with David's servants.

2nd Attempt:

And so, the second thing David did was to invite Uriah for dinner with the intent to make him drunk with the hope that Uriah would then go and lie with his wife, Bathsheba.

But David's plan failed again as Uriah went out to lie in his bed with David's servants as before - not returning home as David had hoped.

3rd Attempt:

Then David sent Uriah back to war with a letter for Joab's attention. Now Uriah was completely unaware of the fact that he was about to deliver a letter to carry out his own death sentence.

The content of this letter stated that Joab was to place Uriah in the forefront where the battle would be the fiercest and then to retreat from him so that he may be killed.

Everything then happened according to plan as Uriah died in battle. And so Bathsheba was married to David and bore him a son. But David's actions greatly displeased God.

3. The Troubles of David:
2 Samuel 12 – 24 (NKJV)

The Parable of Nathan the Prophet and David's confession:
2 Samuel 12,13,14

The Lord then sent Nathan the Prophet to David with the following parable:

² The rich man had exceedingly many flocks and herds.

³ But the poor man had nothing, except one little ewe lamb which he had bought and nourished; and it grew up together with him and with his children. It ate of his own food and drank from his own cup and lay in his bosom; and it was like a daughter to him.

⁴ And a traveler came to the rich man, who refused to take from his own flock and from his own herd to prepare one for the wayfaring man who had come to him; but he took the poor man's lamb and prepared it for the man who had come to him."

2 Samuel 12:2 – 5 (NKJV)

After hearing the parable, David became angry, stating that such a man shall surely die and will have to restore fourfold for the lamb because of his actions and showing no pity.

Nathan then revealed to David that he is the man in the parable, and because he killed Uriah with the sword, David unleashed a sword of judgement over himself that shall never depart from his house.

David's transgression now unlocked the following consequences:

- The child that Bathsheba bore to David became ill and died as spoken by the Prophet Nathan – **2 Samuel 12:16 – 23**
- David then comforts Bathsheba, who bore him another son named Solomon. And the Lord loved Solomon, further instructing the Prophet Nathan that he be called Jedidiah.

- David's son Amnon sexually abused, and so defiled his sister Tamar, David's daughter – **2 Samuel 13:1 – 22**
- Absalom murders Amnon, his brother, in revenge for their sister Tamar – **2 Samuel 13:23 – 33**
- As a result, Absalom fled to Geshur for three years because of his trespass – **2 Samuel 13:34 – 39**
- Absalom then returns to David, his father, who shows him favour – **2 Samuel 14:1 – 33**

Absalom's Treason:
2 Samuel 15

Absalom then conspired against his father David, by turning the hearts of the men of Israel to himself. He successfully accomplished this task by giving the illusion that his heart was more for the people than his father, King David.

This conspiracy continued for over forty years, with those siding with Absalom now continually increasing in numbers. And so, after forty years, Absalom, with the king's approval, travelled to Hebron, stating that he must go and pay a vow he made to the Lord.

At this time, Absalom also sent spies throughout all the tribes of Israel in preparation for the revolt against his father, King David, with Ahithophel the Gilonite, David's counsellor joining him.

When King David gained knowledge of Absalom's conspiracy, he immediately took his servants and fled, making their way over the Brook Kidron where the Cherethites, Pelethites, Gittites and about six hundred men who had followed David from Gath marched before him.

Once they crossed the Brook Kidron, David instructed Zadok, the priest, to take the ark of God back to Jerusalem with Ahimaaz, his son and Jonathan, the son of Abiathar.

And so, King David and all the people with him made their way up the Mount of Olives, weeping as they went up.

It is here that David spoke to the Lord concerning Ahithophel – a conversation that shifted the current course of events entirely into David's favour as he said,

[31] ..."*O Lord, I pray, turn the counsel of Ahithophel into foolishness!*"

2 Samuel 15:31 (NKJV)

It came to pass when King David had reached the top of the mountain that he worshipped God. It was also here that King David was met by Hushai the Archite with his robe torn and dust on his head.

But David instructed Hushai to return to Jerusalem as his informant of all the happenings in the king's house together with Ahimaaz and Jonathan. Hushai was also to confuse and defeat the counsel of Ahithophel for David.

Ahithophel's Advice:
2 Samuel 16:15 – 23 & 2 Samuel 17

Meanwhile, Absalom enquired of Ahithophel for advice on the strategy going forward.

Step #1: 2 Samuel 16:21 – 23

Absalom was to go into his father's concubines that he left behind to tend to the house.

Step #2: 2 Samuel 17:1 – 4

Ahithophel advised that he would take twelve thousand men in pursuit of David and overthrow him while he is weary and weak, making him afraid.

And when all the people flee, he will strike only King David.

Ahithophel's advice was pleasing to Absalom and all the elders of Israel.

Note: *Although this was actually good advice, it was not what God had in mind as His heart was for David and thus the reason for setting up Hushai to confound Ahithophel's good counsel.*

Hushai's Advice:
2 Samuel 17:5 – 29

Absalom then played right into God's plan the moment he summoned for Hushai as a second voice of counsel, unaware that Hushai acts on David's behalf.

Hushai then contradicts the advice given by Ahithophel by speaking in David's favour according to the way that the Lord purposed it.

Hushai's Advice:

Step #1:

[11] 'Therefore I advise that all Israel be fully gathered to you, from Dan to Beersheba, like the sand that is by the sea for multitude, and that you go to battle in person.

[12] So we will come upon him in some place where he may be found, and we will fall on him as the dew falls on the ground. And of him and all the men who are with him there shall not be left so much as one."

2 Samuel 17:11 – 12 (NKJV)

Step #2:

[13] Moreover, if he has withdrawn into a city, then all Israel shall bring ropes to that city; and we will pull it into the river, until there is not one small stone found there."

[14] So Absalom and all the men of Israel said, "The advice of Hushai the Archite is better than the advice of Ahithophel." For the Lord had purposed to defeat the good advice of Ahithophel, to the intent that

the Lord might bring disaster on Absalom.

2 Samuel 17:13-14 (NKJV)

Hushai then, with great haste, sent news to King David, warning him of everything discussed concerning the battle strategy going forward.

Upon receiving the news, David immediately set out with everyone with him, crossed the Jordan River, and pressed on to Mahanaim.

When Ahithophel saw that his advice was not adhered to, he went back home to set his household in order and then committed suicide by hanging himself.

And so Israel and Absalom set out after David and his men encamping in the land of Gilead.

The Defeat & Death of Absalom:
2 Samuel 18

In the following events, we witness one of the most difficult battles David had to face – a battle against his son Absalom.

Now the battle arena was set in the woods of Ephraim, where Joab, Abishai and Ittai received one specific instruction from king David saying,

> *⁵ ... "Deal gently for my sake with the young man Absalom." And all the people heard when the king gave all the captains orders concerning Absalom."*

2 Samuel 18:5 (NKJV)

And so, the battle was fierce that day, causing the death of twenty thousand soldiers. In fact, the woods killed more people that day than the sword.

It is here that Absalom, while riding his mule, got caught up by his hear in a terebinth tree, hopelessly suspended between heaven and earth.

Absalom, now completely vulnerable, found himself in a very dangerous position and at the mercy of David's men.

However, when Joab received news of Absalom, he took three spears and killed Absalom while still alive in the tree by thrusting the spears through his heart.

After this, ten of Joab's armour bearers surrounded Absalom and finished him off.

David Returns to Jerusalem:
2 Samuel 19 – 20

> ² *"So the victory that day was turned into mourning for all the people. For the people heard it said that day, "The king is grieved for his son."*

2 Samuel 19:2 (NKJV)

After these things, King David returned to Jerusalem, where he responded with mercy to Shimei, who mocked and cursed him when he fled from Absalom and left Jerusalem.

King David also met Mephibosheth, Saul's grandson, whom he received with mercy and kindness and finally appointed his government officers.

The Philistine Giants Destroyed:
2 Samuel 21

It then came to pass that the Philistines again laid siege against Israel. This time, the battle almost claimed David's life.

And so it was decided by David's men that he should no longer go out to battle because if he died, then the lamp of Israel would also be quenched.

We then see David's men killing four Philistine giants born to the giant in Gath.

- The 1st giant Ishbi-Benob was killed by Abishai,
- The 2nd giant Saph was killed by Sibbechai,
- The 3rd giant, the brother of Goliath, was killed by Elhanan,
- The 4th giant, a man with six fingers on each hand and six toes on each foot, was killed by Jonathan.

David's Mighty Men:
2 Samuel 23

Besides being a man after God's own heart, David was also known for his exceptional bravery and courage. He was a man that placed his trust entirely in God and, as a result, accomplished some of the most extraordinary feats recorded in the Bible.

David's courage and bravery were contagious - it would rub off upon those surrounding him, as we will see in the lives of those known as David's mighty men, which proves the saying,

"If you want to become a millionaire, then walk with millionaires. If you want to become a giant slayer, then walk with giant slayers."

The list of David's mighty men and their courageous deeds is found in **2 Samuel 23:8 – 39.**

The Census of Israel & Judah:
2 Samuel 24

And so, Israel again stirred the anger of the Lord to come against them in as much that He moved David against Israel to say,

... *"Go and number Israel and Judah."*

2 Samuel 24:1 (NKJV)

David then commanded Joab to go throughout all the tribes of Israel and to take a census of all the people.

Against his better judgment, Joab did as the King commanded – a project that took him nine months and twenty days to complete.

And so, the final report that Joab gave King David stated that in Israel, there were eight hundred thousand men able for war and in Judah, five hundred thousand men.

David then felt the burden of his iniquity weighing down on his heart for having numbered the people. So, David repented of the sin, asking God to forgive him as he acted foolishly.

Unfortunately, in the following events, we see how our actions are never without consequence.

The Lord then spoke to David through the Prophet Gad, leaving David with three choices: **2 Samuel 24:13**

1. Shall seven years of famine come to you in your land or,
2. Shall you flee for three months before your enemies while they pursue you or,
3. Shall there be three days of plague in your land?

And so, David's reply to the Prophet Gad was to be given over into the Lord's hands and not into the hands of men as the Lord is merciful.

The Lord then sent a plague upon Israel from the morning till the appointed time, killing seventy thousand men. And just as the angel of the Lord stretched out his hand over Jerusalem to destroy it, the Lord relented and told the angel to restrain his hand.

David then bought a threshing floor from Araunah the Jebusite, where he built an altar to the Lord upon which David offered burnt and peace offerings.

So, the Lord accepted the prayers and removed the plague from the Land.

Note: *Many people might wonder why it was wrong of David to take a census of all the people. What we need to remember is the motive of the census. The purpose of the census was to see how many able men there were for war. This means that David, for a moment, placed his trust in the strength of his army and not in God.*

179

PROPHETIC DECLARATIONS:

1. 2 Samuel 5:10 (NKJV)

10 "So David went on and became great, and the Lord God of hosts was with him.

I declare and decree in Jesus' Name that I will only go from strength to strength, from anointing to anointing and from glory to glory.

I declare and decree in Jesus Name that I shall see victory upon victory unfold before my eyes all the days of my life.

NOTES

NOTES

NOTES

First Book of **Kings**

"The Divided Kingdom"
Part 1

The book's author is unknown; however, many suggest that it is the Prophet, Jeremiah. The main characters are David, Solomon, Rehoboam, Jeroboam, Elijah, Ahab, and Jezebel.

Just like with the book of Judges, the purpose of this book is to portray the impact of those who heed the Word of God and those who do not. This time, throughout the ruling kings of Judah and Israel.

The book of 1st Kings begins by revealing an act of mutiny against King David when Adonijah, Absalom's brother, tried to take kingship over Israel and Judah through illegitimate authority. Adonijah failed in his attempt to take rule over the kingdom, and so the book commences with David announcing his son Solomon as the successor to reign as king over Israel and Judah.

The book then further unveils the division of the kingdom after Solomon's death.

This book can be divided into two main sections:

1. **Solomon's Reign: 1 Kings 1 – 11**
2. **The Division of The Kingdom: 1 Kings 12 – 22**

HIGHLIGHTED EVENTS IN 1 KINGS:
CHAPTER 1 – CHAPTER 11

1. **Solomon's Reign: 3rd King Over All Israel**

Adonijah's False Presumption to Be King:
1 Kings 1 (NKJV)

In **Chapter 1**, we see Adonijah rising as a self-proclaimed king, completely overruling the authority of King David. With this, Adonijah took chariots, horsemen and fifty men to run before him to proclaim his arrival as the new king.

To strengthen his attempt to take over the kingdom, Adonijah further persuaded Joab, the commander, and Abiathar, the priest, to follow and help him execute this plan.

However, Zadok the priest, Benaiah, Nathan the prophet, Shimei, Rei and the mighty men did not join in this revolt as they remained loyal to King David.

Nathan, the Prophet, then counteracted Adonijah, intercepting his plan by going to Bathsheba, the mother of Solomon. He stated that Adonijah had just made himself king through illegitimate authority, as King David was completely unaware of the current state of affairs.

Nathan further gave Bathsheba clear instructions regarding the matter and how they would go about revealing the situation to King David.

The moment the matter was brought under King David's attention, he immediately summoned for Zadok, the priest, Nathan, the prophet, and Benaiah, instructing them to have Solomon, his son, ride on his donkey — taking him to Gihon.

King David further instructed Zadok and Nathan to anoint Solomon king over Israel and Judah when they arrived at Gihon and then to blow the horn, saying, ***"Long live King Solomon"***.

And so, Solomon was anointed as king over Israel and set upon the throne according to the instructions given by his father, King David.

News of Solomon seated on the throne quickly reached Adonijah, causing him to fear for his life. As a result, he ran and took hold of the horns of the altar, pleading for his life.

Solomon showed mercy towards Adonijah in his first act as king, on the condition that Adonijah must prove himself to be a worthy man. But, if found to be wicked, he shall be put to death.

David's Final Instructions:
1 Kings 2 (NKJV)

David, now near the end of his life, gave Solomon, his son, vital information on maintaining a Godly lifestyle and regarding leadership over the kingdom by leaving him with the following instruction:

a.   **1st Instruction: 1 Kings 2:3 – 4 (NKJV)**

David instructed Solomon to remember the charge of the Lord God, to keep His commandments and to walk in His ways. By doing this, his way will always be prosperous.

b.   **2nd Instruction: 1 King 2:5 – 6 (NKJV)**

David reminded Solomon of what Joab had done to him and the blood of war that Joab shed during a time of peace by killing both Abner and Amasa, two of his commanders.

Later in **1 Kings 2:29 & 34**, we see Solomon give Benaiah the order to strike Joab down for siding with Adonijah. And so, after fulfilling the king's instructions, Benaiah was set in Joab's place over the army.

c.   **3rd Instruction: 1 Kings 2:7 (NKJV)**

David then further instructed Solomon to show kindness to the sons of Barzillai, the Gileadite and to allow them to be among those that eat at the king's table.

d.   **4th Instruction: 1 Kings 2:8 (NKJV)**

Then David's last instruction was to remind Solomon of how Shimei cursed him with a hostile curse. David could not touch Shimei as he swore to him by the Lord that he would not slay him with the sword.

This was an oath between David and Shimei, an agreement that Solomon was not bound by.

Later in **1 Kings 2:36 – 46**, after David's death, Solomon called for Shimei, exiling him to a place in Jerusalem. Solomon further decreed that if Shimei left the boundaries set for him and crossed the Brook Kidron, his blood would be on his own hands, and he shall surely die.

After three years of dwelling in Jerusalem, Shimei seemed to have forgotten about the agreement between him and Solomon when he left Jerusalem to pursue two of his slaves in Gath.

This ignorant act sealed his fate, as Solomon gave Benaiah the order to go strike him down.

Adonijah's Execution:
1 Kings 2:13 – 25 (NKJV)

Just after David's death, we find Adonijah again acting wickedly by scheming behind Solomon's back. Adonijah went to Solomon's mother, Bathsheba, to convince Solomon to give Abishag the Shunamite to him to be his wife.

An act with devastating results, as Solomon gave Benaiah the charge to strike him down because of his wickedness.

And so, Solomon fulfilled all the final instructions of his father David, leaving but one, and that was to keep the commandments of the Lord God.

Solomon's Wisdom:
1 Kings 3:1 – 15 (NKJV)

Now Solomon was at the age of twenty when he became King, tasked with the great responsibility of leading Israel. This task left the young king feeling inferior and unsure if he could fill the shoes of his father, King David.

On a God-appointed night, the Lord appeared unto Solomon in a dream, saying,

"Ask! What shall I give you?"

1 Kings 3:5 (NKJV)

Solomon's request was the exception as he did not ask for long life, riches, or the lives of his enemies but asked for a wise and understanding heart to discern justice.

This was a request so pleasing to God that He even blessed Solomon with riches and honour, further stating that if Solomon kept His commandments as his father David did, He would continue to lengthen his days.

So, we see that God granted Solomon all his heart desires. In the following chapters, we see Solomon judge with great wisdom, becoming the most prosperous and wisest King in all his days. **1 Kings 4:29 – 34**

Solomon's Accomplishments as King:

1. **Solomon's Temple and House:**
   1 Kings 5 – 7 (NKJV)

To build a house for the name of the Lord was always a pressing matter in David's heart, but he could never do so because of all the wars he had to fight. And so, this commission was passed on to Solomon, his son, according to the word of the Lord given to David.

At the age of twenty-four, Solomon began with the construction of the temple, a project that took him seven years to complete.

The Size of the Temple:

Length — 60 cubits (27.432m)
Width — 20 cubits (9.144m)
Height — 30 cubits (13.716m)

After building the temple, Solomon continued with the construction of his own house, a project that took him thirteen years to complete.

The Size of Solomon's House:

Length — 100 cubits (45.72m)
Width — 50 cubits (22.86m)
Height — 30 cubits (13.716m)

Further details on the temple and Solomon's house can be found in **1 Kings 6 – 7.**

2. The Ark Returned to the Temple:
1 Kings 8 (NKJV)

After the temple's completion, Solomon assembled all the elders of Israel and the leaders from every tribe to bring up the ark of the covenant of the Lord from the City of David, which is Zion.

The priest and the Levites brought up the ark of the covenant with all its holy furnishings to the temple with King Solomon. All the congregation of Israel went before the ark, sacrificing sheep and oxen that were so great in number that they could not be counted.

And so, the ark of the covenant was set between the two Cherubim in the most Holy Place with their wings covering the ark. The moment the priest came out of the Holy Place, the cloud filled the house of the Lord to such an extent that *the priest could not continue to minister because of the cloud, for the Glory of the Lord filled the house.* **1 Kings 8:10 – 11 (NKJV)**

¹² Then Solomon spoke:

"The Lord said He would dwell in the dark cloud.
¹³ I have surely built You an exalted house,
And a place for You to dwell in forever."

1 Kings 8:12 – 13 (NKJV)

Solomon further continued to give a prayer of dedication, blessing the assembly and dedicating the temple to the Lord God Almighty — **1 Kings 8:22 – 66 (NKJV)**

God's Second Appearance to Solomon:
1 Kings 9:1 – 9 (NKJV)

After Solomon finished building the temple and his house, the Lord appeared to him a second time, saying:

> [3] *... "I have heard your prayer and your supplication that you have made before Me; I have consecrated this house which you have built to put My name there forever, and My eyes and My heart will be there perpetually."*

> **1 Kings 9:3 (NKJV)**

The Lord further stated the blessings and curses that would be released depending on Israel's choice to either follow the commandments of God or not.

3. **The Queen of Sheba:**
    1 Kings 10:1 – 13 (NKJV)

Now King Solomon reigned over all the kingdoms, from the river to the land of the Philistines, to the border of Egypt, with many coming from all over seeking the wise counsel of King Solomon, bringing many tributes — **1 Kings 4:21 (NKJV).**

And so, when the Queen of Sheba heard of Solomon's fame, she came to test him with difficult questions.

The Queen came with many gifts, such as camels that bore spices, gold and precious stones, and she spoke to Solomon about all that was in her heart.

The Queen was utterly amazed by Solomon's great wisdom, as there was no matter too complicated for him to explain. She was further overwhelmed by the layout of the temple, Solomon's house and by the above-excellent hospitality.

She then gave Solomon one hundred and twenty talents of Gold (*$237 million*), spices in great quantity, and precious stones. Never again was such an amount of spices brought to King Solomon, such as Queen Sheba gave.

And so, the Queen received all that her heart desired and returned to her own country with her servants.

Further records of Solomon's great wealth can be found in **1 Kings 10:14 – 29**

Solomon's Downfall:
1 Kings 11:1 – 13 (NKJV)

Despite all of Solomon's wisdom, in the end, his love for women led him down a path of destruction by marrying many of the strange women in the land.

By doing so, he disobeyed a direct command of God, warning them not to intermarry with the inhabitants of the land because these women would turn their hearts to false gods.

So, despite the stern warnings given by God, Solomon had seven hundred wives and three hundred concubines. All of these were women from the Moabites, Ammonites, Edomites, Sidonians, Hittites and from Egypt.

Now when Solomon was old, it came to pass that his wives did indeed turn his heart to their false gods, exactly like God had warned. His heart was no longer loyal to the Lord his God, like that of his father, David.

Therefore the anger of the Lord was kindled against Solomon because of his idolatry, deliberately disobeying the Lord's commandment not to worship other gods.

These were actions that caused the destruction of a nation. As God said, because of Solomon's doing, He will surely tear the kingdom away from him and give it to his servant.

God further stated that He would leave but one tribe for Solomon's son, for the sake of His servant David, and for the sake of Jerusalem, which He has chosen.

Jeroboam's Revolt Against Solomon:
1 Kings 11:26 – 40 (NKJV)

Now it came to pass that God raised an enemy against that of Solomon by causing Jeroboam – that was a mighty man of valour – and Solomon's servant to rebel against him.

When Jeroboam went out to Jerusalem, he met a prophet named Ahijah alone in a field. Ahijah then took the new garment that was upon him and tore it into twelve pieces, giving ten pieces to Jeroboam, prophesying that thus says the Lord, the God of Israel:

[31] "...Behold, I will tear the kingdom out of the hand of Solomon and will give ten tribes to you
[32] (but he shall have one tribe for the sake of My servant David, and for the sake of Jerusalem, the city which I have chosen out of all the tribes of Israel)..."

1 Kings 11:31 – 32 (NKJV)

And so, God further instructed that if Jeroboam would take heed to all the Lord's commandments, walk in His ways and continually do what is right in the sight of God, God would be with him and give ten Israel tribes into his hands, leaving but one tribe for Solomon's son.

Now it came to pass that Solomon sought to kill Jeroboam, leaving Jeroboam to flee for his life, seeking refuge in Egypt, where he stayed until the death of Solomon.

And so it was that Solomon ruled as king in Jerusalem, over all of Israel, for forty years before he passed on and was buried in the city of David, his father.

4ᵗʰ King over all of Israel – Rehoboam:
1 Kings 11:43 (NKJV)

Rehoboam was the last king over Israel before the division of the kingdom

HIGHLIGHTED EVENTS IN 1 KINGS:
CHAPTER 12 – CHAPTER 22:

> 2. **The Division of the Kingdom:**
>   **1 Kings 12 – 22**

Jeroboam's Revolt Against Rehoboam:
1 Kings 12:1 – 24 (NKJV)

After Solomon's death, his son Rehoboam went to Shechem to be made king over all of Israel, completely unaware that God had already set another plan into motion.

And so, Israel sent and called for Jeroboam, Solomon's servant that fled to Egypt, to come and help them by speaking to Rehoboam on their behalf.

Jeroboam then agreed to go with the assembly of Israel to Rehoboam, presenting him with the following conditions, saying:

> *⁴ "Your father made our yoke heavy; now therefore, lighten the burdensome service of your father, and his heavy yoke which he put on us, and we will serve you." ⁵ So he said to them, "Depart for three days, then come back to me." And the people departed.*

> 1 Kings 12:4 – 5 (NKJV)

Rehoboam then consulted with the elders that served with Solomon on how to respond to the people. They then advised Rehoboam to serve the people and to speak kindly to them because by doing so, he would win their trust, and they will serve him forever.

The choice that Rehoboam made next birthed the division of a nation and, as a result, sealed the plan that God had already set in motion. He rejected their good counsel and went to the young men who had grown up with him, requesting their thoughts on the matter.

The young men, of course, had a completely different outlook towards the situation, advising that Rehoboam should rather make their yoke even heavier. They advised that where Solomon's father chastised them with whips, Rehoboam should chastise them with scourges.

Scripture records that Rehoboam found the counsel of the young men pleasing. He spoke harshly to the people when they returned after three days, declaring that he would be even harder on them, unwilling to meet their requests.

Rehoboam's actions resulted in the division of the kingdom, which fulfilled the Word of the Lord given through the Prophet Ahijah.

16 Now when all Israel saw that the king did not listen to them, the people answered the king, saying:

"What share have we in David?
We have no inheritance in the son of Jesse.
To your tents, O Israel!
Now, see to your own house, O David!"
So Israel departed to their tents.

1 Kings 12:16 (NKJV)

Then Asher, Dan, Ephraim, Gad, Issachar, Manasseh, Naphtali, Reuben, Simeon, and Zebulun — ten tribes in total — went to the North, where they founded the independent Kingdom of Israel, with Jeroboam as their king.

Judah and Benjamin founded the Kingdom of Judah in the South, with Rehoboam as their king.

Now Jeroboam did not heed the commandments given by God but rather did what was evil in the sight of the Lord by building two golden calves, and so history records how Jeroboam led the people into idolatry.

Order of the Kings After the Division of the Kingdom:

The Northern Kingdom — Israel — Ten Tribes
The Southern Kingdom — Judah — Two Tribes

1st King over Israel — Jeroboam I and the Kingdom of Israel's Judgment: 1 Kings 14:1 – 18 (NKJV)

God's anger was greatly stirred because of Jeroboam's actions, bringing terrible judgement upon his household. Jeroboam ruled over Israel for twenty-two years before passing on and was buried with his fathers. After Jeroboam died, his son Nadab was appointed as king over the kingdom of Israel in his place.

1st King over Judah — Rehoboam and the Kingdom of Judah's Judgement: 1 Kings 14:21 – 31 (NKJV)

Rehoboam was forty-one years old when he became king and ruled for seventeen years in Jerusalem. Now Rehoboam also did what was evil in the eyes of God.

And so, Rehoboam passed on and was buried with his fathers in the City of David, and Abijam, his son, was appointed to rule as king over the kingdom of Judah in his place.

The rest of Rehoboam's acts are recorded in **2 Chronicles 11 – 12**

2nd King over Judah — Abijam: 1 Kings 15:1 – 8 (NKJV)

Now Abijam also did what was evil in the sight of God, and there was continuous war between Abijam, king over the kingdom of Judah and Jeroboam, king over the kingdom of Israel.

And so, Abijam reigned for three years in Jerusalem over the kingdom of Judah before he passed on and was buried with his fathers in the City of David. Then Abijah's son, Asa, was appointed to rule as king over the kingdom of Judah in his place.

The rest of Abijam's acts are recorded in **2 Chronicles 13 – 14:1**

3rd **King over Judah — Asa: 1 Kings 15:9 – 24 (NKJV)**

Now Asa did what was right in the eyes of God and so removed all the perverted persons from the land and all the idols that his fathers had made.

Now there was continual war between Asa and Baasha, king of Israel, all the days of their lives.

Asa ruled forty-one years as king over the kingdom of Judah before passing on and was buried with his fathers in the City of David. Asa's son, Jehoshaphat, was appointed king over the kingdom of Judah.

The rest of Asa's acts are recorded in **2 Chronicles 14:2 – 15 & 2 Chronicles 15 – 16**.

2nd **King over Israel — Nadab: 1 Kings 15:25 – 32 (NKJV)**

Now Nadab ruled as king over Israel for two years, and he did what was evil in the sight of God. Then it came to pass that Baasha, the son of Ahijah, killed Asa and reigned in his stead over the kingdom of Israel.

And so, when Baasha became king, he killed all the house of Jeroboam according to the Word of the Lord, which He had spoken through His prophet Ahijah.

3rd **King over Israel – Baasha: 1 Kings 15:33 – 34 & 1 Kings 16:1 – 7 (NKJV)**

Now Baasha ruled as king over Israel for twenty-four years, and he did what was evil in the sight of God.

And so, Baasha passed on and was buried in Tirzah. Baasha's son, Elah, was appointed to rule as king over the kingdom of Israel.

4th King over Israel — Elah: 1 Kings 16:8 – 14 (NKJV)

Elah ruled as king over Israel for two years until Zimri, commander of over half of Elah's chariots, became drunk. He slew Elah, taking his place as king to rule over the kingdom of Israel.

5th King over Israel — Zimri: 1 Kings 16:15 – 20 (NKJV)

Zimri ruled as king for only seven days, as the people of Israel heard that he had killed the king. And so, Israel made Omri, the commander of the army, king over the kingdom of Israel.

Then it came to pass that Omri and all of Israel attacked Tirzah to find Zimri. But Zimri saw that the city was being taken and quickly went to the king's house and burned the house to the ground with him in it, and so he died.

6th King over Israel — Omri: 1 Kings 16:21 – 28 (NKJV)

Omri ruled as king over Israel for twelve years and six years in Tirzah, doing what was evil in the sight of God.

And so it was that Omri passed on and was buried with his fathers in Samaria. Omri's son, Ahab, ruled as king over Israel in his place.

7th King over Israel — Ahab: 1 Kings 16:29 – 34 (NKJV)

Now Ahab ruled as king over Israel for twenty-two years, and like his fathers before him, he did what was evil in the sight of God.

Then Ahab took Jezebel, the daughter of Eth-Baal – king of the Sidonians – to be his wife. History records that he went to serve and worship Baal.

Elijah's Miracles:

Miracle #1 — Elijah Predicts Three & A Half Year Drought:
1 Kings 17:1 (NKJV)

Now Elijah went to Ahab and prophesied that as sure as the Lord God lives, there shall be no dew or rain for all these years, except at his word.

Miracle #2 — Elijah Fed by Ravens:
1 Kings 17:2 – 7 (NKJV)

After Elijah spoke to Ahab, the Word of the Lord came to Elijah, instructing him to go and hide by the brook Cherith, which flows into the Jordan.

There God commanded the ravens to feed Elijah with bread and meat in the morning and evening.

Miracle #3 — Multiplication of Food and Oil:
1 Kings 17:8 – 16 (NKJV)

And so, after the river dried up due to the drought, the Word of the Lord came unto Elijah again. God commanded him to go to Zarephath, where he would meet a widow God had commanded to provide for him.

When Elijah arrived at Zarephath, he found the widow according to the Word of the Lord. He approached her, asking her to please bring him a little water in a cup that he may drink, and also requested a morsel of bread in her hand.

But the widow replied that she only had a little flour in a bin and a little oil in a jar she was about to prepare for herself and her son, that they may eat and then die.

Then Elijah told her not to be afraid but to go and prepare the meal according to his request and afterwards to make some for herself and her son. He assured her that the Lord said that the bin of flour shall not be used up and the oil in the jar shall not run dry until the day that the Lord shall send rain on the earth.

And so, according to the Lord's Word, the bin of flour never finished, and the jar of oil never dried up.

Miracle #4 — Resurrecting the Widows son:
1 Kings 17:17 – 24 (NKJV)

Then it happened after these things that the widow's son died of an illness. She then cried out to Elijah, asking if he came only to remind her of her past sins and to kill her son.

Elijah then took the child upstairs and laid him down on his bed. Here Elijah cried out to God, pleading for the life of the child, before stretching himself out over the child three times, again crying out to God saying,

"O Lord my God, I pray, let this child's soul come back to him"

1 Kings 17:21 (NKJV)

The Lord then heard Elijah's voice, and the child's soul came back to him, and he was revived.

Miracle #5 — Elijah vs the Baal prophets:
1 Kings 18:1 – 40 (NKJV)

After about three years, the Word of the Lord came to Elijah again. This time, God instructed him to go and present himself to Ahab, as the Lord revealed unto Elijah that he would send rain on the earth.

During this time, Jezebel massacred the prophets of the Lord. But Obadiah, who was in charge of Ahab's household, was a God-fearing man. He took one hundred prophets and hid them in two caves – fifty in each – where he fed them with bread and water.

Ahab instructed Obadiah to go into the land and see if he could find any grass to keep the mules alive, as the drought was severe. So, Obadiah went in one direction and Ahab in another direction, searching for food and water.

Here, Obadiah met with Elijah, who then instructed Obadiah to go and tell Ahab that he was here to meet with him.

This was a very dangerous request for Obadiah, as Ahab sought to kill Elijah. He feared that Ahab might execute the messenger that came to give him the news.

But Elijah stated that he was sent by God and will surely present himself to Ahab according to the Lord's instruction. So, Obadiah went and told Ahab, and Ahab went to meet with Elijah saying,

"Is that you, O troubler of Israel"

1 Kings 18:17 (NKJV)

Elijah then answered and said that Ahab and his father's house had abandoned Israel because they had forsaken the commandments of the Lord and chose to follow Baal.

Elijah then challenged Ahab by calling the four hundred and fifty prophets of Baal and the four hundred prophets of Asherah to assemble themselves at Mount Carmel to be put to the test.

And so, Elijah challenged the four hundred and fifty Baal prophets to make two alters and bring two bulls, one for them and one for Elijah. He further instructed that they must cut the bull in pieces and place it on the wood but not to put any fire under it and that he shall do the same.

The challenge was that they were to call upon the name of their gods, and Elijah would call upon the Name of the Lord, and the one who answered by fire would be proven that He is God.

And so, the Baal prophets accepted Elijah's challenge.

201

Now because they were many, Elijah told them to go first, and so to take one bull, prepare it and place it upon the wood, but to place no fire under it. They then did according to the rules set out and started to call upon the name of Baal from morning until evening with no answer.

Later, Elijah began to mock them as they cried even harder, this time cutting themselves with knives and lances, but to no avail.

Then Elijah repaired the altar of the Lord that was broken down by taking twelve stones, according to the number of the tribes, to rebuild the altar in the Name of the Lord.

He then continued to dig a trench around the altar, large enough to hold two seahs of seed. Then he placed the wood in its place, took the bull and cut it into pieces, and placed it on top of the wood, but set no fire under it.

Elijah then instructed them to pour four barrels of water over the burnt sacrifice and wood three times. A total of twelve barrels of water were poured over the burnt sacrifice and wood until everything was drenched in water, also filling the trench.

Elijah then called upon the Name of the Lord God, *and the fire of the Lord fell and consumed the burnt sacrifice, the wood, the stones, and the dust, and further licked up all the water in the trench* — 1 Kings 18:38 (NKJV)

After witnessing this great sign from God, the people fell to their faces and said, *"the Lord, He is God"*, upon which Elijah brought all the Baal prophets to the brook Kishon, where he executed them with a sword.

Miracle #6 and #7 — The Drought Ends and The Thirty Mile Foot Race: 1 Kings 18:41 – 46 (NKJV)

After this, Elijah went up to the top of Carmel and fell to the ground with his face between his knees. He asked his servant to go up and look towards the sea, to which the servant responded that there was nothing. Elijah asked the servant seven times to go and look again.

On the seventh time, a cloud rose from the sea in the shape of a man's hand. At this, Elijah sent his messenger to go and tell Ahab to prepare his horse and chariot before the rain stops him.

Soon after, the sky was black with clouds, and there was heavy rain. Ahab took his chariot and went back to Jezreel, but the hand of the Lord came upon Elijah who then girded up his loins, and out ran Ahab on foot, a thirty-mile journey reaching the entrance of Jezreel before Ahab.

Miracle #8 — Divine Strength:
1 Kings 19:4 – 8 (NKJV)

Ahab immediately told Jezebel all that Elijah had done and how he killed all the Baal prophets with the sword.

Then Jezebel sent a message to Elijah, threatening him with his life, stating that he will surely be like one of them that he has slain.

We then see unexplained behaviour as Elijah was consumed by fear because of the message from Jezebel. This fear was even after witnessing and experiencing the awesome power of God, right before his very eyes, as he got up and fled to Beersheba.

From there, he went on a day's journey into the wilderness, where he sat down under a broom tree completely depressed, praying for the Lord to rather take his life.

As he slept under the tree, an angel touched him and said he must get up and eat. As he looked, there was a cake baked on coals and a jar of water, which he took, ate and drank, then laid down again.

Then the angel came back a second time and touched him, instructing him to eat and drink because the journey ahead was too great for him. Elijah then ate and drank a second time before going on his way. The food given to Elijah gave him strength for forty days and forty nights until he reached Horeb, the mountain of God.

Elijah's New Commission:
1 Kings 19:11 – 21 (NKJV)

It was here that God appeared to Elijah, instructing him to go up the mountain where the Lord passed by him, leaving Elijah with the following commission:

1. Elijah must return to the wilderness of Damascus and must anoint Hazael as king over Syria. **1 Kings 19:15 (NKJV)**
2. Then Elijah was to anoint Jehu as king over Israel. **1 Kings 19:16 (NKJV)**
3. Elisha, the son of Shaphat, was to be anointed as prophet in his place. **1 Kings 19:16 (NKJV)**

God further made it clear to Elijah that he was not the last prophet according to his thinking, but that the Lord had reserved seven thousand in Israel that have not bowed down to Baal.

Birth of a New Prophet:
1 Kings 19:19 – 21 (NKJV)

And so, when Elijah departed from there, he found Elisha ploughing with twelve oxen. Elijah then took his mantle, threw it upon Elisha, and walked on.

Elisha then took the oxen, sacrificed them using their equipment, and then got up and followed Elijah.

The Death of Ahab Prophesied:
1 Kings 21 – 22:1 – 40 (NKJV)

Through the Chapters that follow, we find Ahab defeating the Syrians twice before making a treaty with Ben-Hadad, the king of Syria.

This treaty was an action that condemned Ahab, allowing a man to slip through his hand that God appointed for utter destruction. And so, through one of the sons of the prophets, the Lord spoke unto Ahab saying:

"...therefore your life shall go for his life, and your people for his people."

1 Kings 20:42 (NKJV)

The Vineyard:
1 Kings 21:1 – 16 (NKJV)

And so, it came to pass after all these things that Ahab wanted Naboth's vineyard as it was close to his house. He wanted to make a vegetable garden out of it, stating that he would give Naboth another vineyard even greater or anything else he wanted.

The vineyard, being Naboth's inheritance, declined Ahab's offer. This caused Ahab to go back home, sulking about the situation. When Jezebel saw that he was downcast, she asked him what was wrong, so he explained the story.

At this, Jezebel conspired against Naboth by setting him up as if he blasphemed against God, and Naboth was innocently stoned to death.

When Ahab heard that Naboth was dead, he immediately took possession of the land.

Elijah Prophesies Ahab's and Jezebels Destruction:
1 Kings 21:17 – 29 (NKJV)

In the following verses, we see God releasing a word of destruction through the Prophet Elijah concerning Ahab and Jezebel.

This stated that calamity would come upon them and that God would completely take away their prosperity and cut off every male from Israel — both bond and free, just like with Jeroboam and Baasha.

The Lord furthermore stated that the dogs would eat Jezebel by the wall of Jezreel, and the dogs would also eat whoever belongs to Ahab in the city, and the birds shall eat whoever dies in the field.

When Ahab heard all these things, he fasted, laid sackcloth upon himself, went into mourning and humbled himself before the Lord. The Lord then showed mercy by stating that because he humbled himself, calamity will not come in his days but in his son's days.

Order of the Kings Continue:

4th King over Judah — Jehoshaphat: 1 Kings 22:41 – 50 (NKJV)

Now Jehoshaphat ruled as king over the kingdom of Judah for twenty-five years. He was thirty-five years old when he became king and did what was right in the sight of the Lord, but still leaving all the high places. Thus the Bible records that Jehoshaphat made peace with the king of Israel.

He then passed on and was buried with his fathers in the City of David, and his son, Jehoram, was appointed as king over the kingdom of Judah in his place.

The rest of Jehoshaphat's acts deeds are recorded in **2 Chronicles 17 – 20**

8th King over Israel — Ahaziah: 1 Kings 22:51 – 53 (NKJV)

The book of first Kings ends with Ahab dying in battle and Ahaziah, his son, ruling as king over the kingdom of Israel in his place. Ahaziah reigned for two years over Israel and did what was evil in the sight of God.

PROPHETIC DECLARATIONS:

1.   1 Kings 18:38 & 41(NKJV)

[38] Then the fire of the Lord fell and consumed the burnt sacrifice, and the wood and the stones and the dust, and it licked up the water that was in the trench.

[41] Then Elijah said to Ahab, "Go up, eat and drink; for there is the sound of abundance of rain."

I prophesy that my prayers will be licked up by the fire of God and will so release blessings in abundance over every dimension of my life. My life will continually be steered towards my God-given destiny by the leading of the Holy Spirit of the true Living God.

NOTES

NOTES

Second Book of **Kings**

"The Divided Kingdom"
Part 2

The Second Book of Kings is a direct continuation of the First Book of Kings and should be viewed as one book. Like with the First Book of Kings, scholars speculate that Jeremiah the prophet might be the author; however, it seems that Isaiah and Jeremiah were the final compilers of the book by utilising the records of the kings of Israel.

The main characters include Elijah, Elisha, the Shunamite Woman, Naaman, Jezebel, Jehu, Joash, Hezekiah, Sennacherib, Isaiah, Manasseh, Josiah, Jehoiakim, Zedekiah and Nebuchadnezzar.

The book's purpose is to show the history of the kings of Israel from the time of Solomon to the Babylonian captivity. It further illustrates the blessings connected with those who obey God and the curses connected with those who do not.

HIGHLIGHTED EVENTS IN 2 KINGS:

Elijah's Miracles Continue:

Miracle #9 - Fire from Heaven:
2 Kings 1:1 – 18 (NKJV)

After Ahaziah severely injured himself, he instructed messengers to go and enquire of Baal-Zebub - the god of Ekron - to find out if he would recover from the injury.

While the messengers were on their way, an angel of the Lord instructed Elijah to go and meet with the king's messengers to convey a message concerning the king. This message was that because there is no God in Israel, and they rather inquire of Baal-Zebub, he shall surely die.

The messengers then returned to Ahaziah and told him all that Elijah had said.

Ahaziah, now consumed with anger, commanded a captain with fifty men to go and capture Elijah. And so when they arrived, they called out to Elijah saying,

"...Man of God, the king has said, "Come down!"

2 Kings 1:9 (NKJV)

Elijah boldly stated that fire will come down from heaven and consume the captain and his fifty men if he is a man of God. Then fire came down and consumed them all.

Then Ahaziah sent another captain with his fifty men, and they faced the same fate when fire came down and consumed them all.

Then the king sent a third captain with fifty men, but this time the captain pleaded with Elijah to show them mercy. So, the angel of the Lord told Elijah not to be afraid and to go with them.

Then Elijah personally delivered the Word of the Lord to Ahaziah, that because there is no God in Israel and they inquire of Baal-Zebub, he shall surely die.

Then it came to pass that Ahaziah died according to the Word of the Lord, spoken by Elijah.

Because Ahaziah had no son, Ahab's son — Jehoram — was appointed to rule as king over the kingdom of Israel.

Elisha's Test
2 Kings 2:1 – 7 (NKJV)

Elisha travelled with Elijah from Gilgal to Bethel, from Bethel to Jericho, and from Jericho to the Jordan. During all three journeys, Elijah instructed Elisha to stay behind as he continued on his journey.

Elisha, of course, every time, rejected the instruction to stay behind, stating:

"...As the Lord lives, and as your soul lives, I will not leave you!"

2 Kings 2:2,4 and 6 (NKJV)

Miracle #10 - The Jordan:
2 Kings 2:8 (NKJV)

When Elijah and Elisha came to the Jordan River, Elijah took his mantle, rolled it up and struck the water. Immediately, the water divided, allowing them to go through on dry ground.

Elisha's Difficult Request
2 Kings 2:9 – 12 (NKJV)

Before it came to pass for the Lord to take Elijah, he offered Elisha one last request to which Elisha requested a double portion of Elijah's spirit to be upon him.

Elijah was pleased with the request; however, what Elisha asked was a difficult thing. Nevertheless, Elijah said that if Elisha sees Elijah being taken from him, it will be according to what he asked, but if not, then it will not be.

While they were still busy talking, a chariot and horses of fire suddenly appeared, separating them, and a whirlwind took Elijah up into heaven.

Then Elisha cried out:

"...My father, my father, the chariot of Israel and its horsemen!"

2 Kings 2:12 (NKJV)

Thus, Elijah was translated into heaven, leaving his mantle for Elisha.

Elisha's Miracles:

Miracle #1 — The Division of Jordan:
2 Kings 2:12 – 18 (NKJV)

On his way back to Jericho, Elisha came to the Jordan, where he took Elijah's mantle that fell from him and struck the Jordan, calling upon the Lord God of Elijah so that the water again divided as before, and Elisha crossed over on dry ground.

When Elisha arrived at Jericho, the sons of the prophets saw him, saying that the spirit of Elijah rests upon him.

Miracle #2 — Healing the Water and Land:
2 Kings 2:19 – 22 (NKJV)

Here we see the men of Jericho who came to Elisha, announcing that the city was gratifying but that the water was bad, thus causing the ground to be barren.

Elisha then requested a new bowl with salt in it that he took and cast into the source of the water, prophesying that the Lord had healed the water and that there shall be no more death nor bareness from it.

²² "So the water remains healed to this day, according to the word of Elisha which he spoke."

2 Kings 2:22 (NKJV)

Miracle #3 — Destruction of the Mockers:
2 Kings 2:23 – 25 (NKJV)

Elisha then journeyed from Jericho to Bethel, where some youths came from the city mocking him, and so, Elisha pronounced a curse on them in the name of the Lord.

Then two female bears came out of the woods and mauled forty-two of the youths.

From here, Elisha moved to Mount Carmel and then to Samaria.

9th King over Israel - Jehoram:
2 Kings 3:1 – 3 (NKJV)

Now Jehoram ruled as king over the kingdom of Israel for twelve years and also did what was evil in the sight of God but not like his parents. He took the sacred pillar of Baal that his father had made and put it away but continued with the sins of Jeroboam.

Miracle #4 — Divine Supply of Water:
2 Kings 3:4 – 20 (NKJV)

Now it came to pass that the king of Moab rebelled against the king of Israel, and Jehoram - king of Israel - joined forces with Jehoshaphat, king of Judah and the king of Edom - three kings in total - to lay siege against that of Moab.

But after marching seven days, the army and the animals that followed them had no water, and none could be found anywhere.

Everything seemed to be against the three kings, so Jehoram thought it was God's plan to assemble them so they could be delivered into the hands of Moab, to which Jehoshaphat suggested that they rather find a prophet to enquire of the Lord concerning the situation.

So the three kings went to Elisha, the prophet, that only helped them because of Jehoshaphat.

And so, after Elisha summoned for a musician and he played, the hand of the Lord came upon him, and he prophesied according to the Word of the Lord. Thus saying that they should make the valley full of ditches because it shall be that without rain or water, the trenches shall be divinely filled so that they can drink.

Elisha further prophesied according to the Word of the Lord, stating that God would give the Moabites into their hands.

And it came to pass the next morning after the grain offering that water suddenly came from Edom and filled the land.

Miracle #5 — Water Illusion:
2 Kings 3:21 – 27 (NKJV)

When the Moabites saw that the three kings joined forces against them, they immediately prepared for the attack and assembled every abled body at the border where they camped for the night.

The following day when the Moabites got up, the sun was shining on the water, causing them to see the water as red as blood on the other side, thinking that the kings had now killed each other.

So, the Moabites went to the camp of Israel to collect the spoils but were caught by surprise and completely off guard when they found the Israelites were still alive — now rising against them — thus causing the Moabites to flee from before the Israelites.

The Israelites then went in pursuit of the Moabites — killing them in their own land, destroying the cities, each man throwing a stone on every good piece of land and stopping every spring of water, cutting down all the good trees — all according to the Word of the Lord, spoken by the Prophet Elisha.

Seeing that he would not win this battle, the king of Moab took his son, that was next in line to be king and sacrificed him as a burnt offering on the wall, causing great indignation to be against Israel.

Then Israel departed from Moab, returning to their own land.

Miracle #6 — Divine Multiplication of Oil:
2 Kings 4:1 – 7 (NKJV)

Here we find a testimony of a widow that was the wife of one of the sons of the prophets who died, and her current circumstances were not looking good.

Unable to repay her debt, she was on the verge of losing even her sons to the creditors who wanted to enslave them.

She then cried out to Elisha, that knew her husband, how he was a God-fearing man, to please help her in this situation.

Elisha then asked the widow what she had in the house, to which she responded, nothing but a jar of oil.

This was the perfect setting for God to reveal His mighty power. Elisha then instructed the widow to go and borrow as many empty vessels as possible from everywhere, then to bring the vessels into the house and shut the door behind her and her sons.

He then further instructed her to start filling the empty vessels with oil and continue until all the vessels were filled.

She then did according to the instructions given by Elisha, filling all the empty vessels. It then came to pass that when she filled the last empty vessel, and there were none left to fill, that the oil stopped.

Elisha then instructed the widow to go and sell the oil that was more than enough to repay all her debt and for them to live off of the rest.

Miracle #7 — Prophesying the Shunammite's son:
2 Kings 4:1 – 17 (NKJV)

There was a certain woman in Shunem that hosted the prophet Elisha and his servant every time that they would pass that place.

And so, one day, as they stayed there, he instructed his servant Gehazi to find out if there was anything that he could do for the woman, seeing that she was taking such good care of them.

Gehazi then revealed unto Elisha that she had no son and that her husband was old, to which Elisha prophesied that she would bear a son in the next year at about the same time.

217

This was a prophecy that she thought to be impossible; however, the following year, about the same time, she indeed bore a son according to the words spoken by Elisha the Prophet.

Miracle #8 — Resurrecting the Shunammite's son: 2 Kings 4:18 – 37 (NKJV)

And so, it came to pass that something happened when the child was a little older, causing his death. The child's mother then hastily made her way to Elisha.

When Elisha saw her from a distance, he instructed his servant Gehazi to run ahead before him and meet with her, asking if everything was ok, to which she responded:

"It is well".

2 Kings 4:26 (NKJV)

But when she finally came to Elisha, she cried out, declaring that the boy had died.

Elisha then instructed his servant Gehazi to run ahead and take his staff to lay it upon the child's face. Gehazi did everything according to Elisha's instructions, but the child still did not come back to life.

Now when Elisha came into the house, he prayed to the Lord and then stretched himself over the child, and the child's body became warm.

Elisha then stretched himself over the child for a second time, and suddenly the child sneezed seven times before opening his eyes.

Miracle #9 — Elisha Cures the Poisonous Pot: 2 Kings 4:38 – 41 (NKJV)

Here we see Elisha removing poison from a pot of stew prepared for the sons of the prophets at Gilgal during a time of famine.

One of them went out and took a lapful of wild gourds from an unknown vine and sliced them into the pot, not knowing what they were. However, when some of them ate, they cried out to Elisha that there was death in the pot.

Elisha then instructed them to give him some flour which he placed in the pot so the pot was cured, and the people could eat.

Miracle #10 — Multiplication of Food for a Hundred Men: 2 Kings 4:42 – 44 (NKJV)

This miracle recorded Elisha feeding one hundred men with only twenty loaves of barley bread and newly ripened grain that he received as first fruits from a certain man.

Miracle #11 — Naaman Healed from Leprosy: 2 Kings 5:1 – 27 (NKJV)

Naaman, the commander of the army of Syria, was a leper and received information from a young Israelite girl that was taken captive that there was a man of God — a prophet in Israel — that could heal him.

Naaman then came to Elisha's house, where Elisha sent his messengers to tell Naaman to go and dip himself in the Jordan seven times, and it shall be that after the seventh time, he would be healed.

This angered Naaman at first, but after being persuaded by one of his servants, he went and did according to the instructions given by Elisha, and Naaman was immediately healed.

Naaman then presented Elisha with a gift that he refused, but Gehazi, the servant of Elisha, pursued after Naaman to take the gift for himself.

This was an act of greed and disobedience that brought a great sickness upon Gehazi.

Elisha — knowing of the thing that Gehazi had done - told Gehazi that the leprosy of Naaman shall now be upon him and his descendants forever. Gehazi then left Elisha's presence leprous, as white as snow.

Miracle #12 — The Axe Head Floating:
2 Kings 6:1 – 7 (NKJV)

Now it came to pass that the sons of the prophets went to the Jordan to cut down some of the trees to build a more prominent place for them to dwell in. And so, as one of them was cutting down a tree, the iron axe head came loose and fell into the river.

He then cried out to Elisha for help as the axe was borrowed, so Elisha took a stick and threw it in the river at the location where the axe head had fallen into the water, causing the iron to float.

And so, the man retrieved the lost axe head from the river.

Miracle #13 — Prophetic Espionage:
2 Kings 6:1 – 12 (NKJV)

Here we see the king of Syria unable to hide his battle plans against Israel from the man of God.

Every time the king of Syria met with his servants to discuss their battle strategy, it would be divinely revealed unto Elisha, who then disclosed their plans to the king of Israel.

This caused the king of Syria to think that there was a spy in his camps, so he questioned his people. This was only to discover that the prophet Elisha was the one warning the king of Israel of all that the king of Syria spoke, even in his bedroom.

Miracle #14 — Elisha's Servant Receives Prophetic Sight:
2 Kings 6:13 – 17 (NKJV)

The king of Syria then sent horses and chariots with a great army to Elisha, a multitude so great that they surrounded the entire city of Dothan.

When Elisha's servant saw the great army surrounding the city, he cried out in fear:

"...Alas, my master! What shall we do?"

2 Kings 6:15 (NKJV)

Elisha, however, saw in the spirit and stood unshaken by this great multitude. He then told his servant not to fear, as those with them were more than those with the Syrian army.

Elisha then prayed, asking the Lord to open the eyes of his servant that he may see, and his eyes opened. What he saw in the spirit crushed every form of fear as the mountain was full of horses and chariots of fire surrounding Elisha.

Miracle #15 — Syrian Army Struck with Blindness: 2 Kings 6:18 – 23

As the Syrian army made their way down to Elisha, he prayed to the Lord to strike them with blindness, and the Lord struck them with blindness according to Elisha's word.

Elisha then led the Syrian army to Samaria, where he asked the Lord to open their eyes again, and when the Lord opened their eyes, they were standing surrounded by Israel.

According to Elisha's instructions, the king of Israel showed them mercy by sparing their lives and even feeding them. After this, the Syrians left, and went back to their own land.

The Curse of Cannibalism Over Israel: 2 Kings 6:24 – 31 (NKJV)

It came to pass that Ben-Hadad, king of Syria, gathered his army and came up against Israel during a great famine in Samaria, besieging them to such an extent that they were faced with inhumane circumstances.

An apostate Israel also unlocked one of the curses announced in **Leviticus 26:29** of what would happen if they departed from the Lord, stating:

> ²⁹ *"You shall eat the flesh of your sons, and you shall eat the flesh of your daughters."*

Leviticus 26:29 (NKJV)

We see this curse manifest in Israel when the king was presented with a case of two women who agreed to eat their sons. And so, after having eaten the one and the time came to eat the other, the one woman refused and hid her son.

The king then furiously set out to take Elisha's head upon hearing this.

Miracle #16 — The Revealed Word of Knowledge:
2 Kings 6:32 – 33 (NKJV)

The Lord then revealed to Elisha the king's plan, and so he prophesied, revealing to the elders sitting with him that the son of a murderer had sent his messenger to come and take his head and that his master was following right behind him.

While Elisha was still speaking these words, the messenger came to the door, followed by the king stating:

> ³³ ..."*Surely this calamity is from the Lord; why should I wait for the Lord any longer?"*

2 Kings 6:33 (NKJV)

Miracle #17 — The Divine Plunder:
2 Kings 7:1 – 20 (NKJV)

Elisha then prophesied the Word of the Lord, stating that the next day about the same time, the people would experience great relief from the stronghold of the famine.

Elisha further prophesied that the commander that is with the king shall see this thing happening but shall not partake in it.

So it came to pass that four lepers of Samaria decided to place the fate of their lives in the Syrian army. They reasoned that if they stayed in Samaria, they would die, but if they went to the Syrian camp, the Syrians might take them captive and keep them alive, but if not, they would kill them all the same.

The four lepers were utterly shocked when they arrived at the Syrian camp, only to find it completely deserted. This was because the Lord had caused the Syrian army to hear the sound of many chariots, horses, and a great army.

This caused them to think that the king of Israel had joined forces with other kings against them, so the Syrian army left the camp entirely intact as they fled for their lives in great haste.

The four lepers at first helped themselves to many of the spoils hiding the gold, silver and clothing. After thinking of how Israel was suffering, they knew that it was not right of them to keep this good thing silent, and so revealed the matter unto the king of Israel.

[18] So it happened just as the man of God had spoken to the king, saying, "Two seahs of barley for a shekel, and a seah of fine flour for a shekel, shall be sold tomorrow about this time in the gate of Samaria."

2 Kings 7:18 (NKJV)

And so it came to pass that the commander saw this great victory but did not partake in the spoils thereof, as the people trampled him to death at the gate, according to the words spoken by Elijah the Prophet.

Miracle #18 — Restoration of the Shunammite's Land: 2 Kings 8:1 – 2 (NKJV)

Here we see Elisha prophesying to the Shunammite Woman, the same woman whose son he had raised from the dead. He prophesied that the

Lord was about to cause a famine of seven years, and it would be best for her and her household to move to another location.

Upon receiving this divine warning, this woman immediately did all according to the word of Elisha and dwelled in the land of the Philistines during the seven years of famine.

Miracle #19 — Divine Timing:
2 Kings 8:3 – 6 (NKJV)

When the woman returned after seven years, she went to the king to appeal for her house and land.

It so happened that while Gehazi told the king of all the great things that Elisha had done upon the king's request and shared the testimony of how Elisha had raised the dead, that the Shunammite woman came in.

Gehazi was surprised and told the king that this was the same woman and that it was her son, who Elisha had raised from the dead.

The Shunammite confirmed, so the king restored all that belonged to her.

Order of Kings Continue:

New King over Syria — Hazael:
2 Kings 8:7 – 15 (NKJV)

And so it came to pass that Ben-Hadad, king of Syria, became terminally ill, to which he sent Hazael to Elisha to enquire if he would recover.

Elisha then prophesied the word of the Lord to Hazael, stating that the king will indeed recover from the illness but nonetheless will still die and that Hazael will be king over Syria.

He further prophesied to Hazael and said:

> [12] ... *"Because I know the evil that you will do to the children of Israel: Their strongholds you will set on fire, and their young men you will kill with the sword; and you will dash their children, and rip open their women with child."*

2 Kings 8:12 (NKJV)

Hazael, now in shock because of the words he just heard, denied that he would ever do such a wicked thing. He then returned to Ben-Hadad, king of Syria, with the good news that he would recover but kept silent over the rest.

The king then recovered according to Elisha's word, but the next day, Hazael took a wet cloth and placed it over the king's face, causing him to die. So, Hazael ruled as king over Syria in his place.

5th King over Judah — Jehoram:
2 Kings 8:16 – 24 (NKJV)

Now Jehoram also did what was evil in the sight of God and was married to Ahab's daughter, following all her ways.

Jehoram was thirty-two when he became king and reigned for eight years in Jerusalem over the kingdom of Judah before he passed on and was buried with his fathers in the City of David.

Ahaziah, his son, was then appointed to rule as king over the kingdom of Judah in his place.

The rest of Jehoram's acts and deeds are recorded in **2 Chronicles 21**.

6th King over Judah — Ahaziah:
2 Kings 8:25 – 29 (NKJV)

Now Ahaziah was twenty-two when he was appointed as king over the kingdom of Judah and reigned for one year, and he also did what was evil in the sight of God.

And so, Ahaziah, king over Judah, joined forces with Jehoram, also known as Joram, king over Israel, to lay siege against Hazael, king of Syria.

The rest of Ahaziah's acts and deeds are recorded in **2 Chronicles 22:1 – 9**

10ᵗʰ King over Israel — Jehu:
2 Kings 9:1 – 37 (NKJV)

Jehu's Accomplishments:

1. **The Death Of Jehoram (Joram) the King of Israel:**
    2 Kings 9:1 – 26 (NKJV)

Upon Elisha's instruction, one of the sons of the prophets went to Jehu — commander of the Israelite army — and poured oil over him, prophesying that the Lord God anoints him as king over Israel.

He further prophesied that Jehu would utterly destroy the house of Ahab to be like that of Jeroboam, to avenge the blood of the Lord's servants, His prophets that came by the hand of Jezebel.

And so, Jehu — now driven by a divine assignment — took his chariot and horse and went to Jezreel, where Joram was recovering from his wounds when he fought against the king of Syria. It is here that Jehu also found Ahaziah, the king of Judah, that came to see Joram.

When Joram saw that Jehu came with the intent of war, he tried to flee, but Jehu drew his bow and shot Jehoram so that the arrow came out of his heart, and Jehoram died in his chariot.

2. **The Death of Ahaziah the King of Judah:**
    2 Kings 9:27 – 29 (NKJV)

Ahaziah, who saw that his life was now in danger, also tried to flee, but Jehu set out after Ahaziah, where they finally shot him in his chariot. And so Ahaziah died in Megiddo, where his servants took him and buried him with his fathers in the city of David.

The rest of Ahaziah's acts and deeds are recorded in **2 Chronicles 22:1 – 9**

3. **The Violent Death of Jezebel:**
   2 Kings 9:30 – 37 (NKJV)

Jehu then came to Jezreel, where Jezebel saw him through a window asking if he comes in peace, upon which he asked if there was anyone that stood with him.

Two or three eunuchs then took Jezebel and threw her out of the window so that some of her blood splattered on the wall and on the horses that then trampled her underfoot.

Later, Jehu instructed to take this accursed woman and to bury her as she was the daughter of a king, but when they came to her found nothing but her skull, feet and the palms of her hands.

And so the word of the Lord was fulfilled that said:

> [36] … *"This is the word of the Lord, which He spoke by His servant Elijah the Tishbite, saying, 'On the plot of ground at Jezreel dogs shall eat the flesh of Jezebel;* [37] *and the corpse of Jezebel shall be as refuse on the surface of the field, in the plot at Jezreel, so that they shall not say, "Here lies Jezebel."*

2 Kings 9:36 – 37 (NKJV)

4. **The Death of Ahab's Seventy Sons:**
   2 Kings 10:1 – 11 (NKJV)

Jehu then went after Ahab's seventy sons that dwelled in Samaria by writing letters to elders and those who reared Ahab's sons, instructing them to choose the best qualified of Ahab's sons and appoint him as king to defend their house.

But those in charge of the house and of the city, the elders and those who reared Ahab's sons, were afraid and responded with submission, giving over to be Jehu's servants.

They then took the seventy sons of Ahab and slaughtered them, delivering their heads in baskets to Jezreel upon Jehu's instruction, then laid them out in two heaps at the gate until the next morning.

The next day Jehu continued to execute the rest of those who remained in Ahab's household in Jezreel, from his great men to all close acquaintances and his priests, until no one remained.

And so, the word of the Lord was fulfilled concerning Ahab's household and all that belongs to him, spoken by the prophet Elijah.

5. The Death of Ahaziah's Forty-Two Brothers:
2 Kings 10:12 – 14 (NKJV)

And so, it came to pass that when the brothers of Ahaziah came to greet the sons of the king that, Jehu realised they were the brothers of Ahaziah.

Jehu then ordered that they are taken alive, and so they took them alive and executed them — forty-two in all at the well of Beth-Eked.

6. The Rest of Ahab's Family Killed:
2 Kings 10:15 – 17 (NKJV)

Jehu then went to Samaria, where he executed all who remained of Ahab, fulfilling the word of the Lord spoken by the prophet Elijah.

7. The Death of All the Baal Worshippers:
2 Kings 10:18 – 31 (NKJV)

Here we see Jehu devising a cunning strategy by proclaiming that a great sacrifice will be made for Baal, calling all the Baal priests and worshippers to assemble for this "*great event*", pretending to be for Baal.

Jehu placed such high value on this event, claiming they would be put to death if any missed it. This, of course, was a plan of deception so that Jehu could execute all the worshippers of Baal.

And so, all the Baal priests and worshippers filled the temple of Baal from one end to another. Jehu further instructed that any who stood for the Lord should be removed from the temple.

Now Jehu chose eighty men to stand on the outside of the temple to ensure that no one came out, and so, after the burnt offering, Jehu commanded the guards and the captains to go in and slaughter everyone.

After the guards and captains killed everyone with the edge of the sword, they went into the inner room of the temple of Baal, removing the sacred pillars, tearing down the temple and making it a refuse dump until this day.

And so, Jehu performed everything according to what God had in His heart to do toward Ahab and his household and did what was right in the sight of God by completely removing Baal from Israel.

Because he had done this great thing, the Lord stated that his sons shall sit on the throne of Israel to the fourth generation.

But Jehu did not walk in the law of God with all his heart, for he continued with the sins of Jeroboam that caused Israel to sin.

Jehu Died:
2 Kings 10:32 – 36 (NKJV)

Now the Lord started to give parts of Israel over into the hands of Hazael, the king of Syria, their enemy, because of their continual refusal to turn from their wicked ways.

Jehu ruled over Israel for twenty-eight years before he passed on and was buried with his fathers in Samaria, and then his son Jehoahaz was appointed as king over Israel in his place.

7th Ruler over Judah — Athaliah
(1st and only woman to rule over Judah):
2 Kings 11:1 – 3 (NKJV)

After Ahaziah's death, Athaliah, his mother, executed all the royal heirs, Ahaziah's sons, except for Joash (Jehoash), whom Jehosheba, Ahaziah's sister, took and hid in the house of the Lord for six years while Athaliah ruled over Judah.

Now Athaliah ruled for seven years before she was executed, and Joash, the son of Ahaziah, was appointed as king over Judah.

The rest of Athaliah's acts and deeds are recorded in **2 Chronicles 22:10 – 12 / 2 Chronicles 23:12 – 21**

8th King over Judah — Joash, also known as Jehoash:
2 Kings 11:4 – 21 & 2 Kings 12:1 – 21 (NKJV)

In the seventh year of Athaliah's reign, Jehoiada the priest revealed Joash, the king's son, unto the rulers over hundreds and the captains and the guard in the house of the Lord.

They then surrounded Joash on every side, protecting him so that no harm would come to him, killing anyone who came within range.

The king's son was then brought forth where they placed the crown upon him and gave him the testimony, which is a copy of the law of Moses by which he is to govern and judge the people, further anointing him and announcing him as the new king, shouting:

... "Long live the king!"

2 Kings 11:12 (NKJV)

The noise of the people then attracted Athaliah's attention to the temple of the Lord, where she saw the new king standing by a pillar according to the custom, with the leaders and trumpeters with him.

Upon seeing the celebration of the new king, Athaliah rent her clothes and cried out:

... "Treason! Treason!"

2 Kings 11:14 (NKJV)

And so, Athaliah was removed from the house of the Lord on the instruction given by Jehoiada, the priest, and executed at the entrance of the king's house.

After this, Jehoiada made a covenant between the Lord, the king, and the people that they would serve the Lord and be His people.

So, they went to the temple of Baal and tore it down, completely breaking it into pieces with all of its images and executing Mattan, the priest of Baal, leaving nothing to stand.

Jehoash was seven years old when he became king over Judah and ruled for forty years, doing all that was right in the sight of God under Jehoiada's counsel but still did not remove all the high places.

Jehoash Restores the Temple:
2 Kings 12:1 – 18 (NKJV)

The first thing Jehoash did as king of Judah, recorded in the Bible, was to repair the house of the Lord. All the money that came into the house of the Lord as dedicated gifts were to be used to repair any damage done to the Lord's house.

After Hazael, the king of Syria, besieged and took Gath; he set out to take Jerusalem. And so, to save the city, Jehoash took all his sacred things, including those of his fathers, Jehoshaphat, Jehoram and Ahaziah, with all the gold in the treasuries of the house of the Lord and the king's house and gave them to Hazael king of Syria who then upon receiving this gift, turned away from them.

The Death of Joash:
2 Kings 12:19 – 21 (NKJV)

And so, it came to pass that two of the servants of Joash, Jozachar and Jehozabad, conspired against him and struck him down so that he died in the house of the Millo and so was buried with his fathers in the city of David.

Then Amaziah, son of Joash, was appointed as king over Judah in his place.

The rest of Ahaziah's acts and deeds are recorded in **2 Chronicles 23:1 – 11 & 2 Chronicles 24**

11ᵗʰ King over Israel — Jehoahaz:
2 Kings 13:1 – 9 (NKJV)

Jehoahaz ruled as king over Israel for seventeen years and did what was evil in the sight of God as he followed in the sin of Jeroboam that caused Israel to sin.

Because of their evil, the anger of the Lord was kindled, and so the Lord delivered them into the hands of Hazael, king of Syria and Ben-Hadad, Hazael's son, all the days of their life.

And so, Jehoahaz pleaded with the Lord, who then raised a deliverer to help them escape the hand of oppression of the Syrians, only to continue in the sin of the house of Jeroboam.

The Lord, however, did not allow them to be restored to full as he caused the king of Syria to destroy them, leaving them with only fifty horsemen, ten chariots and ten thousand foot soldiers.

Jehoahaz then passed on and was buried with his fathers in Samaria, and his son Joash (Jehoash) was appointed as king over Israel in his place.

12ᵗʰ King over Israel — Jehoash, also known as Joash:
2 kings 13:10 – 13 (NKJV)

Jehoash ruled as king over Israel for sixteen years and did what was evil in the sight of God, walking in the same sins as Jeroboam that caused Israel to sin.

Jehoash then passed on and was buried with his fathers in Samaria, and his son — Jeroboam II — was appointed as king over Israel in his place.

The Death of Elisha and 20ᵗʰ Miracle:
Dead Bones Raising the Dead:
2 Kings 13:14 – 25 (NKJV)

Now Elisha fell sick with a terminal illness and was about to die when Joash, the king of Israel, came and wept over him, saying:

..."O my father, my father, the chariots of Israel and their horsemen!"

2 Kings 13:14 (NKJV)

Elisha then instructed the king to take a bow and arrow and shoot out of the east window, which Joash did with Elisha's hand upon his own, stating that it was the Lord's arrow of deliverance. The arrow of deliverance from Syria that he must strike until he has destroyed them.

Elisha further instructed the king to strike the ground with the arrow, which he did three times. And so Elisha was angry at Joash for only doing it three times, stating that he should have done it five or six times because now he will not completely destroy the Syrians but will defeat them only three times.

And so Elisha died and was buried, and it came to pass that some people were busy burying their friend and saw a band of Moabites invading the land, causing them to throw the dead body into Elisha's grave. But when the dead body touched the bones of Elisha, life came back into the man, and he stood up on his feet. **2 Kings 13:20 – 21 (NKJV)**

And so it came to pass according to the word of the Lord spoken by Elisha, that Joash defeated Ben-Hadad, the king of Syria, the son of Ahaziah, three times. And so, they recaptured the cities of Israel that were taken by them.

9th King over Judah — Amaziah:
2 Kings 14:4 – 21 & 2 Kings 12:1 – 21 (NKJV)

Now Amaziah became king when he was at the age of twenty-five, and reigned as king over Judah for twenty-nine years, and did what was right in the sight of God but did not remove all the high places.

And so, the moment that Amaziah became king, he avenged his father's death by executing the servants that murdered his father.

233

Ahaziah then killed ten thousand Edomites in the Valley of Salt before turning against Jehoash, the king of Israel.

It then happened that Joash, king of Israel, went to war against Amaziah — the king of Judah — and defeated them, taking Amaziah captive.

Joash further broke down the walls of Jerusalem from the Gate of Ephraim to the Corner Gate, taking all the gold, silver, and articles found in the house of the Lord and the king's house with hostages, and returned to Samaria.

And so, it came to pass that Amaziah was assassinated in Lachish and was brought back on horses to Jerusalem, where he was buried with his fathers in the City of David.

Azariah, also known as Uzziah, the son of Amaziah, was then appointed as king over Judah.

The rest of Amaziah's acts and deeds are recorded in **2 Chronicles 25:1 – 9**

13th King over Israel — Jeroboam II: 2 Kings 14:23 – 29 (NKJV)

Now Jeroboam ruled over the kingdom of Israel for forty-one years and did what was evil in the sight of the Lord as he did not depart from the sins of Jeroboam I that caused Israel to sin.

And so it came to pass that the Lord saw the great oppression of Israel. Because He said that He would never completely blot out their name from under heaven, He chose to save them through the hands of Jeroboam II according to the Word of the Lord that was spoken through His servant Jonah the prophet.

Jeroboam then passed on, and Zechariah, his son, was appointed as king over Israel in his place.

10th King over Judah — Azariah, also known as Uzziah: 2 Kings 15:1 – 7 (NKJV)

Azariah was sixteen years old when he became king over Judah and ruled for fifty-two years, doing what was right in the sight of the Lord, except for removing all the high places.

The Lord then afflicted Azariah with leprosy until the day of his death, and so he was buried with his fathers in the City of David.

Jotham, the son of Azariah, was then appointed as king over Judah in his place.

The rest of Uzziah's acts and deeds are recorded in **2 Chronicles 26.**

14th King over Israel — Zechariah:
2 Kings 15:8 – 12 (NKJV)

Now Zechariah ruled as king over Israel for six months and did what was evil in the sight of the Lord.

It then happened that Shallum conspired against Zechariah, killing him in front of all the people, and so reigned as king over Israel in his place. In doing so, fulfilling the word of the Lord that He spoke to Jehu that his sons shall sit on the throne to the fourth generation.

15th King over Israel — Shallum:
2 Kings 15:13 – 16 (NKJV)

Shallum reigned as king over Israel for one month when Menahem conspired against him and struck him down so that he died. Menahem then ruled as king over Israel in his place.

16th King over Israel — Menahem:
2 Kings 15:17 – 22 (NKJV)

Now Menahem ruled for ten years over Israel and did what was evil in the sight of the Lord.

Menahem also persuaded Pul, the king of Syria, by paying him a thousand pieces of silver when he came up against Israel, upon which he turned back and left Israel in peace.

Menahem rested with his fathers, and Pekahiah, his son, was appointed as king of Israel in his place.

17ˢᵗ King over Israel — Pekahiah:
2 Kings 15:23 – 26 (NKJV)

Pekahiah reigned for two years over the Kingdom of Israel and did what was evil in the sight of the Lord.

And so Pekah, his officer, conspired against him. Pekah killed Pekahiah and then ruled as king over Israel in his place.

18ᵗʰ King over Israel — Pekah:
2 Kings: 15:27 – 31 (NKJV)

Pekah reigned for twenty years over Israel and did what was evil in the sight of God.

During his reign, Tiglath-Pileser, king of Assyria, took Ijon, Abel Beth Maachah, Janoah, Kedesh, Hazor, Gilead and Galilee, all the land of Naphtali and took them captive to Assyria.

Hoshea then conspired against Pekah, killed him, and so took the throne, reigning as king over Israel in his place.

11ᵗʰ King over Judah — Jotham:
2 Kings 15:32 – 38 (NKJV)

Jotham was twenty-five years old when he became king and reigned for sixteen years over Judah in Jerusalem and did what was right in the sight of the Lord but still did not remove the high places.

Jotham then rested with his father in the City of David, and Ahaz, his son, ruled as king over Judah in his place.

The rest of Jotham's acts and deeds are recorded in **2 Chronicles 27**

12ᵗʰ King over Judah: Ahaz:
2 Kings 16:1 – 20 (NKJV)

Ahaz was twenty years old when he became king and reigned for sixteen years in Jerusalem and did what was evil in the sight of God, causing his sons to pass through the fire, according to the wickedness of the evil nations that the Lord had cast out from before them.

Ahaz then rested with his fathers in the City of David, and Hezekiah, his son, ruled as king in his place.

The rest of Ahaziah's acts and deeds are recorded in **2 Chronicles 28**

19ᵗʰ King over Israel — Hoshea:
2 Kings: 17:1 – 4 (NKJV)

Hoshea reigned for nine years over Israel and did what was evil in the sight of the Lord.

Shalmaneser, king of Assyria, came up against Israel, so Hoshea became his servant. But when the king of Assyria came to knowledge that Hoshea was conspiring against him, he took him and bound him in prison.

The Ten Tribes of Israel Taken Captive by Assyria:
2 Kings 17:5 – 23 – 41 (NKJV)

It then came to pass that the king of Assyria attacked Israel throughout all the land and, after three years, took Samaria and carried Israel away to Assyria.

All this happened because Israel sinned greatly against the Lord, refusing to keep His commandments, and turning away from doing what was right in the sight of God.

This now only left the kingdom of Judah that also did not keep the Lord's commandments but continually did what was evil in the sight of the Lord.

So, Assyria placed people from Babylon, Cuthah, Ava, Hamath, and Sepharvaim in Samaria to possess its cities.

13th King over Judah: Hezekiah:
2 Kings 18:1 – 37 (NKJV)

Hezekiah was twenty-five years old when he became king and reigned for twenty-nine years over Judah and did what was right in the sight of the Lord, according to his father, David.

He removed all the high places and destroyed all the sacred pillars, wooden images and the bronze serpent that Moses had made. *(This bronze serpent was more than nine hundred years old by this time).*

Hezekiah trusted in the Lord God of Israel, following steadfast after Him, keeping all His commandments and rebelling against the king of Assyria.

Because of his loyal heart, the Lord caused him to prosper wherever he went.

And so, it came to pass that the king of Assyria sent a great army against Jerusalem to king Hezekiah, presenting him with two options. These were that if they surrendered, they would live, but if not, everyone would be killed.

The king's messenger then spoke on behalf of the king to those on the wall at Jerusalem, stating that they should not trust Hezekiah and allow him to deceive them when he proclaims the Lord shall surely deliver them.

He further told them that they would be rewarded with two thousand horses, taken to a land like their own, *a land of grain and new wine, a land of bread and vineyards, a land of olive groves and honey (2 Kings 18:31)*, so that they would live and not die if they surrender and serve the king of Assyria.

The messenger further boasted of how all the gods of the nations could not save them from the hands of the king of Assyria and so not to think that the Lord would be able to save them from his hands, stating that they would be like all those nations that they have already conquered.

Assyria was now making the biggest mistake of their lives as they challenged the only true living God.

Isaiah Prophesies Deliverance:
2 Kings 19:1 – 37 (NKJV)

Now when the message was delivered to Hezekiah, he immediately brought the matter before the Lord by sending Eliakim, Shebna, and the elders of the priests to Isaiah the prophet to enquire of the Lord, stating:

> *[4] "It may be that the Lord your God will hear all the words of the Rabshakeh, whom his master the king of Assyria has sent to reproach the living God, and will rebuke the words which the Lord your God has heard. Therefore lift up your prayer for the remnant that is left."*

2 Kings 19:4 (NKJV)

And so, Isaiah sends them back to Hezekiah with a message from the Lord stating not to fear the blasphemous word spoken by the king of Assyria and his servants because the Lord will send a spirit upon the king of Assyria that shall cause him to hear a rumour, and he shall then return to his own land where he will fall by the sword.

The king of Assyria then sends the Rabshakeh with a letter to Hezekiah, further provoking the Lord God, stating that they will make a mistake in putting their trust in the Lord, as He will not be able to deliver them from the hands of the king of Assyria.

When Hezekiah received this letter, he took it to the house of the Lord and laid the letter before God, praying that God will see and hear these blasphemous words of the king of Assyria against Him.

Hezekiah further prayed for the Lord to rise and deliver them from the hands of this evil king so that all the kingdoms of the world will know He is the Lord God and Him alone.

Then, Isaiah, the prophet, sent the Word of the Lord to Hezekiah again, stating that because Hezekiah prayed to the Lord against Sennacherib, king of Assyria, that He heard Hezekiah saying:

> *32 "...He shall not come into this city, Nor shoot an arrow there, Nor come before it with shield, Nor build a siege mound against it.*
> *33 By the way that he came, By the same shall he return; And he shall not come into this city,' Says the Lord.*
> *34 'For I will defend this city, to save it For My own sake and for My servant David's sake."*

2 Kings 19:32 – 34 (NKJV)

And so, an angel of the Lord went out through the camp of the Assyrians and killed one hundred and eighty-five thousand people.

So, Sennacherib, king of Assyria, went back home and while worshipping his god in the temple of Nisroch, his two sons, Adrammelech and Sharezer, killed him with the sword and then escaped to the land of Ararat.

Esarhaddon, his son, then became king over Assyria in his place.

Hezekiah Redeeming the Time:
2 Kings 20:1 – 11 (NKJV)

Now it happened that Hezekiah became sick, and when he was near death, Isaiah the prophet came to Hezekiah, instructing him to get his house in order because he would surely die.

Hezekiah — terrified by the news he had just received — turned around, facing the wall weeping bitterly as he brought the matter before God in prayer, reminding God of how he walked in His ways with a loyal heart doing what was right in His sight.

Now it happened that before Isaiah reached the middle court that the Lord told him to go back and tell Hezekiah that He had heard his cry and prayer and would heal him, even adding fifteen more years to his life.

Hezekiah then asked Isaiah for a sign from the Lord that he would indeed be healed.

Then Isaiah asked Hezekiah if the shadow shall go forward or backwards ten degrees. Hezekiah responded that it is natural for the shadow to go forward; instead, let it go back ten degrees because that is impossible.

And so, it came to pass that Isaiah the prophet cried out to the Lord God, bringing the shadow back ten degrees and fifteen more years were added to his life.

The Death of Hezekiah:
2 Kings 20:20 – 21 (NKJV)

Hezekiah rested with his fathers, and Manasseh, his son, was appointed as king over Judah in his place.

The rest of Hezekiah's acts and deeds are recorded in **2 Chronicles 29 – 32**

Order of the Kings Continue:

14ᵗʰ King over Judah — Manasseh:
2 Kings 21:1 – 18 (NKJV)

Now Manasseh was twelve when he became king and ruled over Judah for fifty-five years and did what was evil in the sight of the Lord by following in all the abominations that the Lord had cast out from before the children of Israel.

This provoked the anger of the Lord greatly as he has done even more evil than the Amorites that lived in the land before him.

And so, the Lord spoke by His prophets stating that He will bring great calamity over Jerusalem and Judah and that the Lord will surely deliver them all into the hands of their enemies, turning them completely upside down.

And so, Manasseh passed on and was buried in his own garden in Uzza, and Amon, his son, was appointed as king over Judah in his place.

The rest of Manasseh's acts and deeds are recorded in **2 Chronicles 33:1 – 20**

15th King over Judah — Amon:
2 Kings 21:19 – 26 (NKJV)

Amon was twenty-two when he became king and reigned for two years as king over Judah, doing what was evil in the sight of God, just like his father, Manasseh.

It then happened that Amon's servants conspired against him and killed him. But their fate was quickly sealed as the people of the land then executed those that conspired against the king, appointing Josiah — the son of Amon — as king over Judah.

The rest of Amon's acts and deeds are recorded in **2 Chronicles 33:21 – 25**

16th King over Judah — Josiah:
2 Kings 22:1 – 20 (NKJV)

Josiah was eight when he became king and reigned for thirty-one years over Judah and did what was right in the sight of the Lord, according to his father, David.

Josiah instructed that they repair the house of the Lord upon which Hilkiah the high priest found the book of the law and so gave it to Shaphan the scribe to read.

After reading the book of the law, Shaphan immediately took it to Josiah the king and read the book before him.

When Josiah heard the words recorded in the book of the law, he tore his clothes, instructing Hilkiah, the priest, Ahikam, Achbor, Shaphan and Asaiah to go and inquire of the Lord for the people because God's wrath was greatly aroused against Judah for not obeying the words written in it.

The Lord then sent His word to Josiah, affirming that He would bring great calamity to these people, according to the words that he read in the book of the law, as they had forsaken God and burnt incense to other gods, utterly turning against God.

But the Lord further told Josiah that because he chose to do what was right in His sight and humble himself, he would not see the calamity that would come upon Judah but would go to the grave in peace.

Josiah — (1 Kings 13:1-6 Prophecy Fulfilled):
2 Kings 23:1 – 25 (NKJV)

Josiah then made a covenant before the Lord in the assembly of all of the people reading the book of the law in their hearing as they dedicated themselves to the Lord to follow His Commandments.

Josiah then further purged the temple of the Lord from all the abominations that were brought into the house of the Lord, including the idolatrous priests appointed to burn incense there.

He then purged the land by breaking down all the high places, burning everything to ashes.

Josiah then also took the bones of the tombs in Bethel and burned them on the altar, and so defiled it, further taking the priests, and executed them on the altars, and burned men's bones on them, thus fulfilling the Word of the Lord spoken by the man of God in **1 Kings 13:1 – 6 (NKJV).**

The Death of Josiah:
2 Kings 23:28 – 30 (NKJV)

And so, it came to pass that Josiah fought against Necho, king of Egypt, and Necho killed Josiah at Megiddo, where his servants took his body and buried him in his own tomb.

Then Jehoahaz, the son of Josiah, was appointed as king of Judah in his place.

The rest of Josiah's acts and deeds are recorded in **2 Chronicles 34 – 35**

17th King over Judah Jehoahaz:
2 Kings 23:31 – 34 (NKJV)

Now Jehoahaz was twenty-three years old when he became king, and reigned for three months over Judah, and did what was evil in the sight of God.

It then happened that Pharaoh Necho took Jehoahaz and placed him in prison, taking him back to Egypt, where he later died. He also took over the land of Jehoahaz, making Eliakim the son of Josiah king in his place, but changing his name to Jehoiakim.

The rest of Jehoahaz's acts and deeds are recorded in **2 Chronicles 36:1 – 4**

18th King over Judah — Jehoiakim:
2 Kings 23:35 – 37 & 2 Kings 24:1 – 6 (NKJV)

Jehoiakim was twenty-five years old when he became king and reigned for eleven years over Judah, under the command of Necho the Pharaoh. And he did what was evil in the Lord's sight by following in his father's footsteps.

It then came to pass that Nebuchadnezzar, king of Babylon, came up against Jehoiakim, and Jehoiakim became his servant for three years before he rebelled against Nebuchadnezzar.

But because of the sins of Manasseh and all the innocent blood that he shed, the Lord set out to destroy Judah by setting against Jehoiakim raiding bands of Chaldeans, Syrians, and Moabites, destroying them on every side.

Jehoiakim then passed on and rested with his fathers, and Jehoiachin, his son, was appointed king to rule over a fallen Judah.

The rest of Jehoiakim's acts and deeds are recorded in **2 Chronicles 36:5 – 8**

19th King over Judah — Jehoiachin:
2 Kings 24:8 – 12 (NKJV)

Jehoiachin was eighteen years old when he became king, reigning for three months over Judah, and did what was evil in the sight of the Lord.

At this time, the servants of Nebuchadnezzar - king of Babylon - came up against Jerusalem and besieged the city. At this, Jehoiachin, his mother, servants, princes and officers surrendered to Nebuchadnezzar, and they were taken captive.

The rest of Jehoiachin's acts and deeds are recorded in **2 Chronicles 36:9 – 10**

20ᵗʰ King over Judah — Zedekiah:
2 Kings 24:17 – 20 (NKJV)

And so, the king of Babylon made Mattaniah the uncle of Jehoiachin king and changed his name to Zedekiah.

Zedekiah was twenty-one when he became king and reigned for eleven years under the rule of Nebuchadnezzar.

And Zedekiah also did what was evil in the Lord's sight by walking in his father's footsteps.

Then Zedekiah rebelled against the king of Babylon, and it came to pass that the Lord finally cast Jerusalem and Judah out from His presence, delivering them completely into the hands of their enemies.

Final Fall of Jerusalem and Judah:
2 Kings 25:1 – 21 (NKJV)

And so, Nebuchadnezzar and his army came against Jerusalem and besieged it until the famine in the city was so severe that there was no food left for the people.

And so, the once beautiful city of Jerusalem became a desolate place of ruins as its city walls were now broken down, and all the men fled at night with the king of Judah making his way by way of the plain.

But Zedekiah's attempt to escape was to no avail as his army deserted him, leaving him completely alone. And so, the Chaldeans captured him in the plains of Jericho.

Zedekiah was then taken to the king of Babylon, where they killed his sons in his sight before gorging out his eyes, binding him with bronze fetters, and taking him to Babylon.

After this, the king of Babylon burned the house of the Lord with the king's house and all the houses of Jerusalem with fire, breaking down the city's walls and leaving Jerusalem in complete ruins.

And so, the Word of the Lord was fulfilled that He had spoken concerning an apostate Judah.

The rest of Zedekiah's acts and deeds are recorded in **2 Chronicles 36:11 – 23**

PROPHETIC DECLARATION:

1. **2 Kings 6:17 – 20 (NKJV)**

¹⁷ **And Elisha prayed, and said, "Lord, I pray, open his eyes that he may see." Then the Lord opened the eyes of the young man, and he saw. And behold, the mountain was full of horses and chariots of fire all around Elisha.**

I command my spiritual sight to be opened, aligned and in sync with the Holy Spirit, and so choose to operate from a heavenly perspective. I declare and decree in Jesus' Name that I see myself the way God sees me. I am not defined by what people say but by every word of God. I decree that I am heavenly led and protected, so no harm shall befall my family or me in the name of Jesus.

NOTES

NOTES

First Book of **Chronicles**

"Genealogies"
Part 1

Chronicles were written after the exile, so the authors — or final compilers — of the book of Chronicles seem to be Ezra and Isaiah. They utilised the public records of the nations of Israel.

The main characters are King David and Solomon and capture many parallel events as recorded in 2nd Samuel, making it a book of many repetitions.

The book's purpose is to give the genealogical history of the tribes of Israel, ending with Solomon being anointed as king over Israel.

1. **1 Chronicles 1 – 9:** Through these chapters, we see the break down of families, starting with Adam and continuing through the genealogies of Israel.

    These chapters further reveal the family lines of the twelve tribes of Israel followed by King David before going into the priestly line.

2. **1 Chronicles 10 – 29:** Through these chapters, we find a recap of the death of Saul and his sons, followed by David's reign as king — also covered in the Book of Samuel.

    These chapters further review the ark being brought to Jerusalem, and David, who starts with preparations to build the new temple — also covered in the Book of Samuel.

    The book then ends with a review on Solomon building the new temple and reigning as a new king — as covered in the Book of Kings.

PROPHETIC DECLARATION:

1. 1 Chronicles 4:10 (NKJV)

¹⁰ And Jabez called on the God of Israel saying, "Oh, that You would bless me indeed, and enlarge my territory, that Your hand would be with me, and that You would keep me from evil, that I may not cause pain!" So God granted him what he requested.

I declare and decree in Jesus' name that I will be blessed all the days of my life and that my territory will continually be enlarged with grace and ease as a child of God. I pray that through the Holy Spirit, my spiritual capacity will be increased to have the ability to walk in more that God has ordained for me.

NOTES

Second Book of **Chronicles**

"Genealogies"
Part 2

The Second Book of Chronicles is a continuation of the First Book of Chronicles and should be viewed as one book that was also written after the exile. Like with the First Book of Chronicles, it seems that Isaiah and Jeremiah were the final compilers of the book by utilising the records of the kings of Israel.

The main characters are King Solomon, The Queen of Sheba, Rehoboam, Abijah, Asa, Jehoshaphat, Jehoram, Ahaziah, Athaliah, Jehoash, Amaziah, Uzziah, Jotham, Ahaz, Hezekiah, Manasseh, Amon, Josiah, Jehoahaz, Jehoiakim, Jehoiachin and Zedekiah.

The book's purpose is to show the history of the kings of Judah, from the time of Solomon to the Babylonian captivity. It further illustrates the blessings connected with those who obey God and the curses associated with those who do not. The book contains many parallel events, as recorded in 1 & 2 Kings.

1. **2 Chronicles 1 – 9:** Through these chapters, we find further details regarding the reign of King Soloman, his great wisdom, the design and contruction of the temple and Soloman's house also recorded in the book of 1st Kings.

2. **2 Chronicles 10 – 36:** Through these chapters, we find details regarding the nation's division becoming two Kingdoms. These two Kingdoms are the Northern Kingdom — namely the Kingdom of Israel, consisting of ten of the original tribes of Israel. Secondly, the Southern Kingdom — the Kingdom of Judah, consisted of two of the original tribes of Israel.

However, 2nd Chronicles focuses more on the Southern Kingdom, the Kingdom of Judah and all the events that led up to the Babylonian captivity.

PROPHETIC DECLARATION:

1. 2 Chronicles 20:15 (NKJV)

¹⁵ **And he said, "Listen, all you of Judah and you inhabitants of Jerusalem, and you, King Jehoshaphat! Thus says the Lord to you: 'Do not be afraid nor dismayed because of this great multitude, for the battle is not yours, but God's.**

I declare and decree in the name of Jesus that I will hover over my problems and circumstances. No worry or fear will overcome me by the various storms of life I face because, as a child of God, my battles are fought from a heavenly perspective. I declare that this battle is not mine, but God's.

2. 2 Chronicles 20:20 (NKJV)

²⁰ **So they rose early in the morning and went out into the Wilderness of Tekoa; and as they went out, Jehoshaphat stood and said, "Hear me, O Judah and you inhabitants of Jerusalem: Believe in the Lord your God, and you shall be established; believe His prophets, and you shall prosper."**

I declare and decree in the name of Jesus that I believe and put my trust fully in the Lord God Almighty. I declare and decree that I will prosper in every dimension of my life as I believe in His prophets.

NOTES

The Book of **Ezra**

"A Restored Nation"

The book's author is Ezra, and at first glance, this book might seem insignificant. Still, Ezra's life is preparation for the revealing of the Lord Jesus Christ and, therefore, will require some historical knowledge to understand fully.

The main characters of this book consist of Cyrus, Ezra, Haggai, Zechariah, Darius I, Artaxerxes I, and Zerubbabel.

The purpose of this book is to record all the events that took place when the Jews returned to Jerusalem after their seventy-year Babylonian captivity. The book further records Ezra's involvement in the purification of the priesthood and with Zechariah helping to rebuild the temple.

This carries great spiritual significance as this is the temple that points towards the temple of God that God prepares before the second coming of the Lord Jesus Christ.

The Book of Ezra can be divided into two major sections:

1. The first group of Jews returning to Jerusalem and rebuilding the temple under Zerubbabel: **Ezra 1 – 6**
2. The second group of jews, including Ezra, returns to Jerusalem, where Ezra teaches the law under the governorship of Nehemiah: **Ezra 7 – 10.**

Note: *There are about sixty years between Ezra Chapter 6 and 7.*

HIGHLIGHTED EVENTS IN EZRA:

The Declaration of Cyrus:
Ezra 1:1 – 11

In the very first chapter, we see Cyrus, the king of Persia, making a declaration and signing a decree to bring into fulfilment the Word of the Lord that was spoken by the prophet Jeremiah as found in **Jeremiah 25:9 – 12**

> *⁹ behold, I will send and take all the families of the north,' says the Lord, 'and Nebuchadnezzar the king of Babylon, My servant, and will bring them against this land, against its inhabitants, and against these nations all around, and will utterly destroy them, and make them an astonishment, a hissing, and perpetual desolations. ¹⁰ Moreover I will take from them the voice of mirth and the voice of gladness, the voice of the bridegroom and the voice of the bride, the sound of the millstones and the light of the lamp. ¹¹ And this whole land shall be a desolation and an astonishment, and these nations shall serve the king of Babylon seventy years.*
>
> *¹² 'Then it will come to pass, when seventy years are completed, that I will punish the king of Babylon and that nation, the land of the Chaldeans, for their iniquity,' says the Lord; 'and I will make it a perpetual desolation.*

Jeremiah 25:9 – 12 (NKJV)

The former part of this prophecy has already been fulfilled. So at the start of this very first chapter of Ezra, we stand witness to see the latter part being set into motion when king Cyrus made the following proclamation throughout all of his kingdom.

The decree stated the following:

1. Cyrus, king of Persia, starts by saying that God had commanded him to build Him a house in Jerusalem. This clearly indicates that God was using Cyrus as His servant and in some way revealed His plans unto him as also described in Isaiah:

   > *²⁸ Who says of Cyrus, 'He is My shepherd,*
   > *And he shall perform all My pleasure,*
   > *Saying to Jerusalem, "You shall be built,"*
   > *And to the temple, "Your foundation shall be laid."*

   Isaiah 44:28 (NKJV)

2. In the second part of the king's declaration, Cyrus sets the Jews free with the instruction to go and build the house of the Lord God of Israel in Jerusalem, acknowledging God as the true God in his decree. **Ezra 1:3**

3. The final instruction in the king's declaration stated that the neighbours must help the Jews that would go up to Jerusalem with silver and gold, with goods and livestock, besides freewill offerings for the house of God. **Ezra 1:4**

And so, upon this declaration, all the rulers of the fathers of Judah and Benjamin with the priests, Levites and with all those who God stirred departed to go and build the house of the Lord in Jerusalem.

Cyrus then also took all the articles that were in the house of the Lord that were brought to Babylon by Nebuchadnezzar and gave them to Sheshbazzar to return to Jerusalem.

Return to Jerusalem:
Ezra 2

Now king Cyrus made Zerubbabel governor of Judah. So under his governance, all those who God stirred to return to Jerusalem, that were taken captive by Nebuchadnezzar, the king of Babylon, returned to Jerusalem and Judah, everyone to his own city.

Now Nehemiah was among those who returned to Jerusalem.

Restoration of the Temple Begins:
Ezra 3 – 4

The people now driven with purpose quickly discovered that the assignment set before them would be no easy feat.

They started by implementing all the offerings and feasts according to what was written in the Law of Moses, indicating that the returning exiles had the law with them.

261

This was followed by the restoration of the temple where Levites of twenty years and older were appointed to oversee the house of the Lord and Jeshua with his sons and brothers to oversee those working on the house of the Lord.

And so, when the foundation of the temple was completed, the priests stood with trumpets and the Levites with cymbals to praise and give thanks to the Lord, singing:

11 ..."For He is good, For His mercy endures forever toward Israel."

Ezra 3:11 (NKJV)

It was after this great accomplishment that Judah started to face resistance from their adversaries that came to them and claimed that they now also wanted to help with the building of the temple, further claiming that they too seek the Lord God and so wanted to partake in the worship, but they intended to hinder and delay the progress of Judah.

Zerubbabel and Jeshua, of course, rejected their offer, stating that they did not need their help and that they could build the house of the Lord God of Israel by themselves as Cyrus the king of Persia had commanded them.

The adversaries of Judah then persistently mocked, troubled and discouraged the people of Judah, frustrating their assignment all the days of Cyrus until the reign of Darius, king of Persia.

In an attempt to stop the work being done in Jerusalem, letters were sent to Artaxerxes, the current reigning king of Persia, written by Judah's adversaries in such a persuasive manner that it convinced the king of Persia to stop the work immediately until he gave the command to continue.

The Completion of the Temple:
Ezra 5 – 6

And so, in the second year of the reign of Darius, king of Persia, the prophets Haggai and Zechariah prophesied to the Jews in Judah and Jerusalem in the name of the God of Israel encouraging them to continue with the work on the temple regardless of whether the decree would be confirmed.

Tattenai then sent a letter to Darius stating that they found the people of Judah in Jerusalem continuing with the work on the temple and confronted them concerning on whose authority they were doing the work.

However, the people of Judah responded with an answer stating that the work was being done according to a decree that Cyrus, king of Persia, set and that if king Darius searched his records, he would find that he did indeed establish this decree.

Darius then immediately ordered that the records be searched and found that this statement from the people of Judah was indeed true.

King Darius then gave the following decree:
Ezra 5:6 – 12

1. Tattenai, the governor, and Shethar-Boznai and all their companions are to stay away from Jerusalem and let the governor of the Jews continue their work.

2. All costs involving the building of the house of God were for the king's expense and to be taken from the region's taxes beyond the river.

3. Further, the people of Judah were to be supplied with everything they needed concerning burnt offerings.

4. Anyone who defies this decree shall be hanged from a piece of timber pulled from their own house, and their house shall be completely destroyed.

And so, the temple was completed, and the people dedicated the house of the Lord with sacrifices and assigned priests and Levites to their different divisions over the service of God according to what was written in the Book of Moses.

Ezra's Arrival:
Ezra 7 – 8

It then came to pass after sixty years during the reign of Artaxerxes, king of Persia, that Ezra came up from Babylon to Jerusalem.

Now Artaxerxes, king of Persia, sent Ezra with a decree written in the same manner according to the previous decree established by Darius, king of Persia, that Ezra be given everything that he needed to fulfil the assignment set before him.

And so the hand of the Lord truly was upon Ezra as he found favour from the king, blessing his journey and assignment upon which Ezra gathered leading men of Israel to go up with him to Jerusalem.

Now Ezra was well trained in the Law of Moses and prepared his heart to teach the statutes and ordinances to Israel in Jerusalem.

Ezra then further appointed leaders for the service of the Levites, two hundred and twenty in total.

Now upon their return to Jerusalem, it was later revealed that the people of Israel, priests and the Levites had not separated themselves from the people of the land according to the Word of the Lord that stated not to mix with the people from the land lest they fall into their abominations and so have indeed taken pagan women as wives.
Ezra 9:1 – 2

Pagan Wives Removed:
Ezra 9 – 10

When Ezra received knowledge of this, he tore his clothes and repented, wept and mourned before God for their great iniquity and all the wrong they have done in the eyes of God.

Ezra then began to examine the matter by questioning all the men who had taken pagan wives and brought them forth. These men then gave their promise that they would put their wives away.

And so, because they were guilty of this, they also offered a ram as a trespass offering to cleanse them of the guilt they have brought upon themselves.

PROPHETIC DECLARATION:

1. Ezra 7:10 (NKJV)

[10] **"For Ezra had prepared his heart to seek the Law of the Lord, and to do it, and to teach statutes and ordinances in Israel."**

I declare and decree in the name of Jesus that I set my heart to understanding every Word of God and to set the very course of my life according to His perfect will. I surrender to everything that God has for me and so choose to proclaim the Gospel wherever I may go.

NOTES

The Book of **Nehemiah**

"Re-Birth of a Nation"

The Book of Ezra and Nehemiah were originally one book, called the Book of Ezra, and was later divided into two distinct books, called the first and second Book of Ezra. Then, once again, during the 4th century, the book was changed and called the Book of Nehemiah by Jerome.

The book's main characters consist of Nehemiah, Ezra, Sanballat, and Tobiah.

This is a book of history, of which Nehemiah is the author and was written to record the events of Nehemiah's return to Jerusalem, the rebuilding of the walls of Jerusalem and the many challenges they faced in their re-birth as a nation. It also shows how God, through His faithfulness, always carried them through these many difficult challenges.

The Book of Nehemiah can be divided into two main sections:

1. History of Nehemiah in Babylon and the construction of the walls of Jerusalem — **Nehemiah 1 – 7**
2. The implementation and dedication of certain principles according to the Law of Moses — **Nehemiah 8 – 13**

HIGHLIGHTED EVENTS IN NEHEMIAH:

The Power of Prayer and Fasting:
Nehemiah 1:1 – 11

Nehemiah revealed his heart through these verses when he received information regarding the current state of Jerusalem, how the survivors in the region were in great distress, and that the once glorious city is now nothing but ruins, with its walls broken down and gates burned with fire.

This situation was a pressing matter on Nehemiah's heart that caused him to weep and mourn for many days as he fasted and prayed before the Lord God Almighty to redeem them once again as a nation.

He further prayed and asked the Lord to give him favour with Artaxerxes, king of Persia, to release him from his duties so that he could return to Jerusalem and rebuild it.

Nehemiah returns to Judah:
Nehemiah 2:1 – 10

Nehemiah was the king's cupbearer, which was a very important duty and no easy task.

Note: *To be the king's cupbearer was considered a highly classified position, as the king would deal with sensitive and confidential matters in your presence, and often the cupbearer would be regarded as an advisor, making this a position that required a high level of trust.*

And so, one faithful day, Nehemiah brought wine before the king, and the king noted that Nehemiah was sad. Now the Bible says that Nehemiah became dreadfully afraid when he saw that the king took note of his state of emotions — **Nehemiah 2:2 (NKJV)**

Note: *It was unlawful to come into the king's presence with any emotion that might cause the king to feel uncomfortable. This was an offence punishable by death, which explains why Nehemiah became dreadfully afraid when the king took note of his countenance.*

Nonetheless, Nehemiah's prayer request that he brought before the Lord caused the king to respond in a way that opened the door for Nehemiah to be able to return to Jerusalem when Artaxerxes, king of Persia, asked him the reason for being sad.

And so, after Nehemiah explained to the king the matter pressing upon his heart, and the urgency for him to return and start with the work in Jerusalem, the king granted Nehemiah his request upon the condition that he gave him a set time of his return.

Nehemiah then further requested that the king provide him with letters for the governors behind the river to allow him safe passage until he reaches Judah, and also a letter for Asaph — the keeper of the forest — to supply him with all the beams that he will need to rebuild the city and its walls.

Now because the hand of the Lord was upon Nehemiah, the king granted him all that he asked — even sending captains of his army and horsemen with Nehemiah to ensure his safety, causing his journey to be prosperous.

Nehemiah Assesses the Wall:
Nehemiah 2:11 – 20 (NKJV)

When Nehemiah arrived at Jerusalem, he kept the matter that God had set upon his heart concerning Jerusalem private for three days, to first scout the wall and measure the damage to be repaired.

After having gone out on the third night assessing the wall, Nehemiah came back and told the Jews, priests, nobles and all the officials how the hand of the Lord was upon him and caused him to have favour with the king and how God blessed his journey up until now.

He further instructed them that it was time to rise and rebuild the walls of Jerusalem so that they would no longer be a reproach among all of the nations, to which everyone agreed, so they rose and started the work.

Now when Sanballat the Horonite, Tobiah the Ammonite official and Geshem the Arab heard of what they were doing, they came up against the Jews and tried to discourage them with threats saying:

"Will you now rebel against the king"

Nehemiah 2:19 (NKJV)

Defending the Wall Against Enemies:
Nehemiah 4

And so it happened that when the Israelites restored the wall up to half its height that Sanballat, Tobiah, the Arabs, the Ammonites and the Ashdodites, came up and attacked Jerusalem to distract the Israelites from doing their work.

The Israelites then brought the matter before God in prayer where Nehemiah reminded the people to remember the Lord God, encouraging them to fight for their brethren, sons, daughters, wives, and houses and so set the following measures in place:

1. Nehemiah placed men behind the lower parts of the wall and openings — **Nehemiah 4:13**
2. Each family were strategically placed with their swords, spears and their bows —**Nehemiah 4:13**
3. Half of the servants were appointed to do the work, while the other half was assigned to protect, girded with spears, shields, bows and armour — **Nehemiah 4:16**
4. Those building the wall were to carry a weapon in one hand and build with the other — **Nehemiah 4:17**
5. Then whenever the trumpet sounded, everyone was to rally to that point and assist in the battle, and so the Lord fought for Israel — **Nehemiah 4:20**

The Oppression Lifted:
Nehemiah 5

Through chapter 5, Nehemiah set specific measures in place to lift the oppression that was upon the people by instructing that all their debt be cancelled and their lands, vineyards, olive groves, houses and a hundredth of the money, grain and new wine they have given be restored to them.

Nehemiah did not lay heavy burdens upon the people like the governors before him but led by example. He also physically helped rebuild the wall and gave provisions to the people, as he feared the Lord.

The Wall Completed:
Nehemiah 6:15 – 19 & Nehemiah 7:1 – 5

Finally, after fifty-two days and through all of the persecution and distractions from surrounding enemies, the wall was constructed.

Below are further appointments done by Nehemiah after the completion of the wall:

1. Appointment of gatekeepers, Levites and singers. **Nehemiah 7:1**
2. Nehemiah gave Hanani charge over Jerusalem. **Nehemiah 7:2**
3. Nehemiah made Hananiah the leader of the citadel. **Nehemiah 7:2**
4. Guards were appointed to stand at specified stations and others in front of their houses. **Nehemiah 7:3**
5. The nobles, rulers and people who were taken captive and returned to Jerusalem were to be registered by genealogy. **Nehemiah 7:4 – 73**

Ezra Establishes the Law:
Nehemiah 8:1 – 12

Now Ezra, the scribe, was charged with the very important assignment to establish and teach the law, and so all the people who were able to understand, gathered in the street before the water gate, to hear the law read by Ezra.

Confession of Sins:
Nehemiah 9:1 – 38

And so, in the process of restoration and according to the law of the Lord, those of Israelite lineage removed themselves from all foreigners and came together fasting and covered with sackcloth, with dust on their heads, confessing their sins and the iniquities of their fathers.

The Levites then led the assembly in confession and prayer, making a sure written covenant that the leaders, Levites and priests sealed.

Inhabitants of Jerusalem:
Nehemiah 11:1 – 36

And so, a once lost nation was reborn with the leaders of the people living in Jerusalem. The rest had to cast lots where one out of ten could also live in Jerusalem, and the rest were to live in other cities outside of Jerusalem.

Nehemiah's Second Return to Jerusalem:
Nehemiah 13

After Nehemiah assigned all the priests and Levites, dedicated the wall and gave through all of the temple responsibilities, he returned to Artaxerxes — king of Persia — according to the time he set for the king.

Then while Nehemiah was in Babylon, Eliashib, the priest who had authority over the house of God's storerooms, prepared a room for Tobiah to dwell.

And so, when Nehemiah returned to Jerusalem for the second time on leave, granted him by Artaxerxes king of Persia, and came of knowledge that a room was prepared for Tobiah in the house of God, he was furious.

Nehemiah immediately threw out all of Tobiah's belongings and commanded that the room be cleansed before he brought back all the articles of the house of God, with all the grain offerings and frankincense.

Nehemiah further noted that the people of Judah were still not obeying the law in many ways. For example, the Levites were neglected and did not receive their portions as they were supposed to, and many still traded and worked on the Sabbath day.

Nehemiah then pleaded with the rulers and nobles of Judah not to provoke the anger of the Lord as their fathers had done, causing them to be utterly destroyed.

And so, Nehemiah set the necessary measures in place with all urgency to ensure that the appointing treasurers would appropriately conduct things over the storehouse and close the city gates one night before the Sabbath and only open them after the Sabbath.

Nehemiah further saw Jews who had married pagan women. Understanding the severity and danger of this, he pleaded with them, cursed them, beat some of them and pulled their hair out, making them swear that they would not give their daughters as wives to their sons, nor will they take the pagan daughters as wives for the sons of Judah.

And so Nehemiah cleansed all of Judah from everything Pagan ending with the following words saying:

> [31] ..."*Remember me, O my God, for good!*"

Nehemiah 13:31 (NKJV)

PROPHETIC DECLARATION:

1. **Nehemiah 1:10 – 11 (NKJV)**

¹⁰ Now these are Your servants and Your people, whom You have redeemed by Your great power, and by Your strong hand. ¹¹ O Lord, I pray, please let Your ear be attentive to the prayer of Your servant, and to the prayer of Your servants who desire to fear Your name; and let Your servant prosper this day, I pray, and grant him mercy in the sight of this man."

I declare and decree in Jesus' name that the mighty hand of God is upon me, and so I will have favour wherever I might go. I declare and decree in the name of Jesus that I have the skill and understanding to build His Kingdom everywhere my feet touch the ground.

NOTES

The Book of **Esther**

"The Great Conspiracy"

The author of the book is anonymous. However, there are many speculations that it might be Ezra, Nehemiah or even Mordecai. Esther is a history book in which the main characters consist of Esther, Mordecai, King Ahasuerus (Xerxes) and Haman.

The story of Esther shows how prayer, fasting, faith, courage and a selfless attitude cause the supernatural power of God to go into operation, liberating the entire Jewish nation from a conspiracy of genocide.

Through the chapters of this book, we will see how God is a Master strategist, fighting for His people when Esther miraculously becomes queen, thus setting the stage to save her people.

The Book of Esther can be divided into three main sections:

1. Esther becoming the queen of Persia: **Esther 1 – 2**
2. The discovery of a conspiracy against the Jewish nation: **Esther 3 – 4**
3. Esther divinely outmaneuvers Haman, causing him to fall into his own trap, and so saves her people as a result: **Esther 5 – 10**

HIGHLIGHTED EVENTS IN ESTHER:

1. **Esther Made Queen:**
   Esther 1 – 2

The book of Esther begins with Ahasuerus, king of Persia, hosting a great feast that lasted for six months.

And so, when the king was merry with wine, he commanded his servants to bring Queen Vashti to him so that she could parade before all of his subjects, as she was a very beautiful woman.

Queen Vashti unknowingly triggered a divine strategy plan designed by God to be set into motion when she declined the king's command to come out.

The king — now furious because of Vashti's rebellion — consulted with his wise men, who understood the law and justice, on what do to with Vashti's disobedience.

They advised the king that it would be best to dethrone Queen Vashti, as she had set a rebellious example that might cause all the women throughout the kingdom to dishonour their husbands.

Ahasuerus, king of Persia, approved and then signed a decree. He sent letters throughout his provinces that each man is master of his own house and that all wives must honour their husbands, both great and small.

The Beauty Contest:
Esther 2

After these things, the king's servants suggested that a search be done for a new queen to replace Vashti, to which the king agreed.

And so, the plan that was set out to find a new queen was to be conducted in the following manner:

1. A beautiful young virgin was to be found for the king. **Esther 2:2**

2. The king was to appoint officers in all the provinces of his kingdom. **Esther 2:3**

3. The officers were to gather all the young woman to Shushan the citadel. **Esther 2:3**

4. The young women were to be placed in the women's quarters under the care of Hegai, the king's eunuch. **Esther 2:3**

5. The women was to receive all things necessary for purification. **Esther 2:3**

6. After the twelve-month preparation period was fulfilled, each woman was to be presented to the king. The one most beautiful and talented that pleased the king was to be chosen and appointed as the new queen. **Esther 2:4 &12 – 14**

Now there was a man known as Mordecai who took care of Hadassah, which was Esther, as she was an orphan. Mordecai entered Esther into this beauty contest as she was a beautiful woman.

Now, this beauty pageant was the first of its kind, and nowhere else in scripture has it mentioned any such event that ever took place — both before and after it.

And so, Esther was placed under the care of Hegai, the custodian of the woman, who highly favoured Esther and soon moved her to the best part of the house, with seven maidservants to assist her.

And so, after ten months of preparation, it was the moment of truth as Esther was to be presented to the king. The Bible records that the king loved her more than any other woman, for she had found favour and grace in his sight. So the king crowned her as the new queen in Vashti's place.

Mordecai Uncovers a Conspiracy Against the King:
Esther 2:19 – 23

Here we see how God strategically placed Mordecai at the right location at the right time, sitting at the king's gate, when a conspiracy was unveiled of how two of the king's eunuchs planned to kill the king. This knowledge would later save Mordecai's life and redeem him into an exalted position over his enemy.

Mordecai immediately reported the matter to Esther, who then conveyed this extremely valuable information to the king in Mordecai's name.

After investigating the matter and the information was found to be true, both the eunuchs were sentenced to death by being hanged on the gallows.

The matter was then documented in the Book of the Chronicles in the king's presence.

2. Haman's Conspiracy Against the Jews: Esther 3:1 – 15

In the following verses, we see the lives of the entire Jewish nation in great jeopardy when an adversary rises by the name of Haman.

Now Haman was promoted by Ahasuerus, king of Persia, and set as second in charge over the king's kingdom.

The king then further commanded that everyone at the king's gate must bow and pay homage to Haman every time he made his way through the gate.

And so, every time Haman came through the king's gate, everyone would bow down and pay homage to him, except for Mordecai.

This, of course, infuriated Haman to such an extent that he conspired against the Jews by going to the king, explaining that there is a nation in his kingdom that did not submit to the king's law or his commands, and that it would be best if they rid the kingdom of this nation.

And so, after conspiring for a year and paying the king a bribe of more than $19, 200, 000.00 — the king finally agreed to sign the decree for the execution of the entire Jewish nation.

¹³ And the letters were sent by couriers into all the king's provinces, to destroy, to kill, and to annihilate all the Jews, both young and old, little children and women, in one day, on the thirteenth day of the twelfth month, which is the month of Adar, and to plunder their possessions. ¹⁴ A copy of the document was to be issued as law in every province, being published for all people, that they should be ready for that day"

Esther 3:13 – 14 (NKJV)

Esther's Selfless Act:
Esther 4:1 – 17

The moment when Mordecai received news of the genocide planned against the Jews on the thirteenth day of the twelve-month, he immediately sent a message to Esther to go and plead for their lives before the king.

This was a life-threatening request, as it was unlawful for anyone to come before the king without being summoned — including the queen. This was seen as an offence punishable by death unless the king chose to extend his golden sceptre, which pardoned the violation.

And so, Esther decides to take the battle into the supernatural when she sends a message to Mordecai to instruct the people to pray and fast for three days — not to eat nor drink anything, as she will go before the king. She showed outstanding courage, saying that if she dies, she dies. But if she finds favour in the king's sight, will make her petition known.

3. **Esther Divinely Outmaneuvers Haman:**
   Esther 5 – 10

The Banquet:
Esther 5:1 – 8

On the third day, Esther presented herself to the king without being summoned, anxiously awaiting her fate to be decided.

But the Bible says that when the king saw Esther, she found favour in his sight, so the king held out his golden sceptre, and Esther went near and touched the top of the sceptre.

The king then asked Esther to state her request, even up to half of the kingdom, and it shall be given unto her, to which Esther invited the king and Haman to a banquet the following day, where she would make her petition known.

Haman's Conspires to Kill Mordecai:
Esther 5:9 – 14

When Haman saw Mordechai at the king's gate and that Mordecai was not afraid of him, he became even more infuriated but restrained himself from doing Mordecai any harm.

And so, when Haman came home, he called for his wife and friends, boasting about his riches, the multitude of his children and how the king promoted him above all the other officials. Then he boasted that he was invited to Queen Ether's banquet with the king but that this meant nothing as long as he saw Mordecai sitting at the king's gate.

Haman's wife told him to build gallows fifty cubits high and suggest to the king the following day that Mordecai be hanged.

Haman's Plan Backfires:
Esther 6:1 – 14

It then happened that the king could not sleep that night and so ordered that the record of the Chronicles be read before him.

It was then found written in the Chronicles that Mordecai saved the king's life after unveiling a conspiracy of two eunuchs that wanted to kill the king, and the matter was reported by Mordecai, who was not rewarded for this great deed.

At the exact moment when this recorded event was being read in the king's presence, it happened that Haman came into the king's court to suggest that Mordecai be hanged on the gallows that he had prepared for him.

And so, the king called for Haman and asked him:

⁶ ... "What shall be done for the man whom the king delights to honor?" Now Haman thought in his heart, "Whom would the king delight to honor more than me?"

Esther 6:6 (NKJV)

Haman, who thought that the king was referring to him, suggested that such a man be clothed with the king's royal robe, which the king wore, and to let that man be paraded on the king's horse with the royal crest on its head.

Haman further suggested for all these things to be delivered by the king's most trusted noble princes and be proclaimed before the man, saying:

"Thus shall it be done to the man whom the king delights to honor"

Esther 6:9

Then to Haman's shock, the king responded and told Haman to hurry and do all these things to Mordecai, who sits at the king's gate, and to make sure that nothing he suggested is left undone.

Haman, now completely humiliated, went back home and told his wife and wise men everything that happened, and while he was still speaking, the king's eunuchs came to fetch him for the banquet with the king and Queen Esther.

Haman Hanged on His on Gallows:
Esther 7:1 – 10

At the banquet, the king again asks Esther about her petition, to which she requested that her life and the life of her people be spared as they have been sold to be killed.

The king, now furious, asked Esther who is the man that would devise such a thing in his heart and that will dare to do such a thing, to which Esther pointed at Haman and said:

6 ... "The adversary and enemy is this wicked Haman!"

So Haman was terrified before the king and queen.

Esther 7:6 (NKJV)

Now to further strengthen Esther's case, it happened that while the king went out to the palace garden out of anger, that Haman pleaded for his life before Esther, but in the process stumbled and fell onto the bed where Esther was.

And so, when the king returned from the garden found Haman there on the bed, with Esther, giving the illusion that he was assaulting the queen.

Haman was then taken with his face covered, ordered by the king to be hung on the same gallows he prepared for Mordecai.

And so, the king took Haman's signet ring and gave it to Mordecai, and Esther further instated Mordechai over Haman's household.

The king further instructed that a new decree be written in the king's name by Mordecai and Esther concerning their people and to seal the decree with the king's signet ring, which no one can revoke.

And so, the Jews were redeemed, and when the time came for the king's original decree to be carried out, the decree was overturned towards their tormentors, and the Jews instead overpowered those who hated them.

Mordecai's Achievement:
Esther 10

Now Mordechai grew great in stature and was highly favoured, second to king Ahasuerus, and he was seen as a great man among the Jews and well received by the multitudes of his brethren, keeping the peace of all his countrymen.

PROPHETIC DECLARATION:

1. **Esther 5:2 (NKJV)**

[2] **"So it was, when the king saw Queen Esther standing in the court, that she found favor in his sight, and the king held out to Esther the golden scepter that was in his hand. Then Esther went near and touched the top of the scepter."**

I declare and decree in the name of Jesus that the Lord's favour will remain upon me, where every gift that God has placed inside of me will be activated, and the measure of these gifts shall only increase with every passing day. I pray that the Holy Spirit will teach me how to operate with the spiritual gifts I have been given and so to help me never step out of my measure of grace in the mighty Name of Jesus.

NOTES

NOTES

SECTION 4

THE POETIC BOOKS

Table of Contents

Job — The Book of Ultimate Testing and Deliverance
Psalms — The Book of Prayer and Praise
Proverbs — The Book of Wisdom
Ecclesiastes — The Preacher
Song of Solomon — The Book of Covenant Love

The Book of **Job**

"The Ultimate Test"

The author of the book of Job is uncertain; some scholars say Job, some Moses. Due to a mixed view on authorship, the dates on the book of Job are varied from the Mosaic era to the exile.

The main characters of this book consist of Job, Eliphaz, Bildad, Zophar and Elihu.

The main theme of this book is about a series of trials specifically designed to test Job's faith as he suffers a terrible loss in the area of finances, witnesses the death of his children, and suffers severely in his health while being persecuted by family and friends.

All of this causes his friends to ask a powerful question,

"Why does Job Suffer?"

And so, as the four friends deliberate Jobs great misfortune, three of the four friends come to the same conclusion — Job must have done something wrong in the sight of God and must have fallen into sin to receive such terrible loss. The fourth friend, however, has a different view — rather one of faith, stating that a relationship with God is better than trying to understand why life has gone wrong.

And so, after the four friends presented their case, God then answered Job with a series of questions that only God could answer — questions with answers that not only contradict the bad counsel of his friends but also bring Job to the understanding that believers do not always comprehend what God is busy doing in their lives.

The book's purpose is to reveal various powerful lessons from Jobs personal life and the painful transformation that he goes through.

Note: *Although Job believed in God, we find that his belief was based on what he heard about God, and this further reveals that Job required a personal revelation of who God is.*

As we go through this book, it is evident that our walk with God is dangerously limited if all we know about God is what we have heard and not what we have personally experienced.

And so, later in chapter 42, we see Job repent of this very thing, causing Satan's plan to backfire. In fact, God took Job's tests and turned them into a blessing by refining him and turning him into the best version of himself.

There is another powerful truth in this book that reveals our opinions of others dealing with struggles in their lives should be reserved and not assumed to be sin or wrongful doing.

Note: *The greatest value in this book is the display of God's Goodness and Majesty in such a way that we see clearly how God is incapable of doing us wrong. He is not wicked and has no bad intention toward us but loves us unconditionally.*

We need to understand that sickness is not from God, nor is financial loss or death; this is a truth that is revealed in this book in a compelling way, further indicating how God uses these tragedies to transform Job's life and the lives of those around him.

God is in the restoration business.

The Book of Job can be divided into seven main sections:

1. **The Introduction to Job**
2. **The Attacks**
3. **Job Grieves**
4. **Jobs Three Friends Provide Their View**
   4.1 First View
   4.2 Second View
   4.3 Third View

4.4 **Conclusion Of All Three Views**
5. **Jobs Reply to His Friends**
6. **The Fourth View**
7. **The Lord Reveals Himself to Job**

HIGHLIGHTED EVENTS IN JOB:

The Introduction to Job:
Job 1:1 – 5 (NKJV)

Job's character is first described as blameless and upright, fearing God and rejecting evil. The Bible further states that Job was a man with seven sons and three daughters and wealthy to such a degree that he was the greatest man of all the men in the east.

Note: *A common way of defining wealth in this time was by means of livestock and children. As seen in* **Job 1:2 – 4.**

The Attacks:
Job 1:6 – 22 & 2:1 – 10 (NKJV)

In chapter one, we see Job through God's eyes as He said:

> *"...Have you considered My servant Job, that there is none like him on earth, a blameless and upright man, one who fears God and shuns evil?"*

> **Job 1:8 (NKJV)**

Satan then states that Job's perfect character is only a result of God's blessings and protection in his life, suggesting that if God allows him to sift Job, he will surely curse God to His face?

And so, God agrees to put Job to the test as He said to Satan:

> *"...Behold all that he has is in your power; only do not lay a hand on his person. So Satan went out from the presence of the LORD."*

> **Job 1:12 (NKJV)**

We then see how in an instant, Job receives horrific news in quick successions of the following events one after another:

Attack #1 — The Sabeans took Job's oxen and donkeys and killed the servants — **Job 1:14 – 15 (NKJV)**

Attack #2 — Then the fire of God fell from heaven and consumed the sheep and servants — **Job 1:16 (NKJV)**

Attack #3 — The Chaldeans took Job's camels and killed the servants with the edge of the sword — **Job 1:17 (NKJV)**

Attack #4 — While all this was going on, another servant came and explained how a great wind destroyed Job's house and that his children were inside, killing them all — **Job 1:18 – 19 (NKJV)**

Directly after all these unthinkable events took place, we find Job acting completely contrary to what Satan expected as the Bible says that;

"...²⁰ Job arose, tore his robe, and shaved his head; and he fell to the ground and worshipped. ²¹ And he said:

Naked I came from my mother's womb, and naked shall I return there. The LORD gave, and the LORD has taken away; Blessed be the name of the LORD."

²² In all this Job did not sin nor charge God with wrong.

Job 1:20 – 22 (NKJV)

And so, at a second appointed time when the sons of God presented themselves before the Lord, Satan also came and requested that Job be sifted, even more, this time in his own health, to which the Lord approved on the condition that Satan is not allowed to kill him.

Attack #5 — Job gets struck with painful boils from the sole of his feet to the crown of his head — **Job 2:7 (NKJV)**

Attack #6 - Jobs wife taunts him and responds with a very dis respectful question saying,

> *"Do you still hold fast to your integrity? Curse God and die!"*
> **Job 2:9 (NKJV)**

In **Job 1:11**, Satan suggests that Job will curse God to His face, which then does not happen, so the second time around, Satan tries to use Job's wife to tempt him to sin.

Yet again, this backfires in Satan's face as Job responds perfectly to his wife, affirming a powerful point by saying,

> *"...¹⁰ you speak as one of the foolish women speaks. Shall we indeed accept good from God, and shall we not accept adversity?"*

> **Job 2:10 (NKJV)**

And so, when Job's four friends heard about the terrible calamity that came upon him, they set out to comfort and mourn with him during this time.

Now the Bible says that when Job's four friends arrived at the scene, they could not recognise him because of the terrible state that he was in. This dreadful sight caused them to weep, tear their robes and sprinkle dust on their heads, and so they stayed with Job for seven days and seven nights in silence as they saw that his grief was great.

Job Grieves:
Job 3 – 4 (NKJV)

Following the aftermath of Jobs grief, Job opens his mouth, cursing the day he was born and further questions God and becomes vocal in his feelings and thoughts. After Jobs outcry of despair, we see that Job feared this very thing.

Note: *It might be that Satan's entry point against Job was fear, as we see in **Job 1:9** and **Job 3:25**.*

Job's Three Friends Provide Their View:
Job 4 – 26

First View:

- Eliphaz founded his argument on experience, suggesting that Job must have sinned, later even accusing him of being foolish — **Job 4:8 & Job 15**
- And so, Eliphaz charges Job with sin stating that he should repent so that God could restore him — **Job 22:21 – 30**

Second View:

- Bildad suggests out of his traditional view that Job is a hypocrite — **Job 8:6-8, 11 – 13.**
- Later, Bildad adds to his view that the wicked are punished; therefore, Job must have been wicked — **Job 18:21**

Third View:

- Zophar also presumes that Job's circumstances must be due to sin, thus getting what he deserves — **Job 11:2, 6.**
- Zophar further suggest that Job is wicked and a hypocrite — **Job 20:5**

And so, the three friends conclude that this misfortune that befell Job can only be due to sin and wickedness.

However, Job defends himself by standing firm on his belief that he is innocent, claiming that both the godly and ungodly experience success and loss.

Jobs Reply to His Friends:
Job 27:1 – 31:40 (NKJV)

It is clear in Job's reply to his friends that he is not at all impressed with their counsel but rather feels ridiculed and persecuted by their scornful words saying:

"I am one mocked by his friends"

Job 12:4 (NKJV)

"Miserable comforters are you all"!

Job 16:2 (NKJV)

"My friends scorn me"

Job 16:20 (NKJV)

"Why do you persecute me as God does,"

Job 18:21 (NKJV)

Finally, Job reflects on Gods Majesty as he is frustrated with his friend's counsel saying:

"Indeed these are the mere edges of His ways, and how small a whisper we hear of Him!"

Job 26:14 (NKJV)

Job further describes his integrity and the price that he is prepared to pay if he has not lived a life where he was blameless and upright and remained one who feared God and shunned evil. Based on this knowledge, he confirms that he will not allow his mouth to sin – **Job 1:1 and Job 31.**

The Fourth View:
Job 32 – 37 (NKJV)

Different Approach:

Elihu takes a different approach towards Job, and so, at first, we see how he gets angry with Job because it seems like he is justifying himself – **Job 32:2 (NKJV)**

Then secondly, we see how Elihu rebukes all three of Jobs friends because,

"...they had found no answer, and yet had condemned Job."

Job 32:3 (NKJV)

Note: *Elihu was present during the entire discussion, listening quietly to Job and his three friends, patiently waiting for them to finish their arguments. Once they were finished and had nothing further to say, then only Elihu spoke out from a place of wrath [anger].*

"Now because they were years older than he, Elihu had waited to speak to Job. When Elihu saw that there was no answer in the mouth of these three men, his wrath was aroused."

Job 32:4 – 5 (NKJV)

We then see Elihu giving Job another perspective, defending God's way of dealing with Job saying:

"Far be it from God to do wickedness, and from the Almighty to commit iniquity."

Job 34:10 (NKJV)

And so, Elihu's argument states that God is teaching Job something — words that encourage Job, who then decides not to harden his heart towards God's educational discipline but rather to seek humility during this time.

"For has anyone said to God, 'I have borne chastening; I will offend no more; Teach me what I do not see; If I have done iniquity, I will do no more'?"

Job 34:31-32 (NKJV)

Elihu's argument is further based on the fact that God will not answer the pride of evil men. Thus, one of the reasons why God is not responding to Job's outcry is because of his pride, saying:

"But no one says, where is God my Maker, who gives songs in the night, who teaches us more than beasts of the earth, and makes us wiser than the birds of heaven? There they cry out, but He does not answer, because of the pride of evil men."

Job 35:10 – 12 (NKJV)

Furthermore, Elihu feels Job is running his mouth out of foolishness,

"And now, because He has not punished in His anger, nor taken much notice of folly, therefore Job opens his mouth in vain; he multiples words without knowledge."

Job 35:15 – 16 (NKJV)

Elihu Concludes His Message:

Finally, Elihu, through his conviction, speaks to Job describing God's Goodness - explaining that Job should rather look at what he has gone through as an advanced process through which God has a divine plan — **Job 36:5 – 12 (NKJV)**

He further describes to Job that what he is going through is the *"ULTIMATE TEST"* designed to teach him various lessons about himself and that the way he responds to this process will be pivotal to his success or failure — **Job 36:1 – 37:23**

The Lord Reveals Himself to Job:
Job 38 – 42 (NKJV)

We then see a complete turnaround when the LORD decides to intervene regarding the situation and so answers Job in a whirlwind rebuking Eliphaz, Bildad, and Zophar for their false counsel and misrepresenting Him — **Job 42:7 (NKJV)**

Note how God spoke with Job in front of his friends:
Job 38:1 to 42:6

1. God answers out of the whirlwind,
2. God does not address Jobs circumstances,
3. God demonstrates to Job that He has created the earth and manages it effortlessly with love,
4. Yet above all else, He loves Job more than His creation, challenging Job to answer Him as to why he doubts Him — **Job 38:1 – 40:2 (NKJV)**
5. Job is then rebuked for arrogance in assuming that he knows God's ways - when God created all creatures, the heavens, and the earth and all its complexities. Who then is Job to question God? — **Job 38:1 – 39:30 (NKJV)**
6. We see that Job's knowledge of God was based on what he heard and not out of a personal relationship with Him. And so, it was only after God spoke to Job through the whirlwind that Job now had a true revelation of God saying: **"But now my eyes see You"** — Job 42:5 (NKJV)
7. God defends Job and rebukes three of his friends — **Job 42:7 (NKJV)**
8. The Lord then commands Eliphaz, Bildad and Zophar to prepare an offering and for Job to pray for them.

The Great Restoration:
Job 42:10 – 17 (NKJV)

"And the LORD restored Job's losses when he prayed for his friends. Indeed the LORD gave Job twice as much as he had before."

Job 42:10 (NKJV)

Note: *The ability to obey God at this point is crucial as we see how God only restores Job after he prayed for his friends — Job 42:10 (NKJV)*

We also see God was not the One who made Job sick but rather allowed Satan to sift him.

And so, through these tests, we see how Job's attitude and self-centeredness were corrected, resulting in humility, forgiveness, and obedience.

Satan took from Job, but God was the One who restored to him double what the enemy took.

And so, in conclusion, it is important for us to understand that despite severe loss through a series of tests, we must still trust in God and rely only on Him.

Understand that trials do not last, and the ***Ultimate Test*** is to have faith in God despite what's happening around you.

"KNOW THAT GOD IS FOR YOU EVEN IN THE MIDST OF THE ULTIMATE TEST."

Remember that throughout this process, Job never cursed God. This is an example well worth following.

Before the Tests	God's Restoration
7 Sons	7 Sons
3 Daughters	3 Daughters
7,000 Sheep	14,000 Sheep
3,000 Camels	6,000 Camels
500 Yoke of Oxen	1,000 Yoke of Oxen
500 Female Donkeys	1,000 Female Donkeys
Very Large Household	Family Restored
7 Sons	Increased Silver
7 Sons	Increased Gold

[16] *"After this Job lived one hundred and forty years, and saw his children and grandchildren for four generations.*

[17] *So Job died, old and full of days."*

Job 42:16 – 17 (NKJV)

PROPHETIC DECLARATION:

1. **Job 22:28 (NKJV)**

[27] **"You will make your prayer to Him,
He will hear you,
And you will pay your vows."**

[28] **"You will also declare a thing,
And it will be established for you;
So light will shine on your ways."**

I declare and decree in Jesus' name that my prayers will be birthed in the presence of the Almighty and so be led by the Holy Spirit to accomplish every task and assignment according to God's perfect will and according to the way that God has ordained it.

I declare and decree in Jesus' name the light of God's Word will continually be a lamp unto my feet and a light unto my path.

NOTES

_____

_____

_____

_____

_____

_____

_____

_____

_____

_____

_____

_____

_____

_____

_____

_____

_____

_____

_____

_____

_____

_____

_____

_____

_____

_____

_____

_____

NOTES

The Book of **Psalms**

"The Book of Prayer and Praise"

Psalms is the longest book in the Bible and comprises various songs and poetry written over approximately nine hundred years. The book contains many different topics and themes, written by multiple authors.

The Book of Psalms carries the ability to uplift, inspire and motivate the reader as it shows us how to seek and worship the Lord no matter the circumstances around us.

The book further reveals how we praise God for all He has done and how we worship Him for who He is.

The book of Psalms is made up of the following authors:

1. Moses wrote 1 Psalm.
2. David wrote 73 Psalms.
3. Solomon wrote 2 Psalms.
4. Asaph wrote 12 Psalms.
5. Heman wrote 1 Psalm.
6. Ethan wrote 1 Psalm.
7. The sons of Korah wrote 10 Psalms.
8. The authors of the remaining 50 Psalms remain anonymous and are known as *"orphan"* Psalms.

The book of Psalms can be divided into five major books and possibly reflects the first five books of Moses.

Book #1: The Genesis Book — Psalm 1 – 41

Book 1 starts the same as Genesis with the blessing of God upon man, further revealing that man's blessedness is locked up in his obedience to the Word of God — **Psalm 1**

It further expounds on man's continual rebellion but how God remains faithful to His Word when we cry out to Him in times of distress.

It reveals how He will raise a standard against our enemies when we return to Him with repentant hearts, continually keeping our eyes fixated upon Him, the Author of everlasting salvation — **Psalms 2 – 15**

It then ends with hope, salvation, and deliverance in the Lord God Almighty as we lean upon His Word through faith — **Psalm 16 – 41**

Book #2: The Exodus Book — Psalm 42 – 72

The second book deals with the nation of Israel and starts like Exodus with an outcry to God to remember His people and save them from the midst of distress, destruction, and despair — **Psalm 42 – 43**

It then continues to reveal God as a Mighty Rock and a place of refuge for those who continually believe and trust in Him. It shows how God mightily delivers and restores His people as the Righteous Judge when they cry out to Him, repenting and placing their trust and hope only in Him – the True Living God — **Psalm 44 – 72**

Book #3: The Leviticus Book — Psalm 73 – 89

Through the chapters of this book, we see the results of the redeemed as they walk before God. Almost every chapter reveals how God is a place of refuge for man.

Book #4: The Numbers Book — Psalm 90 – 106

This book starts like Numbers with Israel, as they take account of their generations. It further reveals instructions regarding thanksgiving, praise, worship, and the importance of remaining obedient and faithful to God. It shows how God's mercies and kindness will always be with those who abide in His presence.

Book #5: The Deuteronomy Book — Psalm 107 – 150

The chapters in this book are a revision of the previous four books and mainly focus on God and His Word and how those who keep His Word in their heart will continually live a life of prosperity and will always have good success.

This book also contains the longest Psalm, which is **Psalm 119**, which evidently reveals the impact on man's life when they meditate on the excellencies of God's Word.

This is also the only one of the five books with an equal number of Psalms.

Note: *Although Psalms is divided into five distinct sections, it was still thought of as a whole book, with an introduction* **(Psalm 1 – 2)** *and a conclusion* **(Psalm 146 – 150).**

Major themes covered in Psalms:

1. **Praise:**

Psalm 8:1 – 9	Psalm 106
Psalm 34:1 – 22	Psalm 138
Psalm 103:1 – 22	Psalm 145:1 – 21
Psalm 69	Psalm 100:1 – 5
Psalm 105	Psalm 150

2. **Thanksgiving:**

Psalm 7:17	Psalm 95:1 – 2 & 6 – 7
Psalm 9	Psalm 100:3 – 4
Psalm 28:6 – 7	Psalm 105:1 – 4
Psalm 30:1 & 11 – 12	Psalm 106
Psalm 44	Psalm 107:1 & 13 – 15
Psalm 56	Psalm 116
Psalm 69:30	Psalm 118:1 – 6 & 28 – 29
Psalm 75	Psalm 136:1 – 9 & 26
Psalm 86	Psalm 138
Psalm 92:1 – 2 & 4 – 5	Psalm 47:1 & 3 – 5

3. **Love:**

Psalm 13:5	Psalm 40:11
Psalm 17:7	Psalm 51:1

Psalm 25:10
Psalm 26:2 – 3
Psalm 31:7
Psalm 36:5
Psalm 85:10
Psalm 86:5
Psalm 89:1 – 2
Psalm 94:18
Psalm 103:11 &1 3

Psalm 57:10
Psalm 59:16
Psalm 63:3
Psalm 107:8 – 9
Psalm 119:64
Psalm 136:1 – 3
Psalm 143:8

4. Protection and Warfare:

Psalm 4:8
Psalm 16:1
Psalm18:1 – 3
Psalm 18:16 – 19
Psalm 23:1 – 4
Psalm 25:20 – 21
Psalm 27:1 & 5
Psalm 28:6 – 9
Psalm 31:1 – 5
Psalm 40:1 – 3

Psalm 46:1 – 2
Psalm 55:16 –1 7
Psalm 69:29
Psalm 91:1 – 2 & 4
Psalm 94:18
Psalm 121:1 – 8
Psalm 116:1 – 9
Psalm 138:3 & 7
Psalm 144:1

5. Inspirational:

Psalm 3:3
Psalm 8:4 – 6
Psalm 17:2
Psalm 18:47
Psalm 23:1 – 6
Psalm 25:12 – 14

Psalm 37:23 – 24
Psalm 62:5 – 8
Psalm 97:1 – 6
Psalm 103:20
Psalm 107:17 – 20
Psalm 109:29

6. Hope:

Psalm 5:1 – 3
Psalm 9:18
Psalm 25:3
Psalm 30:5

Psalm 42:5
Psalm 62:5 – 6
Psalm 119:49 – 50
Psalm 126: 5 – 6

Psalm 31:24

Psalm 33:18 & 20 – 22

Psalm 39:7

Psalm 130:7

Psalm 143:8

7. Faith:

Psalm 3:3 – 5

Psalm 16:7 – 8 & 11

Psalm 17:6 – 8

Psalm 23:4

Psalm 27:1 & 10

Psalm 31:5 & 14 – 15

Psalm 34:4 – 5

Psalm 37:3 – 4

Psalm 43:3

Psalm 46:10

Psalm 62:5 – 8

Psalm 71:1 – 6

Psalm 91:4

Psalm 119:105

Psalm 121:1 – 2

Psalm 143:8

PROPHETIC DECLARATION:

1. Psalm 23:1 – 6 (NKJV)

I declare and decree in Jesus' name that,

[1] **The Lord is my shepherd;**
I shall not want.
[2] **He makes me to lie down in green pastures;**
He leads me beside the still waters.
[3] **He restores my soul;**
He leads me in the paths of righteousness
For His name's sake.
[4] **Yea, though I walk through the valley of the shadow of death,**
I will fear no evil;
For You are with me;
Your rod and Your staff, they comfort me.
[5] **You prepare a table before me in the presence of my enemies;**
You anoint my head with oil;
My cup runs over.
[6] **Surely goodness and mercy shall follow me**
All the days of my life;
And I will dwell in the house of the Lord Forever.

NOTES

The Book of **Proverbs**

"The Book of Wisdom"

The main author of Proverbs is Solomon, who wrote the first twenty-nine chapters, leaving the last two chapters to be compiled by Hezekiah.

Now the Bible states that one night the Lord appeared to Solomon in a dream, saying:

"Ask! What shall I give you?"

1 Kings 3:5 (NKJV)

Solomon's response was the exception, as he did not ask for long life, riches, or the lives of his enemies as others do, but asked for a ***wise and understanding heart to discern justice.***

This request gave Solomon the power to generate wealth beyond anything imaginable, as his wisdom and riches were incomparable, living a life of prosperity beyond measure.

Solomon's infallible wisdom and secrets in living such a life of prosperity was recorded and compiled into a book known as Proverbs, making this a well of knowledge and power readily available at every believer's fingertips.

Note: *Knowledge is the acquisition of information, and wisdom is having the ability to apply that knowledge in an intelligent manner.*

Therefore, the book's main purpose is to equip every believer, by the leading of the Holy Spirit, with the necessary skillset to conduct their lives with God's intelligence.

We also see how all wisdom is locked up in God and how those who fear God — walking faithfully and blameless with Him, continually doing what is right in the eyes of God — shall tap into these dimensions of great wisdom.

The Book of Proverbs, therefore, conveys practical, moral and spiritual truths in the form of short but intelligent explanations for God's children.

The Book of Proverbs can be divided into two main sections:

1. **Wisdom concerning a son taking heed to his parent's words, thus focusing on the younger generation: Proverbs 1 – 9**

In the first section of the Book of Proverbs, Solomon gives instructions, guidance, and wise counsel on how to live Godly lifestyles by covering major themes such as:

- How to recognise and receive wise counsel and the importance thereof — **Proverbs 1:1 – 7**

- How to recognise, reject and shun evil counsel and the importance thereof — **Proverbs 1:8 – 19**

- How to live a life of wisdom and the many benefits connected with such a life — **Proverbs 1:20 – 33, Proverbs 9:1 – 12**

- The great value of wisdom — **Proverbs 2, Proverbs 8**

- The blessings connected to when we place all our trust in the Lord and learn not to lean on our own understanding — **Proverbs 3**

- Wisdom as security and how to use wisdom to guard our hearts — **Proverbs 4**

- Guidance regarding important moral values like making dangerous promises — **Proverbs 6:1 – 5**

- The traits of a wicked man and the dangers thereof — **Proverbs 6:12 – 19**

- Warnings and dangers of adultery and how to deal with such wickedness when it presents itself — **Proverbs 5, Proverbs 6:20 – 35, Proverbs 7, Proverbs 9:13 – 18**

2. **Wisdom in general - covering various topics: Proverbs 10 – 31**

In the second section of the Book of Proverbs, the style changes dramatically from where one main theme is covered per chapter into various two or three-line sayings about life and how we should conduct our lives in a Godly manner making many contrasts between various topics.

This section is made up of three hundred and eighty-eight short poems, and each poem is one verse long. Each poem is called a proverb, making it difficult to distinguish a common theme that connects an entire chapter.

Therefore, it will be easier to divide these chapters into major topics that are covered, such as:

1. **The contrast between the Wise and the Foolish:**

Proverbs 10:1,8,21,23   Proverbs 19:1,8,13,29
Proverbs 11:12,29   Proverbs 21:30
Proverbs 12:15,16,23   Proverbs 22:15,17
Proverbs 13:16,20   Proverbs 23:9,23
Proverbs 14:9,16   Proverbs 24:7,23
Proverbs 15:5,14   Proverbs 26:1,3 – 5,8,11,12
Proverbs 17:10,16,25,28   Proverbs 27:2
Proverbs 18:2,6,7   Proverbs 28:11,26
                                       Proverbs 29:9,15

2. **The contrast between Pride and Humbleness:**

Proverbs 11:2   Proverbs 22:4
Proverbs 13:10   Proverbs 21:4
Proverbs 15:25   Proverbs 25:25,27

Proverbs 16:18,19   Proverbs 27:1
Proverbs 18:12   Proverbs 29:23
Proverbs 20:6   Proverbs 30:2

3. The contrast between the Righteous (Upright) and the Wicked:

Proverbs 11:4,7,8   Proverbs 17:23
Proverbs 12:2,3,10,26   Proverbs 20:26
Proverbs 13:5,25   Proverbs 21:10,18,29
Proverbs 14:2,34   Proverbs 24:16
Proverbs 15:8,28,29   Proverbs 28:1,4
Proverbs 16:17,31   Proverbs 29:10,27

4. The contrast between Truth and Lying:

Proverbs 12:22   Proverbs 21:28
Proverbs 14:5,22,25   Proverbs 22:21
Proverbs 17:4   Proverbs 23:23
Proverbs 16:6   Proverbs 24:26
Proverbs 19:5,28   Proverbs 28:4

5. The contrast between Love, Strife and Hatred:

Proverbs 10:1,12   Proverbs 20:3,20
Proverbs 11:13   Proverbs 25:21,8
Proverbs 15:17   Proverbs 26:20,21,22,25
Proverbs 17:1,9,14   Proverbs 28:25
Proverbs 18:8   Proverbs 30:33

6. Husbands (men) and Wives (women):

Proverbs 11:16,22   Proverbs 21:19
Proverbs 12:4   Proverbs 27:16
Proverbs 14:1   Proverbs 30:23
Proverbs 18:22   Proverbs 31:10 – 31
Proverbs 19:13,14

7. **Fathers, Mothers, and Children:**

Proverbs 10:1
Proverbs 13:1,22,24
Proverbs 14:26
Proverbs 17:6,25
Proverbs 19:13,14,18

Proverbs 23:14
Proverbs 28:24
Proverbs 29:15,17
Proverbs 30:17
Proverbs 31:2

8. **The Fear of the Lord:**

Proverbs 9:10
Proverbs 10:27
Proverbs 14:26,27
Proverbs 15:16
Proverbs 16:16

Proverbs 19:23
Proverbs 22:4
Proverbs 24:21
Proverbs 28:14

9. **Authority:**

Proverbs 20:2,8,26
Proverbs 24:22,25
Proverbs 25:5,15
Proverbs 29:26
Proverbs 31:4

10. **Drunkenness and Slothfulness (Sluggard)**

Proverbs 10:26
Proverbs 12:27
Proverbs 13:4
Proverbs 18:9
Proverbs 19:15,24
Proverbs 22:13
Proverbs 26:13 – 16

Notes:

- *A person with wisdom becomes a person of influence, and a person of influence becomes a person of value, and a person of value will always generate great success.*
- *Above all else, remember that the first lesson in "Wisdom" is that we fear and respect God.* ***Proverbs 9:10 – 11***

PROPHETIC DECLARATION:

1. Proverbs 10:28 (NKJV)

[28] **"The hope of the righteous will be gladness,
But the expectation of the wicked will perish."**

I declare and decree in Jesus' name that my prayers will be like weapons of mass destruction that rain down upon the headquarters of the wicked where they come together and scheme, causing them to be scattered in every direction.

I declare and decree in Jesus' name that every plan, weapon, device and assignment formed against me, my loved ones and my calling shall be permanently dismantled and be destroyed and shall not come nigh my dwelling place.

I declare and decree in Jesus' name that I shall walk in the Wisdom of God all the days of my life — Amen.

NOTES

The Book of **Ecclesiastes**

"The Preacher"

Solomon must have written Ecclesiastes as he was the only son of David that ruled over Israel from Jerusalem. We see the evidence of this throughout the book of Ecclesiastes.

The main character of this book is Solomon, the son of David. It can be seen throughout this book that Solomon transcribed this late in his life between 931 to 971 B.C. If it is not understood correctly, it might cause discouragement.

"Ecclesiastes" comes from the Greek word *"ekklesia"*, meaning a person who calls an assembly. The Hebrew Name for Ecclesiastes is "Qoheleth", meaning "the preacher" — someone who either assembles people or addresses them once assembled.

In **Ecclesiastes 1:1**, the author refers to himself as a preacher. Therefore, the book of Ecclesiastes can be viewed as the Preacher who calls an Assembly.

The writer seems to be searching for the meaning and value of life and the role God plays in this, both in the natural and eternal realms.

There is a consistent theme throughout this book reflecting on life with God and without God. The theme and conclusion carry great relevance to the meaning of life, making this a book that is rich in lessons.

Vanity is a significant word commonly found throughout the book and comes from the Hebrew word *"hebel"*, which means *"breath"*.

Therefore, the main theme of this book could be summarised as follow:

"God gives true meaning to life — not living for Him makes every aspect of our lives futile and vanity..."

This book's secondary theme shows Solomon expressing that he should have enjoyed life and the things that God had blessed him with — **Ecclesiastes 5:18 – 20 (NKJV).**

Solomon was blessed, and he realises that he will be judged on the way he managed his blessings — **Ecclesiastes 7 – 10 (NKJV)**

And so, the intention of this book is to present us with a realistic vision of life where the emphasis is to identify the instruction and sovereignty of God in this life. Solomon seeks to understand and see life through a human experience and uses his personal experiences to refine his conclusion regarding true value "*under the sun*".

The book is broken down into four main sections:

1. **Solomon's search — Ecclesiastes 1:1 – 11 & 13 (NKJV)**
2. **Investigations and findings — Ecclesiastes 1:12 – 11:6 (NKJV)**
3. **Cautioning — Ecclesiastes 11:8 – 12:8 (NKJV)**
4. **Solomon's conclusion — Ecclesiastes 12:9 – 14 (NKJV)**

1. **Solomon's Search:**
   Ecclesiastes 1:1 – 11 & 13 (NKJV)

Here the writer is questioning what gives true value to life and if it can be found in this present-day, further examining what that looks like. Solomon is teaching us wisdom after reflecting on his life, using his life experience to provide a frame for his research.

"And I set my heart to seek and search out by wisdom concerning all that is done under heaven; this burdensome task God has given to the sons of man, by which they may be exercised."

Ecclesiastes 1:13 (NKJV)

2. **Investigations and findings:**
   Ecclesiastes 1:12 – 11:10 (NKJV)

Investigations:
Ecclesiastes 1:12 – 11:10

- Seek and search by wisdom all that is done under heaven — **Ecclesiastes 1:3 – 13**
- Philosophy — **Ecclesiastes 1:12 – 6:12**
- Greed — **Ecclesiastes 2:1 – 11, 18 – 26, 4:4 – 6; 5:8 – 14**
- Possessions — **Ecclesiastes 2:4 – 9**
- Labour — **Ecclesiastes 2:10 – 11, 18 – 24**
- Madness and folly — **Ecclesiastes 2:12**
- Everything has a time — **Ecclesiastes 3:1 – 8**
- God organised the universe — **Ecclesiastes 3:1 – 14**
- Enjoyment — **Ecclesiastes 3:11, 12; 5:18 – 20; 9:7 – 10**
- Not all dreams are from God — **Ecclesiastes 5:3**
- Riches — **Ecclesiastes 5:10 – 20 – 6:1 – 2**
- Judgement — **Ecclesiastes 11:7 – 10**

Findings:
Ecclesiastes 7:1 – 11:6

- **Without God's help,** we will fail to determine what is the right thing to do.
- **Without God's revelation**, people do not know what will come after them.

3. **Cautioning:**
   Ecclesiastes 11:8 – 12:8

Caution to the Young:

- We are encouraged to always rejoice in God's blessings — **Ecclesiastes 11:8**
- A warning to the young to seek God early in life, with the understanding that God will judge all things, which should encourage us to live moral lives — **Ecclesiastes 11:9**

Caution to the Elderly:

- Life is short, which is why we should remember God in our youth — **Ecclesiastes 12:1 – 7**
- Frailty comes at some point in old age affecting your body and appearances — **Ecclesiastes 12:1 – 7**
- We are reminded in **Ecclesiastes 12:1 & 6** to *"Remember your creator"*. The writer here encourages us to continually build and work on our relationship with God throughout our lives up until death where:

> *"The dust will return to the earth as it was,*
> *And the spirit will return to God who gave it."*

Ecclesiastes 12:7 (NKJV)

A Final Admission:

- Solomon tried every possible practice that the world said would bring pleasure but found it all to be fruitless and meaningless — **Ecclesiastes 12:8**

4. **Solomon's conclusion:**
   Ecclesiastes 12:9 – 14

The book of Ecclesiastes was given to teach us the meaning of life, keeping in mind that Solomon was the wisest man on the earth at that time, where he had everything in life to the fullest level of success, wealth, women, pleasure, power, status, fame, and great accomplishments.

And so, in Solomon's reflection, he noted two ways in which we could live life — one with God and the other without God.

Now, as Solomon looks back on his life, he finally comes to the following conclusion about life under the sun as we know it:

1. Fear God
2. Keep His commandments
3. God will ultimately judge all, whether good or evil.

Note: *It is essential to have a devoted relationship with God so that your relationship will stand in the day of judgment. It is not enough just to know about Him; WE MUST HAVE A PERSONAL RELATIONSHIP WITH HIM WHERE WE TRULY KNOW AND FOLLOW HIM.*

The Duty of Mankind:

Reverence for God and obeying Him is the whole duty of mankind. While fulfilling this quest, it should be done fully knowing there is no fairness in this world. However, God will ultimately judge all and set it right.

PROPHETIC DECLARATION:

1. Ecclesiastes 4:12 (NKJV)

[12] **"Though one may be overpowered by another, two can withstand him. And a threefold cord is not quickly broken."**

I declare and decree in Jesus' name that as I am yoked with the Living God, no evil shall befall me.

My heavenly Father, I pray, may You help through the leading of Your Holy Spirit to build and strengthen my relationship with You. May You continue to lead me into all truth that I may know You more fully and continue to enjoy your favour — Amen

NOTES

The Book of **Song of Solomon**

"The Book of Covenant Love"

This book is also well known as Song of Songs, of which Solomon is the author and was written sometime during his reign between 970-930 B.C.

The book of Song of Solomon consists of small poems to make up one complete poem and mainly revolves around two main characters – King Solomon and the Shulamite woman.

Scholars have different views regarding the purpose of the book:

a. Some are of the opinion that it represents an allegorical picture of the love of God for Israel,
b. Others are of the opinion that it represents an allegory of Christ's love for His church,
c. Yet others view this book as a practical handbook on sexual intercourse between husband and wife.

Regardless of the purpose, the theme throughout the book is ultimate love.

The Book of Song of Solomon can be divided into three main categories:

1. The Engagement — **Song of Solomon 1 – 3**
2. The Wedding Ceremony — **Song of Solomon 4**
3. Relationship Between Husband and Wife — **Song of Solomon 5 – 8**

HIGHLIGHTED EVENTS:

1. **The Engagement:**
    Song of Solomon 1 – 3

Through these chapters, Solomon writes of the courtship process and engagement between the beloved, which is Solomon and his lover, the Shulamite woman.

These chapters end with the Shulamite woman being summoned for the wedding.

2. The Wedding Ceremony: Song of Solomon 4

This Chapter reveals Solomon's heart and emotions toward his bride and expresses his thoughts when he sees her.

3. Relationship Between Husband and Wife: Song of Solomon 5 – 8

These chapters reveal the power of the love that exists between a husband and wife.

> *⁶ "Set me as a seal upon your heart,*
> *As a seal upon your arm;*
> *For love is as strong as death,*
> *Jealousy as cruel as the grave;*
> *Its flames are flames of fire,*
> *A most vehement flame.*
>
> *⁷ Many waters cannot quench love,*
> *Nor can the floods drown it.*
> *If a man would give for love*
> *All the wealth of his house,*
> *It would be utterly despised."*

Song of Solomon 8:6 – 7 (NKJV)

PROPHETIC DECLARATION:

1. Song of Solomon 2:4 (NKJV)

⁴ **"He brought me to the banqueting house,
And his banner over me was love."**

I declare and decree in Jesus' name that as a child of God, I will reflect nothing but the love of the Father. My mindset continually will be to keep peace and unity in the body of Christ.

NOTES

NOTES

SECTION 5

THE MAJOR PROPHETS

Table of Contents

Book of **Prophet Isaiah**

"The Evangelical Prophet"

The Prophet Isaiah is the book's author, and his name means "Salvation of the Lord". The events of this book were recorded and written in Palestine about 792-722 B.C.

The book of Isaiah reflects the entire Bible as it consists of sixty-six chapters divided into two main sections.

The first section has thirty-nine chapters corresponding with the first thirty-nine books of the Old Testament and deals with law and judgement.

The second section has twenty-seven chapters that correspond with the twenty-seven books of the New Testament and deal with comfort, hope and salvation through Christ.

In this book, we see how God, through many visions and prophecies, reveals His judgement concerning Israel and Judah through the Prophet Isaiah to warn them because of their continual rebellion and sin, repeatedly doing what is wrong in the sight of God.

We then further discover how God reveals to the prophet Isaiah the Lord Jesus Christ that shall be born of a virgin and suffer great persecution, but how God, through His great suffering, shall bring complete restoration and everlasting salvation.

And so, the Prophet Isaiah prophesied everlasting redemption that shall come through Christ Jesus seven hundred years before His birth, making Isaiah an evangelical prophet.

The book of Isaiah is one of the books that are quoted the most in the New Testament and reveals great spiritual significance.

HIGHLIGHTED EVENTS IN ISAIAH:

1. Judah's Continual Rebellion:
   Isaiah 1

The first verse of chapter one reveals Isaiah prophesying during a time when four kings reigned and ruled over Judah and Jerusalem, known as Uzziah, Jotham, Ahaz, and Hezekiah. This tells us that Isaiah's ministry lasted for more than fifty years.

In the first chapter of this book, we see God stating His case against an apostate Judah, charging them with the following offences: **Isaiah 1:4 (NKJV)**

- Sinful nation.
- A people who are laden with iniquity.
- A brood of evildoers.
- Children who are corrupters.
- They have forsaken the Lord.
- They have provoked the Lord to anger.
- They have turned away backward from the Holy One of Israel.

We then see God, through His unconditional love, always presenting Judah and Jerusalem with opportunities to repent by sending many warnings of judgement through the Prophet Isaiah.

In doing so, hoping that a fallen Judah will turn from their continual rebellion so that He can restore and heal them, this time leaving them with the following commandments as found in **Isaiah 1:16 & 17:**

- Wash yourselves.
- Make yourselves clean.
- Put away your evil doings from before My eyes.
- Cease doing evil.
- Learn to do good.
- Seek justice.
- Rebuke the oppressor.
- Defend the fatherless.
- Plead for the widows.

If obeyed, these divine instructions would unlock the favour of God over their lives, causing them to eat the good of the land, but if denied and they continue in their rebellion, it will cause their utter destruction.

2. **Prophecy of Hope and Waring:**
   Isaiah 2 – 5

Chapter two opens up with a promise concerning the end times stating in verse two that these things shall come to pass in the latter days. The **(KJV)** says, *"in the last days."*

This is the 3rd prophecy in Isaiah that shall only be fulfilled in the Millennial reign — **Isaiah 2:1 — 4**

3. **Isaiah's Vision and Call:**
   Isaiah 6

The chapter gives us a glimpse through the Prophet's eyes as he sees the Lord sitting on a throne with the train of His robe filling the temple.

We also find the revealing of six-winged angels known as Seraphim standing above the temple as described in **Isaiah 6:2.**

"And one cried to another and said:
Holy, holy, holy Is the Lord of hosts; The whole earth is full of His glory!"

Isaiah 6:3 (NKJV)

One of the seraphim then took a live coal from the altar and touched Isaiah's mouth with it. The explanation for doing this is found in **Isaiah 6:7**

We then come to one of the most profound occurrences in scripture as Isaiah overhears a meeting taking place in heaven and the Lord asking,

"...Whom shall I send,
And who will go for Us?"...

Isaiah 6:8a (NKJV)

343

And so, without delay, Isaiah reveals his availability saying,

"...Here am I! Send me."

Isaiah 6:8b (NKJV)

And so, Isaiah, ordained by God as a Prophet, was mandated with a specific message from the Lord, not only to prophesy judgement but also everlasting redemption that shall come through Christ for all.

4. **Isaiah's 1ˢᵗ Prophecy of Christ:**
   Isaiah 7:1 – 25

In the former part of this chapter, the Lord gives Isaiah specific instructions regarding a prophecy for Ahaz.

And so the Lord commanded Isaiah the following: **Isaiah 7:2**

- He must go and meet Ahaz,
- He was to take his son, Shear-Jashub, with him,
- He was to meet Ahaz at the end of the aqueduct from the upper pool on the highway to the Fuller's Field.

The above information confirms the legitimacy and realness of what is taking place. These were real people, real places and actual events, and therefore, not some make-belief fairy-tale as many may suppose.

We then see how the Lord, through the Prophet Isaiah, in the latter part of this prophecy, reveals the birth of Jesus Christ, stating,

"Therefore the Lord Himself will give you a sign: Behold, the virgin shall conceive and bear a Son, and shall call His name Immanuel."

Isaiah 7:14 (NKJV)

5. **Isaiah's 2ⁿᵈ Prophecy of Christ:**
   Isaiah 9:1 – 7

Where the first prophecy touched on the birth of the Messiah, the second prophecy focused more on His government, as seen in **Isaiah 9:6 – 7.**

The Returning Remnant:
Isaiah 10:20 – 34

The Prophet then continues to reveal that a time will come when the yoke of bondage and oppression will be removed from the remnant of Israel, further declaring that this remnant shall once again return to the Lord, the Holy One of Israel.

We then come to a powerful passage of scripture that reveals how the burden will be removed and how the yoke will be destroyed, stating,

"It shall come to pass in that day
That his burden will be taken away from your shoulder,
And his yoke from your neck,
And the yoke will be destroyed because of the anointing oil."

Isaiah 10:27 (NKJV)

6. **Isaiah's 3ʳᵈ Prophecy of Christ:**
   Isaiah 11:1 – 16

A prophetic picture of Christ and a future Kingdom is further revealed in this chapter.

Here the coming Christ is made mention of as a Rod that will stem from Jesse, followed by the revealing of the Seven Spirits that shall rest upon Him,

- The Spirit of the Lord — **Isaiah 11:2**
- The Spirit of Wisdom — **Isaiah 11:2**
- The Spirit of Understanding — **Isaiah 11:2**
- The Spirit of Counsel — **Isaiah 11:2**
- The Spirit of Might — **Isaiah 11:2**

- The Spirit of Knowledge — **Isaiah 11:2**
- The Spirit of the Fear of the Lord — **Isaiah 11:2**

7. Judgement Upon the Nations:
   Isaiah 13:1 — 23:18

From **Isaiah 13 — 23**, we see the oracles of judgement and salvation targeted toward foreign nations whose wealth affected Judah and Jerusalem. Among the prophecies are the following nations:

1. Babylon — **Isaiah 13:1 - 14:23**
2. Assyria — **Isaiah 14:24 - 27**
3. Philistia — **Isaiah 14:28 - 32**
4. Moab — **Isaiah 15:1-16:14**
5. Damascus (Syria) and Israel — **Isaiah 17:1 - 14**
6. Ethiopia — **Isaiah 18:1 - 7**
7. Egypt — **Isaiah 19:1-20:6**
8. Fall of Babylon — **Isaiah 21:1 - 10**
9. Edom — **Isaiah 21:11 - 12**
10. Arabia — **Isaiah 21:13 - 17**
11. Jerusalem — **Isaiah 22:1 - 14**
12. Shebna — **Isaiah 22:15 - 25**
13. Tyre — **Isaiah 23:1 - 18**

Isaiah 14:12 - 21 also thoroughly describes Lucifer and his fall due to pride and rebellion.

The pride of Lucifer is revealed through the familiar five "I Will's" found in **Isaiah 14:13 - 14**

8. Isaiah's Apocalyptic Prophecy:
   Isaiah 24 - 27

Chapter 24 - 27 is many times seen as one prophecy sometimes called the *"Isaiah Apocalypse"*.

The first part of the prophecy marks the total destruction of humankind. We see how God, through the Prophet Isaiah, turn His focus from judging individual nations to the judgement of the entire earth due to sin and rebellion against Him.

We also note how this judgement is not only focused on the human race but also against evil principalities and powers — **Isaiah 24:21 – 23**

The final part of the prophecy shifts focus from judgement to Israel's deliverance, noted four times by the phrase *"in that day"*.

    A.   In that day, the Lord will punish Leviathan — **Isaiah 27:1**
    B.   In that day, sing to her... **Isaiah 27:2**
    C.   In that day, the Lord will thresh... **Isaiah 27:12**
    D.   In that day, the great trumpet will be blown... **Isaiah 27:13**

9. Prophecies of Judgment and Blessing: Isaiah 28:1 – 35:10

A. Woe to Ephraim — Isaiah 28:1 – 15

Ephraim's leader's had become drunkards refusing the warnings from Yahweh, which caused their fall.

B. Woe to Ariel [Jerusalem] — Isaiah 29:1 – 16

Here we find a spiritually blind Israel whose words do not align with their actions. They serve and honour God with futile words, yet their hearts are far from Him.

C. Woe to the Egyptian Alliance — Isaiah 30 – 31

God had given Judah divine guidance, which they rejected, seeking an alliance with Egypt in defence against Assyria. At this point, Judah had been placing their trust in Egypt's horses instead of God.

"Woe to those who go down to Egypt for help, And rely on horses, Who trust in chariots because they are many, And in horsemen because they are very strong, But who do not look to the Holy One of Israel, Nor seek the Lord!"

Isaiah 31:1 (NKJV)

D. Woe to the Spoiler of Jerusalem — Isaiah 33:1

This prophecy revealed how this supposedly unstoppable army would, in fact, be stopped as the Lord states that those plundering will be plundered.

We further see how the Lord will stand as Judge over Jerusalem, saying,

"The Lord is our Judge, The Lord is our Lawgiver, The Lord is our King; He will save us)"

Isaiah 33:22 (NKJV)

10. Judah's Deliverance and Hezekiah's Restoration: Isaiah 36:1 – 39:8

Refer to **2 Kings 18 – 20** to see the remarkable events of how the Lord God not only fought for Hezekiah but also restored and extended his life.

11. Isaiah's 4th Prophecy of Christ: Isaiah 40:1 – 31

From this chapter going forward, we see how the theme changes dramatically from many burdens, woes, and judgement to restoration, comfort, blessings, and peace.

The prophecy opens up with the revealing of a messenger whom we know is John the Baptist that shall come to prepare the way for the Messiah and so, it's through the Messiah, that God will make His glory known — **Isaiah 40:3 – 5**

Note: *We see John quoting the Prophet Isaiah's words in* **John 1:23**.

The Chapter then ends off with a well-known promise for those who wait upon the Lord, stating,

> *"But those who wait on the Lord*
> *Shall renew their strength;*
> *They shall mount up with wings like eagles,*
> *They shall run and not be weary,*
> *They shall walk and not faint."*

Isaiah 40:31 (NKJV)

12. Isaiah's 5th Prophecy of Christ:
Isaiah 42:1 – 9

Through this prophecy, we see the Messiah revealed as the gentle redeemer Who will uphold justice and bring healing to those who are broken — **Isaiah 42:1 – 4**

13. Isaiah's 6th Prophecy of Christ:
Isaiah 52:13-53:12

These two Messianic predictions reveal the Lord Jesus Christ as the Servant and point to the person and work of Jesus Christ.

This prophecy paints a picture where the Lord Jesus Christ is revealed as a Priest, Suffering Servant, Intercessor, Conqueror, and The Way for God's grace to sinners. It is through Him that we shall receive a renewed spirit of holiness.

In almost every verse, we see how the prophecy discloses great detail about Jesus's life, purpose, and crucifixion.

14. Isaiah's 7th Prophecy of Christ:
Isaiah 56:1 – 8

The Lord reveals through the Prophet Isaiah that salvation will be for everyone who believes in Him, who follows His statutes and laws, keeping the commandments of the Lord by doing what is right in His sight — for Jew and Gentile.

15. Isaiah's 8th Prophecy of Christ:
Isaiah 61:1 – 3

This prophecy reveals the main purpose that Jesus was mandated with, which was to bring healing and restoration to those who believe.

As we read the first three verses of this prophecy, we find that every statement has to do with healing and restoration.

The prophecy further reveals how Jesus was to accomplish this very crucial task stating that the Spirit of the Lord is upon Him.

Note: *We see the Lord Jesus reading from **Isaiah 61:1 – 2** in the synagogue found in **Luke 4:18 – 19**. However, He leaves out the last part of **Isaiah 61:2**, stating, "And the day of vengeance of our God."*

Jesus the *"Anointed One"* is highlighted throughout the final prophecies of Isaiah.

The book of Isaiah then ends with a prophecy concerning the New heavens and earth — **Isaiah 66:22 – 24**

PROPHETIC DECLARATION:

1. Isaiah 40:28 – 31(NKJV)

28 "Have you not known?
Have you not heard?
The everlasting God, the Lord,
The Creator of the ends of the earth,
Neither faints nor is weary.
His understanding is unsearchable.
29 He gives power to the weak,
And to those who have no might He increases strength.
30 Even the youths shall faint and be weary,
And the young men shall utterly fall,
31 But those who wait on the Lord
Shall renew their strength;
They shall mount up with wings like eagles,
They shall run and not be weary,
They shall walk and not faint."

I declare and decree in Jesus' name that as I wait upon the Lord through prayer and supplication, I will continually renew my strength, I will run and not be weary, I will walk and not be faint.

NOTES

NOTES

Book of **Jeremiah**

"A Call to Repentance"

Jeremiah is one of the major prophets of the Bible and was written by prophet Jeremiah himself. Jeremiah, the son of Hilkiah, was a prophet from a priestly town of Anathoth and perhaps was a descendant from Abiathar. There is no certainty to the meaning of Jeremiah's name, but scholars suggest it can either mean *"Yahweh Exalts"* or *"Yahweh Throws"*.

Because of Jeremiah's lineage, he would have been raised a priest, though no record of his priestly service exists. Instead, God chose this man of undeniable courage to speak to the people of Judah on the Lord's behalf — even though they would not listen.

In his writings Jeremiah is very transparent regarding his personal life. There is more known of the personal life of prophet Jeremiah than any other in the Old Testament as he has given us many glimpses into his thinking, concerns, and frustrations.

Jeremiah was commanded not to marry or have children to illustrate his message that judgement was pending, and that the next generation would be swept away. Because of His message of judgement, it would seem that the prophet Jeremiah had few friends. Only Ahikam, Ahikam's son Gedaliah, and Ebed-Melech seem to qualify but the closest of them all was his associate and scribe Baruch. The prophet Jeremiah also dictated his prophecies from the Lord to Baruch.

Jeremiah proclaimed a message of doom and was a message contrary to the hope of the people. His message would have included a suggestion to surrender to the Babylonians. Regardless of his message of doom, his critical rebuke of the leaders, and contempt for idolatry, Jeremiah's heart still ached for his people, as he knew that Israel's salvation could not be divorced from faith in God and a right covenantal relationship expressed by obedience.

Jeremiah was nearly twenty years old when he began to prophesy, and he continued in that office for the rest of his adult life — some forty years or more scholars would suggest. Because his message held little weight with the people, Jeremiah's prophecies reveal a substantial amount of emotional depth — often sorrow over the plight of God's people or his own troubles — **Jeremiah 12:1 – 4; 15:10**

Jeremiah's ministry therefore began in 627 B.C. and ended sometime around 582 B.C. with his prophecy to the Jews who fled to Egypt **(Jeremiah 44:1)** shortly after the fall of Jerusalem in 586 B.C. For the majority of this time, Jeremiah based his ministry out of Jerusalem, prophesying to Judah during the reigns of Josiah, Jehoahaz, Jehoiakim, Jehoiachin, and Zedekiah.

The Southern Kingdom of Judah fell during Jeremiah's prophetic ministry (586 B.C.), having been threatened for many years by outside powers — first Assyria and Egypt and then by their eventual conquerors, Babylon.

Jeremiah found himself addressing a nation hurtling headlong toward judgment from God. The Israelites may have feared the future as the outside powers drew near, but rather than respond with humility and repentance, the people of Judah primarily lived as islands unto themselves, disregarding both the Lord's commandments and the increasing danger that resulted from their disobedience.

The book of Jeremiah can be divided into the following 6 main categories:

Note: *The prophecies in this book was not written in chronological order.*

The call of the Prophet
Jeremiah 1

Warnings & Exhortations to Judah
Jeremiah 2 – 35

This category speaks about the following major events.

1. **Earliest Discourses: Jeremiah 2 – 6**
2. **Temple Message: Jeremiah 7 – 10**

3. Covenant & Conspiracy: Jeremiah 11 – 13
4. Messages concerning the Drought: Jeremiah 14 – 15
5. Disaster & Comfort: Jeremiah 16:1 – 17:18
6. Command to Keep the Sabbath Holy: Jeremiah 17:19 – 27
7. Lessons from The Potter: Jeremiah 18 – 20
8. Condemnation of Kings, Prophets & People: Jeremiah 21 – 24
9. Foretelling the Babylonian Exile: Jeremiah 25 – 29
10. Promises of Restoration: Jeremiah 30 – 33
11. Historical Appendix: Jeremiah 34 – 35
    a. Warning to Zedekiah: Jeremiah 34:1 – 7
    b. Manumission of Slaves Revoked: Jeremiah 34:8 – 22
    c. The Symbol of The Rechabites: Jeremiah 35:1 – 19

Sufferings & Persecutions of the Prophet
Jeremiah 36 – 38

This category speaks about the following major events.

1. Burning Jeremiah's Roll: Jeremiah 36
2. Imprisoning of Jeremiah: Jeremiah 37 – 38

The Fall of Jerusalem and Its Aftermath
Jeremiah 39 – 45

This category speaks about the following major events.

1. The Fall Itself: Jeremiah 39
2. Accession & Assassination of Gedaliah: Jeremiah 40:1 – 41:15
3. Migration to Egypt: Jeremiah 41:16 – 43:13
4. Prophecy against Those in Egypt: Jeremiah 44
5. Historical Appendix - A Promise to Baruch: Jeremiah 45

Judgement Against The Nations
Jeremiah 46 – 51

This category speaks about the following major events.

1. Judgement Against Egypt: Jeremiah 46
2. Judgement Against Philistia: Jeremiah 47
3. Judgement Against Moab: Jeremiah 48
4. Judgement Against Ammon: Jeremiah 49:1 – 6
5. Judgement Against Edom: Jeremiah 49:7 – 22
6. Judgement Against Damascus: Jeremiah 49:23 – 27
7. Judgement Against Kedar & Hazor (Arabia): Jeremiah 49:28 – 33
8. Judgement Against Elam: Jeremiah 49:34 – 39
9. Judgement Against Babylon: Jeremiah 50 – 51

Historical Appendix
Jeremiah 52

This category speaks about the following major events.

1. Zedekiah's Reign: Jeremiah 52:1 – 3
2. Siege & Fall of Jerusalem: Jeremiah 52:4 – 27
3. Summary of Three Deportations: Jeremiah 52:28 – 30
4. Release of Jehoiachin From Prison: Jeremiah 52:31 – 34

HIGHLIGHTED EVENTS IN JEREMIAH

1. The Call of the Prophet:
   Jeremiah 1 (NKJV)

The book of Jeremiah begins with the calling of Jeremiah by God. The introduction of Jeremiah tells us a great deal about Jeremiah. He was a preacher's son, for his father Hilkiah was a priest. He was born in the village of Anathoth, close enough to Jerusalem to see the city walls, but at the edge of the wilderness, where the land slopes down to the Dead Sea. He labored as God's prophet for forty years or more, from 627 B.C. to sometime after 586 B.C. — **Jeremiah 1:1 – 3**

Jeremiah's sufferings began with a divine call:

The word of the Lord came to me, saying,

"Before I formed you in the womb I knew you,

before you were born I set you apart;
I appointed you as a prophet to the nations."

Jeremiah 1:4 – 5 (NKJV)

Jeremiah's life did not start with Jeremiah. Jeremiah's salvation did not start with Jeremiah. Jeremiah's truth did not start with Jeremiah. He entered the world in which the essential parts of his existence were already ancient history.

God knew Jeremiah before he was even born. He knew him. He formed him. He set him apart and appointed him as a prophet to the nations. He did all this long before Jeremiah drew his first breath or shed his first tear. The word *"knew"* in the Hebrew in verse 4 is also used to describe sexual intimacy between husband and wife. This is the relationship God had with Jeremiah, even before he was born.

Jeremiah was not just set apart for salvation, he was set apart for vocation. God had work for him to do. The prophet had a mission to accomplish and a message to deliver to his generation.

Jeremiah's unique appointment was to be a prophet to the nations. God intended his ministry to be international in scope. Part of Jeremiah's job was to promise God's grace to the nations, proclaiming, *"all nations will gather in Jerusalem to honor the name of the Lord"* — Jeremiah **3:17.**

But to be a prophet to the nations also includes announcing God's judgment. By the time he reached the end of his ministry, Jeremiah had pronounced a divine sentence of judgment upon every nation from Ammon to Babylon. Just as all nations receive God's sovereign grace, all nations are subject to God's severe justice.

Jeremiah knew what God wanted him to do. Yet even after he received the revelation of his divine call, he was still in doubt of it:

"Ah, Sovereign Lord," he said, *"I do not know how to speak; I am only a child"* — **Jeremiah 1:6**. Jeremiah was in doubt of two things, his youth and his inexperience as a prophet.

But God rebuked Jeremiah and reassured him of the Call:

"Do not say, 'I am only a child.' You must go to everyone I send you to and say whatever I command you'"

Jeremiah 1:7 (NKJV)

God did not disqualify Jeremiah based on his youth and inexperience. In fact, he treated him the same way he treated Moses. He did not deny the basis for the prophet's objection. He did not argue with Jeremiah about his speaking credentials or quibble with him about his age. Jeremiah may have had reasonable doubts. But God exposed his false humility for what it really was: a lack of faith.

"Then the Lord reached out his hand and touched my mouth and said to me, 'Now, I have put my words in your mouth"

Jeremiah 1:9 (NKJV)

God then took Jeremiah and equipped him with the prophetic. The words that Jeremiah was speaking now were not words from Jeremiah, but it was now the words and breath of God coming out of the mouth of Jeremiah.

Once God dealt with the doubtful Jeremiah, He then gave him a dangerous commission:

"You must go to everyone I send you to and say whatever I command you. Do not be afraid of them, for I am with you and will rescue you"

Jeremiah 1:7 – 8 (NKJV)

It is here where God started training Jeremiah to become a prophet. God will train Jeremiah from verse 10 to 19 by asking him, *"Jeremiah, what do you see?"* (v.11)

Note: *God did not show Jeremiah wat He saw, rather God wanted Jeremiah to tell Him what he sees.*

Out of these training sessions with God Jeremiah got equipped and trained to be the Prophet for the Nations as God called him to be.

Jeremiah sees two visions: the branch of an almond tree, and a boiling pot tilting away from the north.

God unveils these visions to Jeremiah and explains the symbolism of the last image: he's going to send an army of tribes from the North (meaning the Babylonians) to besiege Jerusalem and conquer it.

God assures Jeremiah that he will need to stand strong and be like a fortified city or pillar because the people will not like what he will say, yet, whatever God commands, he needs to speak.

God warns Jeremiah, saying that the people will oppose him, but God will save and sustain him as long as he does not give in to their demands.

2. **Warnings & Exhortations to Judah: Jeremiah 2 – 35 (NKJV)**

- **Earliest Discourses — Jeremiah 2 – 6**

In **Chapter 2 to 6** we see the early discourses of the people of God. **Chapter 2** starts off where the word of God came to Jeremiah saying that he needs to speak to Jerusalem. Through Jeremiah, the voice of God compares Israel to a bride who used to be devoted to Him when they were together in the wilderness.

But now Israel has become like a field where the fruits were eaten by robbers, who were put to death for trespassing on the harvest. Or like a runaway bride.

God accuses the people and their descendants of abandoning Him. God had to remind them of how He led them out of Egypt and into their own land. Even the rulers and prophets forgot their sacred covenant with God and started worshipping Baal and doing other unholy rituals.

The people turn from the Living Water and built themselves cisterns that are cracked and cannot hold their water. This symbolises the new religious practices they have adopted that won't work. God then asks them to look at other nations to see if they've ever abandoned *their* gods.

Israel is beginning to enslave herself by serving gods of other nations. Foreign powers like the Egyptian cities of Memphis and Tahphanhes have had a bad influence on Israel.

Instead of repenting and returning to God, the Israelites continue to pay more attention to the *"fancy"* lifestyles of foreign empires like Egypt and Assyria.

Israel broke their covenant with the True Living God as they started prostituting themselves to other gods, participating in pagan rituals involving worshipping trees and hills, turning their faces towards trees and stones, which they now worship as father and mother — **Jeremiah 2:27**. They have clearly lost the fear of God.

They would soon find out what bad idea this was. The moment they would cry out to God, He would tell them to go ask their new gods for help — **Jeremiah 2:28.**

God would continue by asking if He has been like a wilderness of darkness to them — **Jeremiah 2:31**, strongly implying that He has been free and available the whole time.

The people killed their own prophets, and obviously did not learn a thing from the punishment God already directed at them. God says that the people have played around with wicked women and killed the innocent poor **(2:30)**. They imagine that God will still have mercy on them, but this will not be the case, as His grace has run out on them. Now it is time for vengeanc as the people of Israel are still putting their trust in Egypt, eliminating them from prospering.

In **Chapter 3**, God's Word continues through Jeremiah saying that Israel won't even return to Him, that she's like a wife that He's already divorced. She has moved on to other lovers, other gods. This has caused Israel a terrible drought, but they still refused to be ashamed.

Jeremiah sees that Judah has learned nothing from watching Israel's adultery and punishment from the Northern Kingdom. Instead of refusing to follow false gods, Judah dove right into them.

Judah would now return to God in a carnal and falsely state — her heart still attached to the stones and trees. God would make the comparison saying that Northern Israel wasn't even in such a bad state as what Judah is right now.

God would then offer the Northern Israelites the opportunity to repent from their adulterous ways and turn back to Him, saying He would give them back their land and lead them back to Zion if they repent — **Jeremiah 3:12 – 14**

Jeremiah then continues prophesying saying that God will then send them pastors and prophets after His own heart to teach the people knowledge and understanding. In that day Israel and Judah will be united together, and all the nations will gather at Jerusalem, the *"Throne of the Lord"* — **Jeremiah 3:15 – 17**. Even The Ark of the Covenant will not be remembered in those future days as it will not form part of worship anymore.

Jeremiah would continue, saying how God Is comparing Israel both to a child who failed to acknowledge Him as a parent, and like a faithless wife.

Regardless of what God said about being too late to repent, God still gives the Israelites an opportunity to forgive His faithless children if they repent and actually mean it.

PROPHETIC DECLARATION:

1. Jeremiah 29:11 (NKJV)

[11] "**For I know the thoughts that I think toward you, says the Lord, thoughts of peace and not of evil, to give you a future and a hope.**"

I declare and decree in Jesus' Name that the plans and thoughts of God for my life will be realised swiftly.

I declare and decree in Jesus' Name that I will prosper and have a good future as God has declared over me.

NOTES

_____

_____

_____

_____

_____

_____

_____

_____

_____

_____

_____

_____

_____

_____

_____

_____

_____

_____

_____

_____

_____

_____

_____

_____

_____

_____

_____

_____

NOTES

NOTES

Book of **Lamentations**

"The Sorrows of a Prophet"

Scholars suggest that the book of Lamentations was written by the Prophet Jeremiah. We find strong evidence of this from within the book itself and other books in scripture that indicate that the Prophet Jeremiah was most probably the author of Lamentations, even though the author remains nameless within the book itself.

We see, for example, in **2 Chronicles 35:25** how Jeremiah was known for writing laments, so the idea of *"lamenting"* links the book of Lamentation to Jeremiah.

We can conclude from scripture that the author witnessed the invasion, as seen in **Lamentations 1:13 – 15**.

Jeremiah was also present for both events, as seen in the Book of Jeremiah.

The word *"lament"* means to express sorrow or grief, as evident in this book.

The book of Lamentations was composed and written in a poetic form and can be divided into the following five poems:

1. **The First Poem: The misery, sin, and prayer of Jerusalem — Lamentations 1:1 – 22**

2. **The Second Poem: God's destruction and the Prophet's reaction — Lamentations 2:1 – 22**

3. **The Third Poem: God's severity and mercy; man's submis siveness and prayer — Lamentations 3:1 – 66**

4. **The Fourth Poem: Devastation, the result of disobedience — Lamentations 4:1 – 22**

6. **The Fifth Poem: A prayer recording Jerusalem's suffering and final plea — Lamentations 5:1 – 22**

Lamentations also feature six significant themes, and all the themes link with the concept of affliction.

1. Their Affliction Was the Consequence of Their Sin: Lamentations 1:1 – 22 (NKJV)

This theme is strongly supported and acknowledged in each chapter of Lamentations, as seen in,

Lamentations 1:5,
Lamentations 2:14,
Lamentations 3:42,
Lamentations 4:13,
Lamentations 5:16.

When these poems were written, Israel had already accepted their fate. Even the Babylonians knew Israel's affliction was due to their wicked actions, as seen in **Jeremiah 40:3.** Israel continually provoked God's anger with their disobedient and rebellious hearts and therefore has brought this calamity upon themselves, as seen in **Lamentations 2:1.**

2. Their Affliction Was Coming from God and not from Man: Lamentations 2:1 – 22 (NKJV)

God was merely using the Babylonians as an instrument in His hands. The fact that God was the ultimate cause is clear in the book of Lamentations. A few examples of this can be seen in,

Lamentations 1:13 & 15
Lamentations 2:1 & 4
Lamentations 3:1, 37 & 38

3. Their Affliction Could Lead Them Back to God: Lamentations 3:1 – 66 (NKJV)

The Prophet Jeremiah was continually conscious of God's purposes and the way that God dealt with His people. Therefore, there is nothing that indicates total abandonment of God or complete removal of His principles from their minds.

4. **Affliction, Tears, and Prayer Belong Together: Lamentations 4:1 – 22 (NKJV)**

God's children were urged to present their pain, grief, and frustration before God in prayer.

Every chapter, except chapter 4, ends with a prayer. We can assume that Chapter 5 makes up for this, as the entire chapter is a prayer.

The prayers of the author are both detailed and emotional, as seen in,

Lamentations 1:20 – 21,
Lamentations 2:20 – 21,
Lamentations 3: 48 – 51,
Lamentations 5:1 – 10

5. **Prayer Should Always be Birthed from Hope: Lamentations 5:1 – 22 (NKJV)**

Here, the theme shifts to hope and focuses more on God's mercy, compassion, grace, and faithfulness. It's a realisation that God's discipline does not mean His love has ceased entirely.

The correct response to God's discipline would mean a change of circumstances, as seen in **Lamentations 3:31 – 32.**

God might have used Babylon; however, this does not mean they are His elect or that He favours their cruel methods, as seen in **Lamentations 3:34 – 36.**

There was hope that Israel would once again be vindicated from the oppression of their enemies, as seen in **Lamentations 3:58 – 66**

6. **Israel had to Submit to Their Affliction Patiently:**

Their sorrow had to be accepted in patience, with the realisation that it would end when God's will had been accomplished, as seen in **Lamentations 3:26 – 32.**

PROPHETIC DECLARATION:

1. Lamentations 3:22 – 24 (NKJV)

²² Through the Lord's mercies, we are not consumed, Because His compassions fail not.
²³ They are new every morning;
Great is Your faithfulness.
²⁴ "The Lord is my portion," says my soul,
"Therefore, I hope in Him!"

I receive the Lord's mercy and compassion that is new every morning. I declare and decree in the Name of Jesus that I will remain faithful to every Word of God as I place my hope and trust only in Him — Amen.

NOTES

Book of **Ezekiel**

"God Strengthens"

The book's author is Ezekiel and was documented during Ezekiel's captivity in Babylon, where he prophesied from about 593 – 573 B.C. Ezekiel means "God strengthens" or "God is strong".

The book's main characters consist of Ezekiel, Ezekiel's wife, Israel's leaders, King Nebuchadnezzar and "the prince".

The theme of this book focuses on the destruction of Jerusalem and its restoration. It was written to proclaim judgment and allow God's people one last opportunity to repent. God uses Ezekiel to deliver these messages in a time when a demoralised Judah was exiled to Babylon.

This book intends to reveal God's sovereignty over people, nations and the course of history. Upon looking deeper, we see how individual responsibility is required and hiding behind the nation's sin is no longer possible. Instead, each person should consider their own ways and take responsibility for their own life and actions instead of following the masses.

The book of Ezekiel can be divided into four general prophecies:

1. Prophecies concerning Israel's captivity and Jerusalem's destruction — **Ezekiel 1 – 24**
2. Oracles of judgement against foreign nations — **Ezekiel 25 – 32**
3. Prophecies concerning Israel in the last days leading up to the coming of the Messiah — **Ezekiel 33 – 37**
4. Prophecies concerning the destruction of Gog, Israel's restoration and the New City and Temple — **Ezekiel 38 – 48**

HIGHLIGHTED EVENTS IN EZEKIEL:

1. **Prophecies concerning Israel's captivity and Jerusalem's destruction: Ezekiel 1 – 24**

The Revelation of God and Divine Mandate:
Ezekiel 1 – 2

The first chapter opens with Ezekiel having a vision and revelation of God in all His splendour, glory, honour, and power.

This is followed by a powerful encounter with the Spirit of God that enters Ezekiel while God speaks. And so, God addressed Ezekiel as the "Son of man", a title commonly found throughout this book.

It is also here that God ordains Ezekiel as a Prophet and Watchman, commissioning him with a divine mandate concerning Israel's sin and rebellion.

The Lord God then encourages Ezekiel not to be afraid of the children of Israel as his message will not be well received, and just as they did not listen to God, so will they also not listen to him.

Ezekiel's Divine Instruction:

"But you, son of man, hear what I say to you. Do not be rebellious like that rebellious house; open your mouth and eat what I give you."

Ezekiel 2:8 (NKJV)

Ezekiel Eats the Scroll:
Ezekiel 3:1 – 15

We then see God giving Ezekiel a scroll to eat with a specific instruction saying,

... "Son of man, feed your belly, and fill your stomach with this scroll that I give you." So I ate, and it was in my mouth like honey in sweetness."

Ezekiel 3:3 (NKJV)

Note: *Remember that this is a spiritual occurrence; therefore, to feed your belly and fill your stomach is about receiving the Word of God into your spirit. We cannot just read the Word of God – His Word must be received into our hearts. This means that we need to pay close attention to what He says, meaning we must hear, not just listen as God commands Ezekiel, saying,*

"Son of man, receive into your heart all My words that I speak to you, and hear with your ears."

Ezekiel 3:10 (NKJV)

Ezekiel Ordained as Watchmen:
Ezekiel 3:16 – 21

God then declares Ezekiel a watchman for the house of Israel — giving both Ezekiel and Israel the following warnings to be delivered by Ezekiel saying,

a. When I pass judgment on the wicked and you [Ezekiel] have not warned them of their wickedness to save their lives, then their blood will be on your hands — **Ezekiel 3:18**

b. However, if you [Ezekiel] warn the wicked and he does not turn from his wickedness, then he will die in his iniquity, but your soul will be delivered — **Ezekiel 3:19**

c. If a righteous man turns from his righteousness and falls into iniquity of which he shall die in his sin, and you [Ezekiel] did not give him a warning, then I will require his blood of your hands — **Ezekiel 3:20**

d. However, if you [Ezekiel] warn that the righteous do not sin and he does not, then he shall live as he took heed to your warning and as a result, your soul will also be delivered — **Ezekiel 3:21**

Prophecies and Visions Delivered:
Ezekiel 3:22 – 24:27

Through the following events, the Prophet Ezekiel prophesied the Word of the Lord using various illustrations and parables in the representation of Israel's current condition and what is to come as a result of their continual rebellion.

    a.   Siege of Jerusalem Described — **Ezekiel 4:1 – 17**
    b.   A Sword against Jerusalem — **Ezekiel 5:1 – 17**

At this point, God is furious with Israel and states,

> *"And I will do among you what I have never done, and the like of which I will never do again, because of all your abominations."*

Ezekiel 5:9 (NKJV)

    c.   Judgement on Idolatrous Israel — **Ezekiel 6:1 – 14**
    d.   Judgement on Israel Drawing Exceedingly Close — **Ezekiel 7:1 – 27**
    e.   Abomination in the Temple — **Ezekiel 8:1 – 17**
    f.   Judgement Arrives — **Ezekiel 9:1 – 11**
    g.   The Glory Departs from the Temple — **Ezekiel 10:1 – 22**
    h.   Judgement and Restoration — **Ezekiel 11:1 – 25**
    i.   Judah's Captivity Described — **Ezekiel 12:1 – 28**
    j.   Warning to Foolish Prophets — **Ezekiel 13:1 – 23**
    k.   Idolatry Will Be Punished — **Ezekiel 14:1 – 11**
    l.   The Verdict Against Judah — **Ezekiel 14:12 – 19:14**
    m.   Oracles Before Jerusalem's Fall — **Ezekiel 20:1 – 24:27**

Ezekiel brought a message of fate to the captives. He told numerous parables, one that even likened Israel to an adulterous woman — **Ezekiel 16:1 – 63.**

He was illustrating that God was busy cleansing His chosen nation.

    2. **Oracles of Judgement Against Foreign Nations:**
        Ezekiel 25 – 32

The following chapters hold an account of judgement being prophesied over seven nations who ridiculed God because of Israel's captivity — they too, would experience God's wrath.

The Seven Nations:

1. Against Ammon — **Ezekiel 25:1 – 7**
2. Against Moab — **Ezekiel 25:8 – 11**
3. Against Edom — **Ezekiel 25:12 – 14**
4. Against Philistia — **Ezekiel 25:15 – 17**
5. Against Tyre — **Ezekiel 26 – 28:19**
6. Against Sidon — **Ezekiel 28:20 – 26**
7. Against Egypt — **Ezekiel 29:1 – 32:32**

3. Prophecies concerning Israel in the last days leading up to the coming of the Messiah: Ezekiel 33 – 37

Through the following chapters, we see God revealing the fairness of His judgement, stating how He will judge everyone according to their works. Showing that what they go through as a nation is and will continue to be a result of their actions.

And so, the principle of sowing and reaping is evident throughout these chapters as God would continually pour out his mercy and grace — presenting the children of Israel with numerous opportunities to repent through various prophecies and warnings delivered by God's chosen watchman, Ezekiel.

If they heed God's instructions and walk according to the statutes and laws that the Lord has set before them as a nation, they will be blessed beyond measure.

However, if they do not listen and continue their disobedience, they will face the destructive consequences of rebellion.

Note: *This principle is evident for every generation of every age. Whatever you sow, you will reap. Always remember that all actions have a specific consequence locked up in them, which can be either good or bad, and the moment we act, those consequences will be unlocked according to our deeds.*

Unfortunately, Israel's stubbornness blinded their hearts to Ezekiel's prophecies and various warnings. So despite the many opportunities provided by God for them to repent and return to Him, they still refused to submit – a decision with devastating consequences causing their complete destruction.

God, however, would never give up on them as a nation, constantly receiving them with open arms when they would repent and cry out to Him.

And so, we see the Lord delivering a series of powerful promises concerning the restoration of Israel, revealing that they will not be utterly destroyed, saying,

> *"My tabernacle also shall be with them; indeed I will be their God, and they shall be My people."*

Ezekiel 37:27 (NKJV)

The Word of the Lord then further revealed the following unto Ezekiel:

a. **Ezekiel as Watchman:**
   Ezekiel 33:1 – 11

Here, God emphasises the important role and responsibilities of a Watchman — a position that is not to be taken lightly.

God explains to Ezekiel that if a watchman sees calamity and does not warn those to whom it comes, they will die in their iniquity, and their blood will be required from the watchman's hands.

Although, when the watchmen see calamity come and warn those to whom it comes, and they do not heed the watchman's words, their blood will be upon their own heads.

However, the ones who do take heed to the warnings – their lives will indeed be saved.

b. **God's Fair Judgement:**
   Ezekiel 33:12 – 33

God truly is The Most Righteous Judge.

This chapter reveals that what Judah is going through is a result of their choices and actions. As previously stated, you will reap what you sow, which can be either good or bad.

Nonetheless, all God wants for them as a nation is peace and prosperity. Their actions, however, will determine the outcome.

Yet, despite the many warnings, Judah's continual rebellion caused the fall of Jerusalem and the ruin of Judah.

c. **God the True Shepherd:**
   Ezekiel 34:1 – 31

The kings of Israel had failed their people, and God was placing a new shepherd in their place, His servant David who would feed them and be their shepherd. God also refers to Himself as a Shepherd here who will seek out His flock and deliver and feed them.

"I will seek what was lost and bring back what was driven away,
bind up the broken and strengthen what was sick..."

Ezekiel 34:16 (NKJV)

d. **Judgement against Mount Seir and Edom:**
   Ezekiel 35:1 – 15

... 'Thus says the Lord God:
"Behold, O Mount Seir, I am against you;
I will stretch out My hand against you,
And make you most desolate;
⁴ I shall lay your cities waste,
And you shall be desolate.
Then you shall know that I am the Lord"

Ezekiel 35:3 – 4 (NKJV)

e. Blessing and Restoration of Israel:
   Ezekiel 36:1 – 38

Israel's judgement has now reached its pinnacle — Jerusalem is destroyed, and Judah is left in ruins, a situation that seems beyond repair.

And so, we find the presence of God being unbroken and His mercy and grace unending as the Lord yet again reached out, making way for restoration and healing.

The Lord declares through the Prophet Ezekiel that when the house of Israel dwelt in their own land, they defiled it with their own ways and deeds, blood and idol worship which is why God scattered them among the nations and judged them according to their own ways and deeds — **Ezekiel 36:16 – 20**

But the Lord had concern for His Holy Name, stating that the scales shall once again tip into Israel's favour when they walk in the Lord's statutes and laws that He has set before them, revealing the blessing that shall follow because of their obedience — **Ezekiel 36:21 – 38**

f. Resurrection of the Dry Bones:
   Ezekiel 37:1 – 28

This chapter reveals the notable account of Ezekiel and the dry bones where the Lord reveals unto Ezekiel the current state and circumstances of Israel, and the circumstances are not very healthy nor conducive to the will, ways and plans of God.

But it also reveals how God will again place His breath in Israel, and they shall live and know He is the Lord.

Note: *This passage of scripture teaches a powerful principle.*

The current crisis you are facing is not the end - refuse to give in to the circumstances. Never let your circumstances become your reality - your reality should instead be based on what God said. It is of the utmost importance that we say what God says because His Words are the only thing that will stand the test of time. But you can't say what God said if you do not know what He is saying.

And so, the Lord proclaims restoration, stating that Israel will once again be gathered from every Side and become one nation under One King.

"The nations also will know that I, the Lord, sanctify Israel, when My sanctuary is in their midst forevermore."

Ezekiel 37:28 (NKJV)

4. **Prophecies concerning the destruction of Gog, Israel's restoration and the New City and Temple: Ezekiel 38 – 48**

a. **The Destruction of Gog:
Ezekiel 38 – 39**

The following two chapters tell us what will happen after Israel's restoration but before the establishment of the millennium.

Note: *Gog headed up a coalition, and though they thought their plans for the invasion were their own, God controlled the attack.*

We see how God used these attacks to summon severe forces of nature to devastate the land of Gog.

b. **Rebuilding of the temple:
Ezekiel 40 – 46**

The millennial temple is revealed in detail through the following nine chapters. This description also includes a new way of worship. It is interesting to see that not just Jews will worship there but all nations.

The description includes:

a. Eastern Gateway of the Temple — **Ezekiel 40:6 – 16**
b. The Outer Court — **Ezekiel 40:17 – 19**
c. The Northern Gateway — **Ezekiel 40:20 – 23**
d. The Southern Gateway — **Ezekiel 40:24 – 27**

e.   Gateways of the Inner Court — **Ezekiel 40:28 – 37**
f.   Where Sacrifices Were Prepared — **Ezekiel 40:38 – 43**
g.   The Inner Court and Vestibule — **Ezekiel 40:47 – 49**
h.   Dimensions for the Sanctuary — **Ezekiel 41:1 – 4**
i.   The Side Chambers — **Ezekiel 41:5 – 11**
j.   The Western End of the Building — **Ezekiel 41:12 – 26**
k.   The Chambers for the Priests — **Ezekiel 42:1 – 14**
l.   Dimensions for the Outside of the Temple — **Ezekiel 42:15 –20**
m. The Lord's Dwelling Place, The Temple — **Ezekiel 43:1 – 12**
n.   The Altar — **Ezekiel 43:13 – 17**
o.   Consecration of the Altar — **Ezekiel 43:18 – 27**
p.   The Eastern Gate and Prince — **Ezekiel 44:1 – 3**
q.   Admittance to the Temple — **Ezekiel 44:4 – 9**
r.   Governing Laws for Priests — **Ezekiel 44:10 – 31**
s.   Description of the Holy District — **Ezekiel 45:1 – 8**
t.   Governing Laws for the Prince — **Ezekiel 45:9 – 17**
u.   The Feasts — **Ezekiel 45:18 – 25**
v.   Protocol for Worship — **Ezekiel 46:1 – 15**
w.   Laws Concerning Inheritance and the Prince — **Ezekiel 46:16 – 18**
x.   Preparation of Offerings — **Ezekiel 46:19 – 24**
y.   Healing Waters and Trees — **Ezekiel 47:1 – 12**
z.   Borders of the Land — **Ezekiel 47:13 – 23**
aa. Division of the Land — **Ezekiel 48:1 – 29**
ab. The Gates of the City and its Name — **Ezekiel 48:30 – 35**

Rebuilding of the Land:
Ezekiel 47 – 48

Note: *Interestingly, under the temple flowed a sacred river to the east representing healing.*

While rebuilding the land, we see how God promises Israel that they will have a land of their own.

The land is divided from north to south, where each tribe receives an equal portion of land. Seven tribes are north of the temple and city, and five tribes are south of the temple and city. A piece of this land is reserved for holy use.

This city has twelve gates named after the twelve tribes of Israel.

Note: *The name of the city is Yahweh Shammah, meaning;* THE LORD IS THERE:

"The name of the city from that day shall be: THE LORD IS THERE."

Ezekiel 48:35 (NKJV)

PROPHETIC DECLARATION:

1. **Ezekiel 11:19 (NKJV)**

[19] **"Then I will give them one heart, and I will put a new spirit within them, and take the stony heart out of their flesh, and give them a heart of flesh,"**

My heavenly Father, I pray, may you remove from me a heart of stone and replace it with a heart of flesh, with a heart that is after Your own heart.

I receive a new heart and spirit and so declare and decree that I will reflect nothing but the heart of the Father — Amen.

NOTES

NOTES

NOTES

Book of **Daniel**

"God is Sovereign"

The author of this book is Daniel, and the book is suggested to be written around the fifth or sixth century B.C. The genre of the book is an account of history, Prophetic Vision, and includes apocalyptic material.

The main characters of the book are Daniel [Babylonian name; Belteshazzar] and his three friends — 1) Hananiah [Babylonian name; Shadrach], 2) Mishael [Babylonian name; Meshach], 3) Azariah [Babylonian name; Abed-Nego].

Daniel's writing covers five kings: King Nebuchadnezzar (Babylonian King), King Belshazzar (Babylonian King), King Darius, King Cyrus (Persian King), and King Jehoiakim (King of Judah).

The book of Daniel has an all-embracing theme, which weaves itself through each part of this book — GOD IS SOVEREIGN. Although this theme is found throughout scripture, it is at the forefront of the book of Daniel.

The book of Daniel is significant as it is one of few books in the Bible that takes place during a period of judgement, whereas some books predict it while others look back on it. It is remarkable to see Daniel's uncompromising integrity and dedication to God repeatedly displayed through this book. Gods' supernatural abilities are revealed through prophecy in the book of Daniel, some regarding major events hundreds of years in advance. A crucial prophecy in Daniel is the prophecy known as "Daniels Seventy Weeks of Years".

This book intends to demonstrate to us that the God of Israel, the only true God — controls the destiny of all nations, holds our breath in His hands and owns all our ways. God appoints rules in the kingdom of men and appoints over it whomever He chooses.

Note: *Understanding the book of Daniel is essential to understanding end-time prophecies.*

The book of Daniel can be divided into the following sections:

1. Exile (around 560-536 B.C) — **Daniel 1:1 – 17**
2. Daniels Separates Himself — **Daniel 1:18 – 21**
3. Nebuchadnezzar's First Dream — **Daniel 2:1 – 49**
4. Deliverance from the Burning Furnace — **Daniel 3:1 – 30**
5. Nebuchadnezzar is Humbled — **Daniel 4:1 – 37**
6. Belshazzar is Humbled — **Daniel 5:1 – 31**
7. Daniel Delivered from the Lion's Den — **Daniel 6:1 – 28**
8. Daniel's Vision of Four Beasts and Ancient of Days — **Daniel 7:1 – 28**
9. Daniel's Vision of a Ram and Goat with Interpretation — **Daniel 8:1 – 27**
10. Daniel's Prayer and Vision of the Seventy Weeks — **Daniel 9:20 – 27**
11. Daniel's Vision of a Glorious Man, Wars of Kings of the North and South, Prophecy of End Time — **Daniel 10 – 12**

HIGHLIGHTED EVENTS IN DANIEL:

1. **Exile:**
   Daniel 1:1 – 7

"In the third year of the reign of Jehoiakim king of Judah, Nebuchadnezzar king of Babylon came to Jerusalem and besieged it."

Daniel 1:1 (NKJV)

"Then the king instructed Ashpenaz, the master of his eunuchs, to bring some of the children of Israel and some of the king's descendants and some of the nobles, 4 young men in whom there was no blemish, but good-looking, gifted in all wisdom, possessing knowledge and quick to understand, who had ability to serve in the king's palace, and whom they might teach the language and literature of the Chaldeans"

Daniel 1:3 – 4 (NKJV)

Among those taken captive and trained to serve in the king's court were Daniel and his four friends, known as Shadrack, Meshack and Abednego.

2. Daniel Separates Himself:
Daniel 1:8 – 21

"But Daniel purposed in his heart that he would not defile himself with the portion of the king's delicacies, nor with the wine which he drank; therefore he requested of the chief of the eunuchs that he might not defile himself. Now God had brought Daniel into the favor and goodwill of the chief of the eunuchs."

Daniel 1:8 – 9 (NKJV)

Note: *The king's food and drink would have been dedicated to false gods and therefore was unlawful for Daniel and his friends to partake of the king's delicacies.*

The chief of the eunuchs is nervous about granting Daniel his request, but Daniel provides him with another option.

Daniel suggested they be tested by giving them only vegetables and water for ten days. After ten days, their appearances were to be compared with those who eat the portion of the king's delicacies.

And so, the test was done, and after the ten days, it was found that their appearances were indeed healthier than those who shared in the portion of the king's delicacies.

As a result, Daniel and his friends were excused from the king's delicacies.

"As for these four men, God gave them knowledge and skill in all literature and wisdom; and Daniel had understanding in all visions and dreams."

Daniel 1:17 (NKJV)

"Then the king interviewed them, and among them all none was found like Daniel, Hananiah, Mishael, and Azariah; therefore they served before the king."

Daniel 1:19 (NKJV)

"And in all matters of wisdom and understanding about which the king examined them, he found them ten times better than all the magicians and astrologers who were in all his realm."

Daniel 1:20 (NKJV)

3. Nebuchadnezzar's First Dream: Daniel 2:1 – 49

During the second year of Nebuchadnezzar's reign, he had a dream that troubled his spirit to the point where his sleep left him.

As a result, he instructed all the wise men, the astrologers, the magicians, and the soothsayers first to tell him what he dreamt and then, after revealing the dream, to also interpret it.

Inability to complete the task would have severe consequences as Nebuchadnezzar decreed that those who are not able will be cut into pieces, and their houses shall be made an ash heap.

This challenge also included Daniel and his three friends, to which Daniel rises to the challenge to save himself and his three friends, requesting time to tell the king his dream and give the interpretation thereof.

Daniel and his three friends then engage in a prayer meeting, asking God to reveal the matter to them.

And so, Daniel receives understanding of the dream in a night vision, wakes up, blesses God, and requests an audience with the king so that the matter may be made known to him.

And so,

> *"Daniel answered in the presence of the king, and said, the secret*
> *which the king has demanded, the wise men, the astrologers, the*
> *magicians, and the soothsayers cannot declare to the king. But there*
> *is a God in heaven who reveals secrets, and He has made known to*
> *King Nebuchadnezzar what will be in the later days. Your dream,*
> *and the visions of your head upon your bed, were these:"*

Daniel 2:27 – 28 (NKJV)

And so, Daniel, through divine revelation, not only reveals Nebuchadnezzar's dream unto him but also gives the interpretation thereof, stating that it's a dream about the end times as seen in **Daniel 2:29 – 45**

Nebuchadnezzar is so impressed with Daniel that he not only acknowledges God as the God of gods, the Lord of kings, and the Revealer of secrets but also promotes Daniel as ruler over the entire province and sets his three friends over the affairs of Babylon — **Daniel 2:47 – 49**

4. **Deliverance from the Burning Furnace:**
   Daniel 3:1 – 30

The king's other advisors, now obviously embarrassed by the experience, conspire against Daniel by convincing Nebuchadnezzar to build an image of gold which he set in the land of Babylon. The king nominated a herald who cried out to the people communicating that when you hear the sound of a horn, flute, or harp in a symphony with all kinds of music shall fall down and worship the gold image.

Whoever does not fall down and worship shall be cast immediately into a fiery furnace.

Of course, Daniel's three friends refuse to follow the instruction. And so, after being questioned by Nebuchadnezzar, stating that they have one more chance to bow down and worship the golden idol, if not, they will be cast into the fiery furnace.

We then see Shadrack, Meshack and Abed-Nego steadfast and immovable in their faith as they boldly respond by saying,

"...O Nebuchadnezzar, we have no need to answer you in this matter. If that is the case, our God whom we serve is able to deliver us from the burning fiery furnace, and He will deliver us from your hand, O king. But if not, let it be known to you O king, that we do not serve your gods, nor will we worship the gold image which you have set up."

Daniel 3:16 – 18 (NKJV)

Nebuchadnezzar was furious and immediately commanded that the three young men be cast into the fiery furnace heated to seven times its normal temperature. The fire was so hot that it killed the guards who took Shadrach, Meshach, and Abed-Nego.

"Then King Nebuchadnezzar was astonished; and he rose in haste and spoke, saying to his counselors, Did we not cast three men bound into the midst of the fire? They answered and said to the king, True, O king." Look he answered, I see four men loose, walking in the midst of the fire; and they are not hurt, and the form of the fourth is like the Son of God."

Daniel 3:24 – 25 (NKJV)

The only thing that was burnt was the ropes that bound them leaving Nebuchadnezzar again to bless the God of Shadrach, Meshach, and Abed-Nego, who sent His Angel and delivered His servants who trusted in Him.

Following this, the king made a decree that should anyone speak against the God of Shadrach, Meshach, and Abed-Nego, they shall be cut in pieces, and their houses shall be made an ash heap as there is no other God who can deliver like this.

5. Nebuchadnezzar is Humbled:
Daniel 4:1 – 37

Nebuchadnezzar then has another dream of a towering tree reaching heaven being cut down, leaving nothing but the stump and roots in the earth, remaining in this state for seven years.

Daniel then, once again by Divine Inspiration, interprets Nebuchadnezzar's dream. This time, the dream warns Nebuchadnezzar to repent of his pride.

And so, twelve months later, while Nebuchadnezzar was walking in the royal palace, he pridefully boasted, saying,

"...Is not this great Babylon, that I have built for a royal dwelling by my mighty power and for the honor of my majesty?"

Daniel 4:30 (NKJV)

The king's words, now revealing the pride in his heart, unleashed a series of consequences as the Bible states,

"That very hour the word was fulfilled concerning Nebuchadnezzar; he was driven from men and ate grass like oxen; his body was wet with the dew of heaven till his hair had grown like eagles' feathers and his nails like bird claws."

Daniel 4:33 (NKJV)

According to the dream's warning, Nebuchadnezzar remained in this state for seven years.

After the season ran its course, the Bible states that Nebuchadnezzar lifted his eyes to heaven, and his understanding returned to him.

Nebuchadnezzar was then restored to share his testimony here in chapter 4, further acknowledging that the God of Daniel is the God of the universe found in **Daniel 4:34 – 35.**

6. Belshazzar is Humbled:
Daniel 5:1 – 31

Nebuchadnezzar had passed on, leaving Belshazzar as the new king of the Babylonians.

Belshazzar, the king, made a great feast for a thousand lords and drank wine with them. While feasting, Belshazzar commanded that the gold and silver vessels taken from Jerusalem by his father Nebuchadnezzar be brought so they could drink from them.

They brought the gold vessels taken from the temple of God, which had been in Jerusalem. The king, his wives, the lords, and concubines drank from them and praised the gods of gold and silver, bronze and iron, wood, and stone.

"In the same hour the fingers of a man's hand appeared and wrote opposite the lampstand on the plaster of the wall of the king's palace; and the king saw the part of the hand that wrote."

Daniel 5:5 (NKJV)

Then the king's countenance changed. He was troubled in his thinking, his hips loosened, and his knees knocked against each other.

Belshazzar cried aloud, calling for the astrologers, the Chaldeans, and the soothsayers. The king then spoke and said if any of you wise men can interpret this writing, he shall be clothed with purple, have a chain of gold around their neck and be the third ruler in the kingdom.

The wise men came but could not read the writing. Because of the words of the king and the lords, the queen went to the banquet hall. She brought to the attention of Belshazzar that there was a man in the kingdom whom Nebuchadnezzar used as chief over all the magicians, astrologers, Chaldeans, and soothsayers.

"Inasmuch as an excellent spirit, knowledge, understanding, interpreting dreams, solving riddles, and explaining enigmas were found in this Daniel, whom the king named Belteshazzar, now let Daniel be called, and he will give the interpretation."

Daniel 5:12 (NKJV)

Daniel is brought before Belshazzar. The king proceeded to catch up on past services Daniel offered Belshazzar's father, Nebuchadnezzar. Daniel moved to explain to Belshazzar that his father, King Nebuchadnezzar, was given his kingdom by the Most High. The majesty, glory and honour were given to Nebuchadnezzar by God, which is why all peoples, nations, and languages trembled and feared before him. Daniel further explains to Belshazzar that when his father's heart was lifted and his spirit was hardened with pride, he was deposed from his kingly throne and lost his glory.

Daniel makes it clear to the king before he translates the writing that the king should give the rewards to another:

"Then Daniel answered, and said before the king, Let your gifts be for yourself, and give your rewards to another; yet I will read the writing to the king, and make known to him the interpretation."

Daniel 5:17 (NKJV)

Note: *Daniel explains King Nebuchadnezzar's consequences for hardening his heart and being filled with pride.*

Daniel then states to Belshazzar, **"But you his son, Belshazzar, have not humbled your heart, although you knew all this."** — Daniel **5:22 (NKJV)**

Belshazzar had lifted himself up against the Lord of heaven. They brought the vessels from the Lord's house before his lords, wives, concubines and drank wine from them while praising gods of gold, silver, bronze, and iron, wood, and stone.

"And this is the inscription that was written:

MENE. MENE, TEKEL,
UPHARSIN

This is the interpretation of each word.
MENE: God has numbered your kingdom, and finished it;
TEKEL: You have been weighed in the balances, and found wanting;
PERES: Your kingdom has been divided, and given to the Medes and
Persians."

Daniel 5:25 – 28 (NKJV)

Belshazzar honoured his word and rewarded Daniel by clothing him with purple and putting a chain of gold around his neck, proclaiming that Daniel was the third ruler in the kingdom.

"That very night Belshazzar, king of the Chaldeans, was slain. And Darius the Mede received the kingdom, being about sixty-two years old."

Daniel 5:30 – 31 (NKJV)

7. Daniel Delivered from the Lion's Den: Daniel 6:1 – 28

Darius then set one hundred and twenty government officials over his kingdom, with Daniel being one of the three that governed over all of them. Daniel now distinguished himself above the governors because he had an excellent spirit. Due to this, the king thought about setting Daniel over the whole realm.

Jealousy now arising in the governors sought to find some charge against Daniel concerning the kingdom but could find no error or fault in him.

As a result, the governors reverted to other methods in conspiring against Daniel by proposing to King Darius to sign a decree that whoever petitions any god or man within thirty days, except the king, shall be cast into the den of lions.

King Darius, unaware that this was a plan against Daniel, signs the degree in approval.

Note: *According to the law of the Medes and Persians, once the king signs a decree, it cannot be altered or changed.*

Daniel, however, refused to follow the rules written in the decree as it came against everything that he stood for, and obedience to it would mean disobedience towards God.

And so, Daniel would still go home into his upper room, kneel on his knees three times a day and pray before God, giving thanks for all to see.

The men who conspired against Daniel wasted no time reporting him to the king for breaking the decree, reminding the king of the punishment for the offence.

The king was greatly displeased with himself and tried to figure out a way to save Daniel.

Unfortunately, according to their laws, this was impossible, so the king honoured their laws and instructed Daniel to be cast into the lion's den.

"Now the king went to his palace and spent the night fasting; and no musicians were brought before him. Also his sleep went from him. Then the king arose very early in the morning and went in haste to the den of lions."

Daniel 6:18 – 19 (NKJV)

Early the following day, the king cried out to Daniel, asking if his God was able to deliver him from the lions.

And so, to the king's amazement, he heard Daniel respond by saying,

"My God sent His angel and shut the lions' mouths, so that they have not hurt me, because I was found innocent before Him; and also, O king, I have done no wrong before you."

Daniel 6:22 (NKJV)

The king was exceedingly pleased to find that Daniel was still alive and commanded that he be released immediately.

We then see how those who have planned evil against Daniel fall into their wickedness. The king then turned toward those who schemed against Daniel, commanding that they, with the children and wives, be cast into the den of lions.

And so, the Bible states that they were mauled by the lions even before they reached the bottom — **Daniel 6:24**

King Darius then wrote that all people, nations, and languages who dwell on the earth should tremble and fear before the God of Daniel. The king then honoured and praised God for delivering and rescuing Daniel.

8. Daniel's Vision of Four Beasts and Ancient of Days: Daniel 7:1 – 28

In the first part of the vision, Daniel saw four great beasts coming out from the sea:

- The first was like a lion with eagle's wings,
- The second was like a bear with three ribs in its mouth,
- The third was like a leopard with four heads and had four wings of a bird on its back,
- The fourth could not even be compared to an animal, so Daniel called it" the great and terrible beast". This beast had ten horns and iron teeth and was exceptionally strong.

The four beasts were indicative of four empires that would rise but also fall. These were the same four empires revealed in **Daniel 2,**

- Babylon Empire,
- Medo-Persian Empire,
- Greek Empire,
- Roman Empire.

Daniel then has a vision of the Ancient of Days and so also receives an interpretation of the vision as seen in **Daniel 7:9 – 28**

9. **Daniel's Vision of a Ram and Goat and Interpretation of the Vision: Daniel 8:1 – 27**

Daniel had this vision two years after the chapter 7 vision, and in this vision, he saw,

- A ram with two horns, the one horn being higher than the other with the higher one coming up last.
- A male goat with a notable horn between his eyes.

Daniel then saw the male goat attacking the ram with ferocious power defeating the ram. This was a representation of the Greek empire conquering the Persian empire.

The ram's one horn then broke off, and in its place, four new ones came up. This was a representation of four kingdoms that shall come from that nation.

10. **Daniel's Prayer and Vision of the Seventy Weeks: Daniel 9:20 – 27**

The vision opens where Daniel understood the prophecy given by Jeremiah according to the Word of the Lord that after seventy years of Babylonian captivity, Israel will once again be restored and return to Jerusalem.

And so Daniel, now realising that the seventy years were almost over, responded to the prophecy by engaging in one of the most powerful biblical principles. He set his face toward the Lord through prayer and supplications with fasting on behalf of the nation of Israel for this word to be fulfilled.

The Seventy-Weeks Prophecy:
Daniel 9:20 – 27

The latter part of the vision holds the famous account of Daniel's seventy weeks prophecy, which is probably one of the most important chapters to understand concerning the end times, making this a chapter well worth further study.

11. Daniel's Vision of a Glorious Man, Wars of Kings of the North and South, Prophecy of End Time: Daniel 10 – 12

In the third year of Cyrus, king of Persia, a message was revealed to Daniel. This was a factual message and a depiction of events that would take place in the far-off future. Daniel understood this message and vision.

- Vision of a Glorious Man — **Daniel 10:1 – 9**
- Angelic Visitation — **Daniel 10:10 – 21**
- Wars of Kings of North and South — **Daniel 11:1 – 45**
- The Time of Trouble — **Daniel 12:1 – 13**

The book of Daniel ends with a prophecy concerning the end times.

"Although I heard, I did not understand. Then I said, My lord, what shall be the end of these things? And he said, Go your way, Daniel, for the words are closed up and sealed till the time of end."

Daniel 12:8 – 9 (NKJV)

404

PROPHETIC DECLARATION:

1. **Daniel 6:3 (NKJV)**

³**"Then this Daniel distinguished himself above the governors and satraps, because an excellent spirit was in him; and the king gave thought to setting him over the whole realm."**

I declare and decree in the Name of Jesus that I have an excellent spirit as I am filled with the Holy Spirit. I have a Spirit of leadership and will fulfil and multiply all that God has placed under my care with excellence, perfection, and distinction.

NOTES

NOTES

SECTION 6
THE MINOR PROPHETS

Table of Contents

Book of **Hosea**

"The Faithful Husband"

Hosea is the first book of what is known as the Minor Prophets and was written by the Prophet Hosea in approximately 715 B.C. It records the events from 753-715 B.C., including the fall of the Northern Kingdom in 722 B.C.

Note: *The differentiation between major and minor Prophets is not based on the individual's significance but is determined by the book's length. The books of the Major Prophets are much longer in size but fewer in numbers.*

The name Hosea means *"salvation"*, which is most likely a reflection of his position in Israel to bring hope to those who would repent and turn back to God because of his message.

And so, Hosea was commissioned by God to write to the Northern Kingdom during the reign of Jeroboam the second.

The book opens with God instructing the Prophet Hosea to marry a harlot named Gomer.

Gomer illustrated two main things:

    a.   She represented the sinful state of Israel and their spiritual adultery towards God and His Word.

    b.   Irrespective of Israel's continual rebellion against God, He would never give up on His chosen people and, through various warnings, would again allow Israel to repent and return to Him.

And so, the book's central theme seems to revolve around Hosea, Gomer, and their children being compared to the relationship between God and Israel.

HIGHLIGHTED EVENTS IN HOSEA:

1. Hosea & Gomer's Marriage and Their First Born:
Hosea 1:1 – 5 (NKJV)

Upon God's instruction, the Prophet Hosea marries Gomer, the harlot who conceived and bore him a son.

God then further instructs Hosea to name the boy Jezreel.

The name Jezreel represents two things:
Hosea 1:4 (NKJV)

   a.   Jezreel means "*Scattered*". This is concerning the Assyrian army that would soon conquer Israel.
   b.   Jezreel also refers to the Valley of Jezreel, where Jehu slaughtered Ahab, Jezebel and all the descendants of Ahab.

And so, the name was given to the boy to confirm God's promise to **avenge the bloodshed of Jezreel on the house of Israel.**

This is also another powerful comparison to illustrate the fall of the entire house of Israel, just like that of the house of Jehu.

And so, even before the end of Hosea's prophetic ministry, we find all the above come to pass as the Assyrians defeated, destroyed, and took the house of Israel captive.

2. Hosea and Gomer's second-born:
Hosea 1:6 – 7 (NKJV)

Gomer conceived again and this time bore a daughter.

Then upon God's instruction, Hosea named the girl Lo-Ruhamah meaning "*No Mercy*" or "*No Love*". This was done to illustrate that the relationship had reached a state where God would no longer show Israel mercy because of their continual rebellion.

We do, however, find God showing mercy on the house of Judah.

After Assyria completely defeated the house of Israel, they set out against the house of Judah, thinking that it would also be an easy feat.

But this time, God was fighting on behalf of the house of Judah. This is where we find the famous account recorded in scripture where God sent His angel who killed 185,000 Assyrian soldiers delivering a great victory into the hands of Jehoshaphat, the current reigning king over the house of Judah. **(2 Kings 19)**.

3. Hosea and Gomer's Third-Born: Hosea 1:8 – 9 (NKJV)

Gomer then conceived a third time and bore Hosea a second son.

Again, upon God's instruction, Hosea was to name the boy Lo-Ammi, meaning *"Not My People"*. This was done to stand as a reminder of how Israel continually rejected the Lord, not taking heed to His commandments, and so could no longer consider themselves God's people.

4. Hosea; Representing God's Love and Compassion: Hosea 2 – 3 (NKJV)

Through all of this, Gomer continued with her career as a prostitute, displaying Israel's true nature, attitude and character.

Hosea, however, remains faithful, displaying the true nature of God, and so proves his love to Gomer when he restores her through purchase, buying her for fifteen shekels of silver and one and one-half homers of barley, stating the following,

"And I said to her, 'You shall stay with me for many days; you shall not play the harlot, nor shall you have a man — so, too, will I be toward you"

Hosea 3:3 (NKJV)

5. God & Israel:
Hosea 4:1 – 14:9 (NKJV)

Chapters 4-14 clearly describe Israel's unfaithfulness towards God. However, these chapters also reveal how God refuses to give up on His people, continually reaching out to them through various warnings to compel Israel to repent and turn from their wickedness.

We see how Israel's continual failure to repent and continual disobedience towards God unlocks a series of events with devastating results, causing their destruction, and so find God speaking the all too familiar words saying,

> *"My people are destroyed for lack of knowledge. Because you have rejected knowledge, I also will reject you from being priest for Me; Because you have forgotten the law of your God, I also will forget your children"*

Hosea 4:6 (NKJV)

Conclusion:

As we go through the book of Hosea, we recognise a clear repetitious pattern that revolves around five cycles of judgement:

Even though Israel's continual rebellion, God would always be relentless in His pursuit of restoration through various warnings, never giving up on His chosen nation.

As the Lord said,

> *"I will heal their backsliding,*
> *I will love them freely,*
> *For My anger has turned away from him.*

Hosea 14:4 (NKJV)

And so we find that through **chapters 4 — 14**, Hosea paints a picture of the people turning away from the Lord and toward other gods.

The Israelite's inclination toward idolatry meant they lived as if they were not God's people, as God had shown them through the birth of Hosea's third child, Lo-Ammi.

However, God also reminded them that He would restore them, using the intimate and personal language of *"sons"* to describe His stubborn people.

PROPHETIC DECLARATION:

1.   Hosea 4:6 (NKJV)

⁶"My people are destroyed for lack of knowledge. Because you have rejected knowledge, I also will reject you from being priest for Me; Because you have forgotten the law of your God, I also will forget your children"

I dedicate to set my heart to understanding the Word of God and to live my life according to the boundaries set out in scripture. I declare and decree in the Name of Jesus that I will be established in the Knowledge of God all the days of my life — Amen.

NOTES

Book of **Joel**

"Jehovah is God"

Joel is the second book of the Minor Prophets and carries various viewpoints as to exactly when Joel wrote the book. However, we know that the book was written sometime before the fall and exile of the Northern and Southern Kingdoms.

Like with many minor prophets, we know very little about the Prophet Joel except that he was the son of Pethuel and was from the kingdom of Judah, to whom he also prophesied. The name *"Joel"* means *"Jehovah is God"*.

The central theme of the book carries a twofold cord in its meaning. Like most prophets, the book conveys the great need for repentance to avoid complete destruction. And so we find that Joel's prophecies were meant not only for Judah at the time but also for our day and age and things concerning the *"end times"*.

HIGHLIGHTED EVENTS IN JOEL:

1. **The Current State of Israel:**
   Joel 1:1 – 20

The book of Joel opens with an in-depth description of four destructive waves caused by a plague of locusts and a severe famine due to Israel's continual disobedience and rebellion.

Wave 1: The Chewing Locust:
Joel 1:4a (NKJV)

This was the 1st wave to come and cause destruction.

Wave 2: The Swarming Locust:
Joel 1:4b (NKJV)

What was left by the chewing locust was now further consumed by the swarming locusts.

Wave 3: The Crawling Locust:
Joel 1:4c (NKJV)

What was left by the swarming locusts was then further consumed by the crawling locusts.

Wave 4: The Consuming Locust:
Joel 1:4d (NKJV)

What was left by the crawling locusts was then further eaten by the consuming locusts.

2. **The Day of the Lord:**
   Joel 2:1 – 11

Through the verses that follow, the Prophet Joel gives an in-depth description of an army so great and powerful that it overtakes and destroys everything in its path.

Again, this chapter is dualistic in its description, giving information about what was about to happen to Judah but is also aimed toward the end times.

Purpose 1: The Kingdom of Judah Taken Captive:

The previous destructive four waves explained can also be linked to the coming judgement of God about to come on Judah because of their unrepentant hearts.

We find this true as Judah was soon overtaken by the Babylonian army, leaving the once glorious city of Jerusalem in complete ruin.

Then the Medes and Persians further destroyed what was left by the Babylonians, and later the Greeks and Romans destroyed what was left by the Persians.

Purpose 2: The End Times:

The phrase *"The Day of the Lord"* is usually associated with the second coming of the Lord Jesus Christ and everything that will take place during this event, so this chapter seems to focus more on the last days than Joel's day.

3. **A Call to Repentance and a Promise of Restoration:**
   Joel 2:12 – 27

Through His infinite grace, compassion, and love, God again allows Israel to repent by giving instructions on how He wants them to return.

Again, this can also be a call of repentance focused on the last days. The Lord expounds through these verses that instead of rent clothes and sackcloth, God wants them to return with humble, meek hearts.

And so, verses 21-27 paint the picture of complete deliverance for the kingdom of Israel and Judah.

> ²⁵ *"So I will restore to you the years that the swarming locust has*
> *eaten,*
> *The crawling locust,*
> *The consuming locust,*
> *And the chewing locust,*
> *My great army which I sent among you."*

Joel 2:25 (NKJV)

4. **The Outpouring of the Holy Spirit:**
   Joel 2:28:32

We find this part of the prophecy fulfilled in the book of Acts on the day of Pentecost after the resurrection and ascension of the Lord Jesus

Christ when the disciples gathered in the upper room and tongues as of fire sat upon each of them. So they were all filled with the Holy Spirit and began to speak with other tongues.

Peter even explained to the people who thought that they were drunk and quoted the Prophet Joel, stating,

> ¹⁵ *"For these are not drunk, as you suppose, since it is only the third hour of the day.* ¹⁶ *But this is what was spoken by the Prophet Joel:*
>
> ¹⁷ *'And it shall come to pass in the last days, says God,*
>
> *That I will pour out of My Spirit on all flesh;*
> *Your sons and your daughters shall prophesy,*
> *Your young men shall see visions,*
> *Your old men shall dream dreams."*
>
> **Acts 2:15 – 17 (NKJV)**

5. Judgement of All Nations: Joel 3:1 – 21

This chapter further explains end-time events, describing how there will come a time when God will judge all the antichristian nations.

We also see a warning being issued to get ready for the familiar battle of Armageddon, the destruction that will occur in the valley of Jehoshaphat.

The book then ends with the guaranteed security, safety, and peace of those who belong to God.

PROPHETIC DECLARATION:

1. **Joel 2:25 (NKJV)**

²⁵ **"So I will restore to you the years that the swarming locust has eaten,**
The crawling locust,
The consuming locust,
And the chewing locust,
My great army which I sent among you."

I declare and decree in the Name of Jesus that as a child of God, I plunder the gates of hell and take back everything that the enemy has stolen from me with interest.

I declare and decree in the Name of Jesus that all lost time will be restored to me in full - Amen.

NOTES

NOTES

Book of **Amos**

"A Burden-Bearer"

Amos is the third book of the Minor Prophets and was written by Amos.

Amos was a farmer who was quite different from the other prophets. He was not from the school of prophets but an outsider and did not consider himself a prophet saying,

> *14 "...I was no prophet,*
> *Nor was I a son of a prophet,*
> *But I was a sheepbreeder*
> *And a tender of sycamore fruit.*
> *15 Then the Lord took me as I followed the flock,*
> *And the Lord said to me,*
> *'Go, prophesy to My people Israel.'*
> *16 Now therefore, hear the word of the Lord:*
> *You say, 'Do not prophesy against Israel,*
> *And do not spout against the house of Isaac.'*

Amos 7:14 – 16 (NKJV)

A sheep breeder and a tender of sycamore fruit were the lowest and least valuable in the social structure. Amos had no social status, yet God raised him as a prophet.

Amos was from the wilderness of Judea but was called as a prophet to the Northern Kingdom. At that time, Jeroboam was the ruler over the Northern Kingdom, and Uzziah was ruler over the Southern Kingdom.

"The words of Amos, who was among the sheepbreeders of Tekoa, which he saw concerning Israel in the days of Uzziah king of Judah, and in the days of Jeroboam the son of Joash, king of Israel, two years before the earthquake."

Amos 1:1 (NKJV)

The above verse indicates the accuracy of his prophecy two years before the actual event. His outlined message is the ultimate rule of David.

HIGHLIGHTED EVENTS IN AMOS:

In chapters 1 and 2, he prophesied judgement to eight nations:

1. Damascus — **Amos 1:3 – 5**
2. Gaza (The Philistines) — **Amos 1:6 – 8**
3. Tyre — **Amos 1:9 – 10**
4. Edom — **Amos 1:11 – 12**
5. Ammon — **Amos 1:13 – 15**
6. Moab — **Amos 2:1 – 3**
7. Judah — **Amos 2:4 – 5**
8. Israel — **Amos 2:6 – 16**

Amos used one common phrase in his prophecies against the gentile nations — That God will send fire and burning onto the earth. He then turns his focus to Judah and Israel.

The book of Amos has three sermons:

1. The Destruction of Israel — **Amos 3:1 – 15**
2. The Wickedness of Israel — **Amos 4:1 – 13**
3. The Lament of Israel — **Amos 5:1 – 6:14**

And five visions:

1. A Vision of Locust — **Amos 7:1 – 3**
2. A Vision of the Fire — **Amos 7:4 – 6**

3. A Vision of the Plumb Line — **Amos 7:7 – 9**
4. A Vision of the Summer Fruit — **Amos 8:1 – 14**
5. A Vision of the Lord Judging and Future Blessing — **Amos 9:1 – 15**

It's also in the book of Amos that we find the famous statement made by the Prophet Amos stating,

"Surely the Lord God does nothing,
Unless He reveals His secret to His servants the prophets."

Amos 3:7 (NKJV)

PROPHETIC DECLARATION:

1.   Amos 3:7 (NKJV)

[3] **"Surely the Lord God does nothing,**
Unless He reveals His secret to His servants the prophets."

I declare and decree in the Name of Jesus that I submit to every Word that proceeds out of the mouth of God. I align my life to the guidance, help, and council God provides for me through His Prophets.

NOTES

_____
_____
_____
_____
_____
_____
_____
_____
_____
_____
_____
_____
_____
_____
_____
_____
_____
_____
_____
_____
_____
_____
_____
_____
_____
_____
_____

Book of **Obadiah**

"A Servant of The Lord"

Obadiah is the fourth book of the Minor Prophets and was written by Obadiah. His name means *"A Servant of God"*, and his message is a divine prophecy foretelling the fall of Edom, a nation founded by Esau, and the restoration of Israel.

Obadiah is the shortest book in the Old Testament and consists of only one Chapter.

He is from the Southern Kingdom and pronounces judgment on the foreign nation of Edom. Obadiah is one of only three prophets who pronounced judgment primarily on other countries.

We see the law of sowing and reaping evident in this prophecy as,

- Edom had indulged in treachery and would perish through treachery.
- They had seized a chance to rob Judah but will now be robbed themselves.
- Edom had indulged in violence and would perish by slaughter.
- They have sought the utter destruction of Israel but will be utterly destroyed.

Obadiah's message reminds us to place ourselves under God's authority and subject our lives to His purposes.

PROPHETIC DECLARATION:

1.   Obadiah 1:15 (NKJV)

¹⁵ "For the day of the Lord upon all the nations is near;
As you have done, it shall be done to you;
Your reprisal shall return upon your own head."

I declare and decree in the Name of Jesus that everything the enemy has assigned against me for my destruction shall not prosper. Every plan, weapon, device, and assignment our adversary the devil has formed against me shall backfire. He shall step into his own traps and fall under his own weapons — Amen

NOTES

Book of **Jonah**

"The Saviour of a Nation?"

Jonah is the fifth book of the Minor Prophets and was written by Jonah approximately 785-760 B.C. He was from the Northern Kingdom and was commissioned to show the mercy and grace of God to the people of Nineveh.

Nineveh was a quadrangle of cities with a population of about 1 million people and was the Pagan capital of the world. It was an enemy of Israel, as spoken about by **Isaiah 7:17, Hosea 9:3** and **Amos 3:7.**

The book can be divided into four major events:

1. **The Storm — Jonah 1:1 – 17**
2. **The Fish — Jonah 2:1 – 10**
3. **The City — Jonah 3:1 – 10**
4. **The Lord's Grace — Jonah 4:1 – 11**

HIGHLIGHTED EVENTS IN JONAH

1. **The Storm:**
    Jonah 1:1 – 17

Rather than commissioning Jonah to his people, God sends him to the Assyrian capital of Nineveh. Jonah, being the patriot that he was, refused and made his way westward towards Tarshish by getting on a boat in an attempt to flee from the presence of the Lord.

This was a futile attempt as the Lord soon after sent a great storm about to destroy the boat he was on.

After realising that the storm was because of Jonah being on the ship, the men decided to throw him overboard in an attempt to save their lives from the storm.

2. The Fish:
Jonah 2:1 – 10

This chapter holds the famous account of where God commanded a great fish to go and swallow the Prophet, Jonah.

After spending three days and three nights in the belly of the fish, Jonah is finally vomited out unto dry land by instruction of the Lord.

3. The City:
Jonah 3:1 – 10

After God eventually turned Jonah in the right direction, the Prophet obediently prophesied to the people of Nineveh while Ashurdan III sat on the throne of Assyria.

> *[2] "Arise, go to Nineveh, that great city, and preach to it the message that I tell you." [3] So Jonah arose and went to Nineveh, according to the word of the Lord. Now Nineveh was an exceedingly great city, a three-day journey in extent. [4] And Jonah began to enter the city on the first day's walk. Then he cried out and said, "Yet forty days, and Nineveh shall be overthrown!"*

Jonah 3:2 – 4 (NKJV)

We then find the people of Nineveh taking heed to the warning given by God through the Prophet Jonah, repenting and turning from their wicked ways. As a result, God relented the disaster He had planned against them, and the city was spared.

4. The Lord's Grace:
Jonah 4:1 – 11

The Lord's decision to withdraw His judgement was displeasing to Jonah as he knew God would show lovingkindness and goodness towards them if they repented.

We can see how Jonah is selfish, thinking only of himself instead of being in sync with what God is busy doing.

Nonetheless, the book ends with the Lord responding to Jonah with the following,

"And should I not pity Nineveh, that great city, in which are more than one hundred and twenty thousand persons who cannot discern between their right hand and their left—and much livestock?"

Jonah 4:11 (NKJV)

PROPHETIC DECLARATION:

1. **Jonah 4:2 (NKJV)**

² So he prayed to the Lord, and said, "Ah, Lord, was not this what I said when I was still in my country? Therefore I fled previously to Tarshish; for I know that You are a gracious and merciful God, slow to anger and abundant in lovingkindness, One who relents from doing harm."

I declare and decree in the Name of Jesus that I will develop the same character, likeness, and image of the Lord Jesus Christ. I will show mercy, compassion, and grace wherever I go. I will live a life that overflows with the lovingkindness of God - Amen.

NOTES

Book of **Micah**

"The Mighty Evangelist"

Micah, the sixth book of the Minor Prophets, was written by Micah. The name Micah comes from the word *Mikayahu* which means: "*Who is like Yahweh?*".

Micah comes from a town called Moresheth-Gath, near the border of Philistia and Judah, about twenty-five miles southwest of Jerusalem. In the book's introduction, we see that he prophesied during the reigns of Jotham, Ahaz, and Hezekiah, kings of Judah.

Micah focuses most of his prophecies on the leaders of Samaria and Jerusalem, the capital cities of Israel and Judah.

The book can be divided into two primary keys:

1. **The Judgement of Israel and Judah — Micah 1 – 3**
2. **The Restoration of God's People in the Millennial Reign — Micah 4 – 5**

HIGHLIGHTED EVENTS IN MICAH

1. **Prophecy Pointing to the Messiah: Micah 5:2**

Seven hundred years before Christ's birth, Micah prophesied His birthplace, Bethlehem, and gave us a glimpse of His eternal nature.

"But you, Bethlehem Ephrathah,
Though you are little among the thousands of Judah,
Yet out of you shall come forth to Me
The One to be Ruler in Israel,
Whose goings forth are from of old,
From everlasting."

Micah 5:2 (NKJV)

2. **The Requirements of the Lord:**
   Micah 6:8

This verse answers what the Lord required of Israel to return. This can also be seen as an attribute that is well worth taking notes of for all who claim to be children of God.

   a. Do Justly
   b. Love Mercy
   c. Walk Humbly with God

PROPHETIC DECLARATION:

1. **Micah 6:8 (NKJV)**

[8] **"He has shown you, O man, what is good;**
And what does the Lord require of you
But to do justly,
To love mercy,
And to walk humbly with your God?"

I declare and decree in the Name of Jesus that I humble myself before the Lord. I surrender, yield, and submit to the authority of God in my life - Amen

NOTES

NOTES

Book of **Nahum**

"The Righteous Judgement of God"

Nahum is the seventh book of the Minor Prophets and was written by Nahum approximately 663-612 B.C

Nahum came from Capernaum and, like Jonah, was mandated to bring the Lord's judgement against Nineveh for a second time and took place almost a century after Jonah.

The Prophet Nahum preached during the reign of King Manasseh, one of the evilest kings in Judah's history.

At this stage, the Assyrians returned to their evil ways and became one of Israel's worst oppressors.

The book of Nahum can be divided into two major events:

1. **Nahum Warns of Judgment & Describes the Power of God — Nahum 1**
2. **Nahum Predicts the Final Destruction of Nineveh — Nahum 2 – 3**

HIGHLIGHTED EVENTS IN NAHUM

1. **Nahum Warns of Judgment & Describes the Power of God: Nahum 1:1 – 15**

The message of this book is that God will not acquit the wicked. God will forgive sin when there is repentance, but He will not condone sin that is persisted. This text declares and describes the destruction of Nineveh, and we see the fulfilment of that prophecy.

The book of Nahum opens up with God revealing His character saying,

² God is jealous, and the Lord avenges;
The Lord avenges and is furious.
The Lord will take vengeance on His adversaries,
And He reserves wrath for His enemies;
³ The Lord is slow to anger and great in power,
And will not at all acquit the wicked.
The Lord has His way
In the whirlwind and in the storm,
And the clouds are the dust of His feet.

Nahum 1:2 – 3 (NKJV)

Nahum then further warns of judgment and describes the power of God, stating,

⁵ The mountains quake before Him,
The hills melt,
And the earth heaves at His presence,
Yes, the world and all who dwell in it.

Nahum 1:5 (NKJV)

The coming judgement of Nineveh was a message of encouragement and hope for the Southern Kingdom oppressed by the Assyrians. As the Prophet stated,

¹² Thus says the Lord:
"Though they are safe, and likewise many,
Yet in this manner they will be cut down
When he passes through.
Though I have afflicted you,
I will afflict you no more;

Nahum 1:12 (NKJV)

2. Nahum Predicts the Final Destruction of Nineveh: Naham 2 – 3

> *7 It shall come to pass that all who look upon you*
> *Will flee from you, and say,*
> *'Nineveh is laid waste!*
> *Who will bemoan her?'*
> *Where shall I seek comforters for you?"*

Nahum 3:7 (NKJV)

Nineveh's destruction was prophesied, described, and deserved and the test of what was prophesied was its fulfilment.

PROPHETIC DECLARATION:

1. **Nahum 1:15 (NKJV)**

¹⁵ **"Behold, on the mountains**
The feet of him who brings good tidings,
Who proclaims peace!
O Judah, keep your appointed feasts,
Perform your vows.
For the wicked one shall no more pass through you;
He is utterly cut off."

I declare and decree in the Name of Jesus that the wicked one is utterly cut off from my life and that he shall no longer pass through my territories, my finances, my relationship, and my life — Amen.

NOTES

_____

_____

_____

_____

_____

_____

_____

_____

_____

_____

_____

_____

_____

_____

_____

_____

_____

_____

_____

_____

_____

_____

_____

_____

_____

Book of **Habakkuk**

"Fearless Faith"

Habakkuk is the eighth book of the Minor Prophets and was written by Habakkuk approximately 612-589 B.C.

Habakkuk wrote the book just before the Babylonian siege and capture of Jerusalem. Habakkuk lived during the reign of Jehoiakim, king of Judah.

Habakkuk is somewhat unique as it is a dialogue between the prophet and God rather than a prophecy addressing Israel. We see in the first two chapters how Habakkuk argues with God.

Habakkuk was troubled by God's strange silence while wickedness, strife and oppression were rampant in Judah. His perplexity only intensified when told that the Lord was preparing to do something about it through the ruthless Babylonians. How could it be possible that a wicked nation would come and execute justice on the Lord's behalf?

The book of Habakkuk can be divided into three main sections:

1. **The Burden — Habakkuk 1:1 – 17**
2. **The Vision — Habakkuk 2:1 – 20**
3. **The Prayer — Habakkuk 3:1 – 19**

HIGHLIGHTED EVENTS IN HABAKKUK

1. **The Burden:**
   Habakkuk 1:1 – 17

The book opens up with the prophet Habakkuk posing a question to God: Why does the evil in Judah go unpunished?

The Lord's Response: God then gives the prophet Habakkuk an in-detail description of the Babylonian army that was about to come and execute judgement.

Habakkuk's second question: How can God use a wicked nation to bring judgement on those who are more righteous than the Babylonians?

2. The Vision:
Habakkuk 2:1 – 20

This was not to be the end of God's chosen nation. There would come a time that God would restore them once again as a nation, and so we find the famous passage of scripture stating,

² Then the Lord answered me and said:

"Write the vision
And make it plain on tablets,
That he may run who reads it.
³ For the vision is yet for an appointed time;
But at the end it will speak, and it will not lie.
Though it tarries, wait for it;
Because it will surely come,
It will not tarry.
⁴ "Behold the proud,
His soul is not upright in him;
But the just shall live by his faith."

Habakkuk 2:2 – 4 (NKJV)

3. The Prayer:
Habakkuk 3:1 – 19

The prophet Habakkuk then acknowledged the words spoken by the Lord, stating,

² "O Lord, I have heard Your speech and was afraid;
O Lord, revive Your work in the midst of the years!
In the midst of the years make it known;
In wrath remember mercy."

Habakkuk 3:2 (NKJV)

The book ends off with the prophet Habakkuk glorifying God with yet another famous scripture singing,

> *¹⁹ The Lord God is my strength;*
> *He will make my feet like deer's feet,*
> *And He will make me walk on my high hills.*

Habakkuk 3:19 (NKJV)

PROPHETIC DECLARATION:

1. **Habakkuk 2:2 – 3 (NKJV)**

**² Then the Lord answered me and said:
"Write the vision
And make it plain on tablets,
That he may run who reads it.
³ For the vision is yet for an appointed time;
But at the end it will speak, and it will not lie.
Though it tarries, wait for it;
Because it will surely come,
It will not tarry."**

I declare and decree that I will not allow Satan to rob me of the vision over my life. I commit to making my vision plain, to write it down so that I may run with it. I will be fruitful with all that Christ has entrusted me with, in Jesus' Name.

NOTES

Book of **Zephaniah**

"God's Approaching Judgement"

Zephaniah, the ninth book of the Minor Prophets, was written by Zephaniah in approximately 630 B.C.

Zephaniah uniquely introduces himself as the son of Cushi, son of Gedaliah, son of Amariah, son of Hezekiah. He highlights his royal lineage as a descendant of one of Judah's good kings.

The book tells us that Zephaniah prophesied during the reign of Josiah, the king of Judah.

The dominant theme of the book is the day of the Lord which Zephaniah prophesies and predicts as a result of sin, stating,

> *14 The great day of the Lord is near;*
> *It is near and hastens quickly.*
> *The noise of the day of the Lord is bitter;*
> *There the mighty men shall cry out.*
> *15 That day is a day of wrath,*
> *A day of trouble and distress,*
> *A day of devastation and desolation,*
> *A day of darkness and gloominess,*
> *A day of clouds and thick darkness,*

> **Zephaniah 1:14-15 (NKJV)**

He further speaks about Judah's fall to Babylon and the eventual future judgment and restoration of all humanity.

The book of Zephaniah can be divided into three main sections:

1. **The Coming Wrath on Judah — Zephaniah 1:1 – 18**
2. **The Coming Wrath on All Nations — Zephaniah 2:1 – 15**
3. **Healing and Restoration — Zephaniah 3:1 – 20**

HIGHLIGHTED EVENTS IN ZEPHANIAH

1. **The Coming Wrath on Judah and All Nations:
    Zephaniah 1 – 2**

We see yet again the all too familiar wicked cycle of a rebellious Judah continually doing what is wrong in the sight of God. And so the Lord sends a warning through the Prophet Zephaniah confirming the judgement that will come on Judah approximately 20 years before their captivity should they refuse to repent and turn from their wicked ways.

He also predicted the desolation of Nineveh, the capital city of Assyria, as seen in **Zephaniah 2:13**

2. **Healing and Restoration:
    Zephaniah 3:1 – 20**

God shows how He gives the sinner what they do not deserve; mercy.

And so, Zephaniah speaks of a day of hope, when the remnant of Israel would come back out of captivity under God's protection, to fulfil His promise as seen in **Zephaniah 3:15**

PROPHETIC DECLARATION:

1. **Zephaniah 3:17 (NKJV)**

¹⁷ **The Lord your God in your midst,**
The Mighty One, will save;
He will rejoice over you with gladness,
He will quiet you with His love,
He will rejoice over you with singing."

I declare and decree in the Name of Jesus that I will enjoy the peace of the Lord all the days of my life. There is no circumstance too great nor problem too big for the Lord. As such, I bring every part of my life and place it subject under the governance, reign, rule, and command of the Almighty God. The Lord is the One who silences every storm that I am faced with.

NOTES

_____

_____

_____

_____

_____

_____

_____

_____

_____

_____

_____

_____

_____

_____

_____

_____

_____

_____

_____

_____

_____

_____

_____

NOTES

Book of **Haggai**

"The Lord's House"

Haggai is the tenth book of the Minor Prophets and was written by Haggai in approximately 520 B.C.

He recorded four messages to the Jews of Jerusalem eighteen years after their return from exile in Babylon.

Haggai is among the most carefully and precisely dated books in the Bible and is a post-exilic book, meaning it was written after the captivity in Babylon.

Haggai is burdened with rebuilding the temple at a time when the Jews have been humbled by their exile to Babylon, now returning to their land but discouraged by the opposition they encountered.

Haggai's message is one of support, confirmation, and assurance. His message was simple and straightforward but passionate. He encouraged them with future glory and the victory to come.

The book can be divided into the four messages of Haggai:

1. The First Message — Consider Your Ways: Haggai 1:1 – 15
2. The Second Message — Be Strong & Work: Haggai 2:1 – 9
3. The Third Message — I Will Bless You: Haggai 2:10 – 19
4. The Fourth Message — A Promise to Zerubbabel: Haggai 2:20 – 23

HIGHLIGHTED EVENTS IN HAGGAI

1. **The First Message — Consider Your Ways: Haggai 1:1 – 15**

The book opens up where the Word of the Lord came to the Prophet Haggai, stating how they need to get their priorities straight, explaining how they live in comfortable houses while the house of God remains unattended.

467

And so, the Lord instructed the Prophet Haggai to go and rebuild His house.

This time they hearkened unto the voice of God and so began working twenty-four days after Haggai's message, as seen in **Haggai 1:14 – 15.**

2. The Second Message — Be Strong & Work: Haggai 2:1 – 9

However, rebuilding the temple was not an easy task as they faced much opposition.

And so, we see how the Lord, through His mighty words, inspires, encourages and uplifts the people not to lose heart, stating that He is with them and will be the One who protects them.

The Lord then further motivates the people by making a statement that changed the very course of history, stating,

'The glory of this latter temple shall be greater than the former,' says the Lord of hosts. 'And in this place I will give peace,' says the Lord of hosts."

Haggai 2:9 (NKJV)

The book closes with the promise of a blessing and Zerubbabel being chosen as a signet ring, as seen in **Haggai 2:15 – 23.**

PROPHETIC DECLARATION:

1. **Haggai 1:8 (NKJV)**

[8] **"Go up to the mountains and bring wood and build the temple, that I may take pleasure in it and be glorified," says the Lord.**

I declare and decree that I will build God's house, that He may take pleasure in it and be glorified in Jesus' Name.

NOTES

NOTES

Book of **Zechariah**

"Yahweh Remembers"

Zechariah is the eleventh book of the Minor Prophets and was written by Zechariah. His name means *"Yahweh Remembers"*.

Zechariah was the grandson of Iddo and prophesied to the people of Judah after they returned from their seventy years of exile in Babylon under the decree of Cyrus, king of Persia.

He was not just a prophet but also a member of a priestly family. Zechariah was born in Babylon and returned to Judah with about fifty thousand other Jewish captives under the leadership of Zerubbabel.

The book can be divided into two main sections:

1. **Early Prophecies: The Temple Re-Built and Zechariah's Visions — Zechariah 1 – 8**
2. **Later Prophecies: After the Temple Re-Built (The Second Coming) — Zechariah 9 – 14**

HIGHLIGHTED EVENTS IN ZECHARIAH

1. **Zechariah's Visions: Zechariah 1 – 8**

Vision #1: Vision of the Horses
Zechariah 1:7 – 17

Meaning of the Vision:

In this vision, we see how God express His anger towards the nations at ease while Israel is still living under oppression but so also reveals how He will restore Israel and bless them once again, as stated in **Zechariah 1:15 – 17.**

473

Vision #2: Vision of the Four Horns and the Four Craftsmen
Zechariah 1:18 – 21

Meaning of the Vision:

The *"four horns"* in this vision represent the nations who scattered Judah, with the *"four craftsmen"* representing the Lord's judgment that is about to come against these nations.

Vision # 3: The Measuring Line
Zechariah 2:1 – 13

Meaning of the Vision:

Zechariah saw a man with a measuring line surveying Jerusalem in this vision. Then another angel came and spoke with the angel communicating with Zechariah, saying,

> **"...Run, speak to this young man, saying: 'Jerusalem shall be inhabited as towns without walls, because of the multitude of men and livestock in it. 5 For I,' says the Lord, 'will be a wall of fire all around her, and I will be the glory in her midst.'"**

> **Zechariah 2:4 – 5 (NKJV)**

This statement was incredibly prophetic as Zechariah was addressing the returning exiles that were also about to rebuild the walls of Jerusalem.

And so, the vision was to show that a Messianic day would come where Jerusalem would no longer need any walls as they would be heavenly protected by God.

Vision #4: Vision of Joshua, the High Priest
Zechariah 3:1 – 10

The first three visions painted a picture of Israel's external deliverance from Captivity, her expansion, and the material prosperity of the land.

However, in this vision, God is focusing on the internal state of Israel, which needs cleansing from sin and reinstating as a priestly nation.

And so, we find the famous account where God rebukes the devil accusing Joshua, the high priest representing Israel, in this vision.

We also see the Lord commanding Joshua's filthy garments to be replaced with new kingly robes. This represented how God will remove Israel's sin and guilt through His grace and love, bringing complete deliverance.

Vision #5: Vision of the Lampstand and Olive Trees
Zechariah 4:1 – 14

In this vision, Zechariah saw a lampstand made of solid gold with a bowl above it and seven pipes connecting the bowl with the seven lamps to supply them with golden oil.

Zechariah also saw two olive trees standing on each side of the lampstand with two gold pipes continually supplying the bowl with oil.

This was a vision of encouragement for God's people who, through many challenges, thought it impossible to complete the temple's rebuilding.

And so God, through this vision, revealed that the work will be completed not through human might nor strength but by His Spirit stating,

So he answered and said to me:

"This is the word of the Lord to Zerubbabel:

'Not by might nor by power, but by My Spirit,'
Says the Lord of hosts.

Zechariah 4:6 (NKJV)

The vision was also indicative to Zerubbabel to show that through the leading, guidance, help, counsel, and power of the Holy Spirit he will not only see the completion of the temple but will also be the one to complete it.

Vision #6: Vision of the Flying Scroll
Zechariah 5:1 – 4

Until now, all the visions contained peace and restoration and were filled with words of encouragement and hope.

However, in the visions to follow God reveal the harsh punishment towards those who refuse to change their wicked ways and continue to live in rebellion against God and His Word, especially when He is showing mercy and kindness.

And so, in this vision, Zechariah sees a flying scroll, 9.14m in length and 4.57m in width. The scroll was not rolled up but flew open so both sides could be read.

We see the angel explaining the scroll in **Zechariah 5:3 – 4**

The scroll represents the Word and Law of the Lord. We know that the command of the law is in writing first to remove any confusion towards God's expectations and secondly to be a continual reminder of the covenant that God's people stand in.

In the same way, the curse of the law is written, and it speaks harshly against disobedience towards God's Word, as we can see in this vision.

Vision #7: Vision of the Woman in a Basket
Zechariah 5:5 – 11

Zechariah then again is told by the angel to lift his eyes and this time sees a measuring basket with a led disk that is raised with a woman sitting inside of the basket.

The angel interprets the vision stating that this was *"their resemblance throughout the earth"*. The NIV says, *"This is the iniquity of the people throughout the land."*

The angel then further explained the meaning of the woman inside the basket as indicative of *"wickedness"*.

Note: *The Hebrew word for "wickedness" is a feminine form and thus could explain why "wickedness" in the vision was represented as a woman.*

The woman was then pushed back into the basket, covering the basket's mouth with a lead lid. The basket was lifted between heaven and earth by two women with wings like a stork and carried away to the land of Shinar.

The vision was to show wickedness being removed from Israel and taken back to its original starting place, Shinar, which is Babylon.

Putting wickedness and idolatry back in Babylon also sets the stage for her final judgment.

Vision #8: Vision of Four Chariots
Zechariah 6:1 – 8

Zechariah then saw four chariots coming out from between two bronze mountains. In this instance, the bronze mountains could symbolise God's righteous, divine judgment against sin carried out by chariots of war going out into the world.

The first chariot had red horses, the second black, the third white, and the fourth dappled, each powerful.

2. **Physical Description of the Antichrist:**
   Zechariah 11

> *17 "Woe to the worthless shepherd,*
> *, Who leaves the flock!*
> *A sword shall be against his arm*
> *And against his right eye;*
> *His arm shall completely wither,*
> *And his right eye shall be totally blinded."*

Zechariah 11:17 (NKJV)

3. The Prediction of the Crucifixion: Zechariah 12

¹⁰ "And I will pour on the house of David and on the inhabitants of Jerusalem the Spirit of grace and supplication; then they will look on Me whom they pierced. Yes, they will mourn for Him as one mourns for his only son, and grieve for Him as one grieves for a firstborn.

Zechariah 12:10 (NKJV)

PROPHETIC DECLARATION:

1. **Zechariah 4:6 (NKJV)**

⁶ **So he answered and said to me:**
"This is the word of the Lord to Zerubbabel:
'Not by might nor by power, but by My Spirit,
Says the Lord of hosts.

I declare and decree that I surrender to the consistent and continual leading, guidance, help, and counsel of the Holy Spirit.

I declare and decree that through the Holy Spirit, I have the ability to conquer any situation and will overcome any obstacle with grace and ease in the Name of Jesus — Amen.

NOTES

NOTES

Book of **Malachi**

"Sending a Messenger"

Malachi is the last book of the Minor Prophets and was written by the Prophet Malachi approximately 450-430 B.C.

His name means *"messenger,"* which points to Malachi's role as a prophet of the Lord, delivering God's message to His people.

The book of Malachi is a final message to a disobedient nation. The people of Judah were taken captive by the Babylonians and, after seventy years, released to return to their Promised Land to rebuild the temple and the city.

By the time of Malachi, the Jews have been back in the land for more than a hundred years. They were expecting blessings when they returned. Though the temple had been rebuilt, the once-passionate Israelites gave way to a complete apathy for the things of God.

The book's central theme revolves around Israel's continual defiled offerings and how God, through His messenger, explain how they are to return to Him and the blessing connected if they choose to be obedient.

HIGHLIGHTED EVENTS IN MALACHI

The Key to Absolute Prosperity:
Malachi 1 – 3

In **Malachi 1:1**, we find that the Lord is heavily burdened by something, and the answer is found in **Malachi 1:6 – 7**

"⁶ A son honors his father,
And a servant his master.
If then I am the Father,
Where is My honor?
And if I am a Master,
Where is My reverence?
Says the Lord of hosts
To you priests who despise My name.
Yet you say, 'In what way have we despised Your name?'
"⁷ You offer defiled food on My altar,
But say,
'In what way have we defiled You?'
By saying,
'The table of the Lord is contemptible.'

Malachi 1:6 – 7 (NKJV)

Through the above passage of scripture, we find that God is feeling dishonoured not because the people bring their offerings but because of the type of offerings they present.

And so, when we look at **verse 8,** God states that they present the lame and the sick, which is evil in the sight of God, and as a result, the Lord departed from them.

But through God's grace, love, and compassion, He would never forget His people, allowing them to repent and return to Him, as we find yet again in the following passage of scripture,

⁷ Yet from the days of your fathers
You have gone away from My ordinances
And have not kept them.
Return to Me, and I will return to you,"
Says the Lord of hosts.
"But you said,
'In what way shall we return?'

Malachi 3:7 (NKJV)

484

We find the Israelites asking an essential question in the above passage of scripture which God answers in **Malachi 3:8 – 10**

> *Bring all the tithes into the storehouse,*
> *That there may be food in My house,*
> *And try Me now in this,"*
> *Says the Lord of hosts,*
> *"If I will not open for you the windows of heaven*
> *And pour out for you such blessing*
> *That there will not be room enough to receive it.*

Malachi 3:10 (NKJV)

Obedience to the above would unlock a powerful blessing, not only of unending prosperity but would also give God the place in their lives where He can rebuke the devourer on their behalf, as seen in **Malachi 3:11 – 12.**

This is something well worth taking note of for every one of us, even today.

The Silent Years:

We then enter what is known as the four hundred years of silence where there was no prophet, no prophecy, no new revelation, until an angel visits Zechariah, the father of John the Baptist in the New Testament.

PROPHETIC DECLARATION:

1. **Malachi 3:10 (NKJV)**

[10] Bring all the tithes into the storehouse,
That there may be food in My house,
And try Me now in this,"
Says the Lord of hosts,
"If I will not open for you the windows of heaven
And pour out for you such blessing
That there will not be room enough to receive it.

I declare and decree that my tithes will be erected as a memorial in heaven that God will not be able to pass by until every need is met. I further declare that because of my obedience to this instruction, the Lord is the One rebuking the devourer on my behalf.

I declare that my success will know no limits and that I will be blessed beyond measure — my life will never lose value in the Name of Jesus — Amen.

NOTES

28 DAY
READING PLAN

Made in the USA
Middletown, DE
12 September 2023

38349225R00298